The Secrets of Retailing,

Or:
How to Beat Wal-Mart!

The Secrets of Retailing,

Or:
How to Beat Wal-Mart!

Marc Joseph
President and Chief Operating Officer
Dollardays International

with Rusty Fischer

The Secrets of Retailing, Or: How to Beat Wal-Mart!

by Marc Joseph with Rusty Fischer

© 2005 Silverback Books, Inc.

Published by Silverback Books, Inc.

Book Design: Future Studio Los Angeles

Cover Design: Beth Kerschen

ISBN 1-59637-037-8

Printed and bound in Hong Kong

SILVERBACK
BOOKS INC.

Dedication

THIS BOOK IS DEDICATED to the entrepreneurs of my father's generation, those brave men who I grew up watching in action every day. Most of these guys fought in World War II and then came home to build their dreams for their families. None of them had anything handed to them and they built their businesses by hard work, dedication to their dream, and the understanding of what it takes to build and service a loyal customer base. Thanks go out in particular to Stanley, Arthur, Sanford, Irwin, Alvin, Jerome, Jerry, Melvin, Stanford, Fred, and Grandpa Joe.

Special thanks go out to Chris, Paul, Rob, Amy, Martin, Roger, Ron, and Ryan for their belief in the DollarDays vision and their tireless support in making a dream become reality.

And a sincere thanks to Peter for his guidance and insight over the last few years. Especially for his help in bringing this book from a concept idea to actually being published.

And to Cathy, who, despite my turning our world upside down over the last decade, has always been there with patience, understanding, and support. I could never have done any of this without her.

Dedication

Table of Contents

Foreword

I AM AN ENTREPRENEUR. My parents founded our first Service Merchandise store back in 1934 in Pulaski, Tennessee. Through hard work and building the right team, we were able to take this one store and build it into a chain of 413 stores doing $4 billion in sales. We even went public in 1971. Sam Walton did the same thing with his Wal-Mart store and Richard Schulze did the same thing with his Best Buy store.

I guess my message here is anyone of us can turn his or her dream into a reality in the retail business. But like any business, retailing is quite competitive and, although I may respect my competitors like Wal-Mart, you bet I want to beat them just like you do. This is the book to help you do just that.

I wish Marc had written this book back in the 1960s when I was starting to grow my chain. It sure would have saved me a lot of time, money, and energy if he had been around to tell me the secrets of retailing as I know them now. Even an old hand in the retail business like me learned something new chapter after chapter. Sometimes, it was just reinforcing what I already knew; at others, it was reminding me of something I may have forgotten.

As many of you may know, I started another chain of stores back in 1999 called 99 Cent Stuff. It, too, is now a public company. I started it because I saw an opportunity in the dollar store industry. As an entrepreneur, I think that over the next ten years the dollar store business will be the segment of retailing with the fastest growth. Because it is such a young business, there really is not much information out there on how to be successful in it. The chapter about dollar stores alone is worth the price of this book.

Recently, I launched www.servicemerchandise.com because the Internet has proven to be such a powerful retailing avenue. I want to continue satisfying customers with great service and tremendous value for jewelry, electronics, appliances, games and toys, and home and garden products. If you are looking for quality goods at a low price, you should check it out.

Whether you are just getting into retailing, or have been in retailing for most of your career, this is a book that will help you succeed. And it is one you should share with your partners and employees too because it will trigger discussions that will improve your business.

Anyone of us can live the American dream. Retailing has been very good to me. It can be good to you, too.

—RAYMOND ZIMMERMAN

Introduction

J UST AS TWENTY YEARS AGO Wal-Mart beat Sears and J.C. Penney at their own game, so today's entrepreneurs have the ability to carve out their own success stories against all competitors—including the world's largest retailer.

Wal-Mart emerged as the retail leader serving 100 million customers every week because the other major giants of years gone by had lost much of their entrepreneurial spirit. They had become corporate, while Wal-Mart kept its entrepreneurial roots and, facing sleepy competitors, was able to grow explosively. But today Wal-Mart has developed the corporate structure it once battled. To a large extent, they have lost touch with the very consumers they once understood so well.

For example, voters in the Los Angeles suburb of Inglewood defeated by a 2 to 1 margin a referendum that would have bulldozed the city's planning and review process in favor of adding a Wal-Mart supercenter to the town. Inglewood is not a "social issue," upper class town. It is a blue-collar town with relatively high joblessness. So why would a community which represents Wal-Mart's core competency overwhelmingly reject Wal-Mart?

The reasons are complicated. But at their heart lies the fact that Wal-Mart failed to convince the citizens that they would benefit all that much from lower prices, while the small business community convinced Inglewood's working-class people that Wal-Mart's low-wage and limited-benefit jobs would have a ripple effect throughout the area. Voters were led to believe that this impersonal store could play havoc with the fiber of their business community. This same scene has recently played out in Chicago and San Francisco.

Here, on a grand scale, are illustrations of how small businesses, by winning the hearts of their customers, can defeat even the largest and richest of firms.

By cutting expenses and buying in huge quantities Wal-Mart has been able to hold down its prices. As a result, it has had enormous success in building sales and market share. They are China's largest single customer, purchasing $25 billion worth of Chinese products annually. But now their very bigness has slowed them down. They can no longer react quickly to local market conditions as they did when they were smaller and more versatile. They have turned into the mega-corp they fought so hard and successfully against not so many years ago.

Herein lies the opportunity to beat Wal-Mart and, for that matter, every other major chain. In every chapter of this book I talk about the fundamentals of entrepreneurial retailing. I discuss hiring the right people, selecting the right location, working with the right vendors, running the right promotions, and much more. This is a book based on my personal experiences both in competing against Wal-Mart (and other powerful chains) and in being a supplier to Wal-Mart. When you finish this book, you will have learned not only how to survive in the shadow of Wal-Mart and every other major chain, but how to capitalize on their presence, how to feed off the customers they attract, how to win, and how to thrive.

Retailing is an evolution, and today's single store entrepreneur—which could easily be you—could well become tomorrow's chain, or even tomorrow's Wal-Mart. It is the American way . . .

Retail Detail

Virtually all independent retailers who have survived against the onslaught of Wal-Mart and the chains have done so by meeting specialized needs. Independent booksellers have battled successfully to hold on to their market share despite the building of more Borders and Barnes & Nobles. According to Mintel, a market research firm, the number of independent coffeehouses has increased from 8,200 in 1999 to 8,800 in 2003 despite the Starbucks onslaught.

Chapter 1

A (Very) Brief History of Retailing, Or:

Why It's Never Too Late to Open Your First Store

Whoever said money can't buy happiness
simply didn't know where to go shopping.
—BO DEREK

B O HAD IT RIGHT: shopping has been providing people with happiness, not to mention everything from table salt to socks, since time began. For centuries, goods have been hauled across deserts, mountains, fields, and rivers to central marketplaces to be sold or bartered.

Spices, silver, olives, fowl, swords, fruit—you name it, it's been sold; or, more importantly, *bought*. In many countries, vendors, or hawkers as they're more commonly known, still hawk—or sell—their wares while tramping from village to village, encampment to encampment, town to town.

Of course, every village had its share of artisans, each with their own specialty, who sold (or bartered) what they made. There were tanners and vintners; bakers and candlemakers; and farmers selling meat, eggs, vegetables, and fruit. In many European towns and villages, many of the streets designate the place where these producers gathered. Fish Street, Baker Street, and so on are ubiquitous. The difference between these sellers and the peddlers hawking their goods was that the latter did not make what they sold; they bought the goods from the artisan who made them (the ancestor of today's manufacturer) and sold them at more than they paid. Ah, the profit of it!

As civilization took hold and people grew roots, these nomadic peddlers tended to set up shop in marketplaces. Containing tents as well as more permanent structures, marketplaces are still the primary form of retailing in these villages. Nowhere was this trend more evident than in Europe. There is hardly a township or village throughout that continent that does not have a weekly market that sells everything from spit-broiled chicken to hundreds of types of cheese (no fewer than four hundred varieties in France) to inexpensive clothes to household goods to ceramics to. . . well, to everything members of local households like to buy.

Often, of course, rather than packing and unpacking every week, traveling market vendors chose to open permanent market stalls in prime locations. Eventually, these morphed into stores, strip malls, shopping centers, and even entire business districts.

Although retail shops (stores whose owners buy rather than manufacture all or most of their goods) have existed since time immemorial, the retail market we know today really came into its own during the Industrial Revolution of the nineteenth century. By then, factories (often the "dark satanic mills" William Blake described in his poem "Jerusalem") started to mass-produce large quantities of fabric (replacing the unmarried, home-based "spinster") and potters such as Wedgewood learned how to "throw" pottery in mass quantities. These and countless other manufacturers needed widespread retail outlets to disseminate their goods.

By the 1850s, most of the staples that we still shop for today—

shoes, slacks, hats, jackets, furniture, pots, pans, and much more—were supplied not by local manufacturers who dealt directly with their customers but by retailers who acted as middlemen between producers and customers.

Americans are famous for playing catch-up; the development of retail chains was no exception. Throughout the late eighteenth and early nineteenth centuries, the great inventors that energized the industrial revolution contributed to vastly improved manufacturing output. These included Thomas Newcomer with his steam-driven pump in 1705, James Watt with his steam engine in 1781, James Hargraves with his Spinning Jenny in 1764, Richard Arkwright with his waterframe in 1771, and, of course, many more inventors and industrialists.

By the middle of the nineteenth century, the demand for goods throughout the far-flung and fast-expanding United States had motivated the great railroad barons to build their iron roads across the country so goods could move rapidly and inexpensively from the manufacturing centers of New England to every corner of the country. On May 10, 1869, the first transcontinental railroad line was completed, the achievement memorialized with a golden spike driven into the ground where the lines from East and West finally met. The birth of the modern chain store in America occurred in 1859 with the grand opening of the Great Atlantic & Pacific Tea Company, Inc., later shortened to just A&P, in none other than New York City itself. By the 1890s, the Sears catalog became America's wish book.

Of course, buying from a catalog or from a peddler's horse-drawn wagon soon became seen as too slow to satisfy demand. As everyone who's ever seen a Western movie knows, it wasn't long before the small general store started to appear in every town and hamlet and then, as time proceeded, became more and more specialized.

Jump forward to the first half of the twentieth century and independent stores, each specialized in its own line of goods, had popped up across the nation, where they remain to this day. Of course, successful storekeepers of small, specialized stores soon became ambitious and were no longer content with running a single store. Once they found a winning combination, specialty stores tended to multiply their outlets, and chain stores specializing in everything from clothing to office supplies to books to almost every category of purchasable items became ubiquitous. At about the same time came the shopping mall.

Certainly customers enjoyed the excellent customer service and individualized treatment for which the small stores were famous, but as the suburbs and so-called bedroom communities of the 1970s and 80s spread farther and farther from big city downtowns, the inconvenience of running from specialty store to specialty store soon grew tiresome. So, in response to the demand for ever more convenience, shopping centers became the focal point for much retail activity, and the mall became a late twentieth-century improvement on the bustling business districts of yore.

Now, instead of schlepping from parking lot to parking lot, shoppers could leave their cars in one central spot and spend the day under the cover of one spacious roof, browsing from store to store to the sounds of piped-in Muzak, all in the comfort of centralized air and ample lighting.

The mall quickly became a staple of American culture in the 80s and 90s, spawning such popular and enduring terms as *food courts, mall rats,* and even *mall walkers.* Each mall had at least two "anchors," large stores with recognizable brand names such as JCPenney, Sears, and Dillard's, that were often situated at opposite ends of the mall. Like the crafty remora feeding off the shark, smaller stores survived from the shoppers coming and going from these giants.

Today, of course, megastores like Super Wal-Mart, Super-Target, and even Super-Kmart are cutting into the malls' profits. And "category killers" such as mega-sized Office Depots, three-story Barnes & Nobles, PETsMARTs, Best Buys, and all the rest crowd out most of their mom-and-pop competitors.

And today? From Wal-Mart to Dollar Tree to Target to eBay to Amazon.com—we haven't stopped shopping, but we have changed the way we do it. Of course, it's always been thus. New developments are supposed to kill the old, but in the end they simply create new avenues for future retailers. For instance, Amazon used to boast that it would soon put all brick and mortar bookstores out of business, but one can barely drive a block without seeing yet another mega Barnes & Noble, Borders, or Books-A-Million.

American retailers, apparently, are as resilient as American shoppers. What goes around comes around, and the impersonal nature of gigantic department stores like Costco and Sam's Club have given rise to a higher demand for more personal customer service, attention to detail, and other services provided on a decidedly smaller scale.

Enter . . . you? Yes, you too can become a part of the retail revolution sweeping the nation today. Why let the Wal-Marts, Targets, and Barnes & Nobles have all the fun? Retail is here, and it's here to stay. Small, personal, service-dedicated retail. It's a business model that will continue forever. As long as customers are willing to pay for something they need or want—and are willing to pay for the necessary expertise to fill those needs and wants exactly—there will always be somebody willing and able to sell it to them. Why shouldn't that somebody be . . . *you*?

Regardless of where you shop, whether online, at a megastore, or at the local mom-and-pop shop, you are part of the force that drives this country's economy. Think about it: Your shopping dollar helps support that cashier working her way through college, that manager supporting his wife and three kids, that entrepreneur who put her life's savings on the line to open up her brand new store. Your sales tax, those six or seven pennies from each dollar you spend (depending on where you live), builds roads, schools, courthouses, and prisons.

Think shopping doesn't affect every man, woman, and child in this, and most other, countries? Think again.

When the economy was suffering as a result of the terrorist attacks of September 11, what did our President tell us to do? Take up arms? Barricade ourselves? Build bomb shelters? Far from it: Citing America's long and storied entrepreneurial history, he suggested we go out to eat. Buy something. Take a vacation. Go on a trip. His message was loud and clear: America was built on capitalism, and that was the very establishment our enemies were trying to destroy. The best way to retaliate, the best way to fight back, said President Bush, was to revitalize the country's economy by shopping!

Giant companies, many of them retailers, are the fuel that feeds our economic fires. The top Fortune 500 companies? Giant retailers such as Wal-Mart, Home Depot, Kroger, Walgreens, and Target. Names we recognize. Stores we frequent.

Every year *Forbes* magazine publishes its list of 400 richest people. The Walton family consistently comes near the top of the list, this year coming in at number four. Walton patriarch Sam Walton opened his first general store in Rogers, Arkansas just forty-three years ago. His brainchild—Wal-Mart—is now the world's largest retailer, and has been for some time, with some 4,000-plus stores around the globe. If Sam were alive today, he would be worth *twice* as much as Bill Gates. After building barns to pay his way through school, John Menard opened his first hardware store in 1972. Now he has 184 stores and his Midwest-based Menards chain is a big rival of stores like Home Depot and Lowe's. Richard Schulze started his first stereo store in Minnesota 1966. Today there are 566 Best Buy stores.

Think these people are brilliant? Unique? Dynamic? Extraordinary? *Superhuman*? Well, they may have a little of those qualities sprinkled in, but don't we all? Haven't you always dreamed of owning your own store? You must, or you wouldn't be reading this right now. Chances are, you've been a lifelong shopper. (Who hasn't?) The difference between you and most shoppers, however, is that you've probably always said to yourself, "I know I could do this." Chances are, you said something more like, "I know I could do this . . . *better*."

Ever go into a bookstore and leave the shelves looking tidier than when you came in? Ever stuck a size 12 skirt back where it belongs? Ever argued with the cashier that the candy canes should be half-price on Christmas Eve?

Whether you're looking forward to opening your first store (soon to become a chain) because you know you can run it better than other stores selling similar merchandise, or you're investing in an entrepreneurial dream the world has never seen before, you *can* succeed.

They say if you want to make enemies, give them a restaurant to run. Well, it's the same with retail. Employees call in sick. Shipments are late. Property taxes go up just when revenues go down. And those pink bunny slippers you had shipped overnight? They'll probably still be on the clearance rack three months from now.

But have no fear. No endeavor is more rewarding than turning the key in your own store door every morning and turning on those lights. *Your* lights. Be it widgets or women's shoes, books or CDs, coffee or clothes, you are beginning a journey the likes of which you've never experienced before.

The retail industry has a long and storied history that holds few surprises for those willing and able to learn from the past. You've seen the trends, and the future is wide open. All that's left is for you to take that first step.

It really doesn't matter what kind of store you'll be running or what you'll be selling. In the end, it is *people* who will buy from you and make you successful. So, with that in mind, we begin our journey with a tool no shopkeeper, storeowner, or entrepreneur can do without: the art and science of psychology!

Retail Detail

According to Opinion Research Corporation, the average American considers 37% off the original price of an item a bargain. Sale items stimulate purchases—the survey found that 69% of shoppers buy something they had not planned to purchase because it was on sale. Seventy-three percent of consumers comparison shop for brand name items. A study by Leo Shapiro and Associates revealed that every week nearly one third of all consumers are involved in a sizable impulse purchase. The median impulse purchase was $30. Over 25% said their last impulse purchase was an article of clothing.

Chapter 2

The Psychology of Buying, Or:

Why You Want *What* You Want *When* You Want It

Consumers these days are on a mission.
They want to quickly locate a product, evaluate it, pay, and get out.
Yet most do not get what they want. If you want to stop the traffic
flow to competing brands or stores, the best way is
to overwhelm them with a great shopping experience.
—ROBERT KIZER, Walker Information, *American Demographics* 12/03

THERE'S NO DOUBT ABOUT IT: shopping *is* a tonic. Be it browsing in the local bakery for that perfect hot, buttered croissant, or spending hours in the mall clomping from store to store for just the right pair of shoes for the office Christmas party, there's something supremely *satisfying* about making a purchase. *Any* purchase.

Why? The reasons are varied and, admittedly, change from day to day. We shop because we're hungry. We shop because we're bored. We shop because we're lonely. We shop because we're with friends. We shop to kill time. We shop to fill time. We shop because it's the weekend. We shop because it's Friday night. We shop because it's Tuesday morning. We shop to fill the new trick-or-treat bowl we bought last Halloween. We shop to stuff the stockings we bought last Christmas. We shop because we just got a raise. We shop because we just got fired. We shop to spend money. We shop to "save" money. We shop to impress our friends. We shop to satisfy *ourselves*.

As you can see, the reasons why we shop are as varied as the products we shop for. In his groundbreaking book *Why We Buy: The Science of Shopping* (Simon & Schuster; 1999), noted author and retail consultant Paco Underhill relates the following:

> . . . shopping is more than the simple, dutiful acquisition of whatever is absolutely necessary to one's life—you need cornflakes, you go to the cornflakes, you grab the cornflakes, you pay for the cornflakes . . . It's the sensory aspect of the decision-making process that's most intriguing, because how else do we experience anything? But it's especially crucial in this context because virtually all unplanned purchases—and many planned ones, too—come as a result of the shopper seeing, touching, smelling or tasting something that promises pleasure, if not total fulfillment . . .

The point: shopping is an esoteric experience few can explain, though thousands of researchers, scientists, CEOs, retailers, and authors such as Mr. Underhill have tried.

But that's not why *we're* here, right? We're here to sell people things. To do that, you've decided to open a store. That means you're not going to have a lot of time to worry about *why* people buy in general, but why they are going to buy from *you*. On top of that, I can guarantee that you're going to need to pay a lot of attention to when, where, how, and, perhaps most importantly, how much they buy. That's where I come in.

So, what ties Americans together?
We're tied together by our belief in political democracy.
We're tied together by our belief in religious freedom.
We're tied together by our belief in capitalism . . .
We're tied together because we respect human life.
We're tied together because we respect the rule of law.
Those are the group of ideas that make us American.
—RUDY GIULIANI, former mayor of New York City

As we have seen, the "obvious" reason people buy is not always obvious. As a result, retail stores in general, and your retail store in particular, need to be designed for the shoppers who use them, not for the designers, architects, and engineers who build a store to win design awards to place on the mantle.

Don't be afraid to think outside the box in your store, even though every other store up and down the strip is doing things in exactly the opposite way. Sometimes less is more, at other times, well, *more* is more.

Remember, too, that there is a psychology about buying that marries the product and price with perception. For example, if you go to a restaurant you may have no problem paying $5.00 for a yogurt because of the perception created by the surroundings, the service, the ambience, etc. But at the grocery store, if the yogurt's not on sale for $0.69, you may not buy it. Thus, as the retailer, you must understand the nature of marrying products with perception.

A book can only take you so far. At some point your gut must take over and tell you how to do things, what to do, and when to do it. Most often, this epiphany will come when you've been staring at a display for four weeks and it looks exactly the same as the day you put it up. In other words, no one's buying the products.

Why? It could be where the display is. It could be how big it is. Could be its color, its size, its shape, or how high off the floor it is. It could be a myriad of things, but there's one thing you know it is: ineffective.

Years ago, when I was still young enough to be almost perfect (as I've learned more and more over the years, I've been becoming steadily more *im*perfect!), I was working in a grocery store that seemed to my untutored (but, nevertheless, slightly know-it-allish) eye to be untidy, almost (but not quite) messy. To show the boss how to do it right, I decided to build a glorious end-aisle display of some soup we were featuring that week. It was a doozy! I worked on it for hours. When I was done, it looked more like an ice sculpture than a display of cans. I stood back, admiring my work, convinced that, even in the first hour, we'd break all sales records. We did—no one bought a single can!

My boss had been slyly observing. Finally, he approached. Without a word, he removed some of the cans, turned others on their side, and walked away. Almost at once, passing shoppers grabbed cans and threw them into their carts. "Great price," I heard one of them murmur as she bought half a dozen.

"It was too perfect," my boss, sneaking up behind me, whispered in my ear. "No one wants to mess up a perfect display. Maybe they're afraid of knocking it down. Maybe they just don't want to be the first to commit. Who knows? But, the fact is, you often need a little untidiness to get things started."

So, if your display is not working, move it. Up, down, sideways, horizontal, left, right. Try to see if anything works better. Put it on the end cap of Aisle 3 on Monday. Try it on Aisle 6 on Wednesday. Put it on a bottom shelf on Thursday or a top shelf on Sunday. If the display works high, keep it high. If it works low, keep it low.

Remember, it's *your* store. The only rule is this one: do what works. In this chapter, we are going to be discussing several of the most common sense approaches to laying out your retail store. The key is to make your customers comfortable enough to buy from you not just once, but to keep coming back.

Retail Detail

Convenience store industry sales were $337 billion in 2003 according to the National Association of Convenience Stores. This was an overall increase of 16% in sales. There are 132,400 convenience stores in the United States.

Chapter 3

Business Plan and Business Structure:
The Twin Foundations of Any Successful Retail Enterprise

*Wal-Mart last year accounted for nearly 8%
of overall US retail sales.
That leaves 92% for others—for now.*
—ADVERTISING AGE (10/6/03)

I BEGIN THIS CRUCIAL CHAPTER with one of my favorite stories:
Two retailers are located directly across the street from each other, in exactly the same business. One is doing quite well; the other is not. Finally, the one doing poorly says to the other, "I don't understand it. I see people coming and going from your store at all hours. You have nice signs; you're always in the store; you're doing gangbusters. What's your secret?" The second storeowner replies, "My secret is that I have two people watching my store—you and me—and you have none."

Why is this story one of my favorites? The answer is simple. The bottom line is that you can't always be worrying about what others are doing down the block, up the street, on the Web, in the Sunday ads, or across town. You have to worry about one person, and that's you. In the end, the moral of the story is, "Don't spend too much time worrying about the other person."

If you're like most of us, as you're thinking about whether or not to open your own store, you're deep into layers of academic, professional, personal, and even physical soul searching. And you are fully justified because the chances are good that your enterprise really won't amount to much if, once you've finally committed to going into retail as your sole means of financial support, you don't have a solid plan in place.

After all, knowing what you want to buy is worthless if you haven't planned on enough money to buy those items in the first place. As you'll see in the many retail examples sprinkled throughout this book, the greatest successes always came with a plan.

And here is where you get one. This chapter will deal solely with the dual aspects of writing a business plan and creating a basic business structure. I call these vital components the "twin foundations of any successful retail enterprise."

Without them, you may operate a business. With them, you'll operate a business success.

Business Plan

Plans are nothing: planning is everything . . .
—DWIGHT D. EISENHOWER, former President of the United States

The reason you write a business plan is to create a document that you can continually review to help you understand where you and your business have been and where you want to go. It is so much more than just some report that you prepare to secure financing, establish credit, impress your suppliers, or secure a location from a landlord. It cannot be written by someone else; to be useful, it must reflect *your* goals, *your* personality, and *your* dreams. It must be *your* business plan.

Before you sit down to write the business plan, there is an old business exercise you should do to help you formulate your thoughts. It is called S.W.O.T.—**S**trengths, **W**eaknesses, **O**pportunities, and **T**hreats.

To begin, take a piece of paper and form four columns. Across the top of the page, mark each column with one of the four initials: **S, W, O,** and **T.** In the columns, write what you think are your business's strengths, weaknesses, opportunities, and threats. Leave it on your desk, sleep on it, and then re-read it the next day to make sure you have hit all the major issues. Add and subtract at will. If you still feel good about your retail concept after some minor, or major, revisions, then you are finally ready to start the business plan.

Just like this book begins with a cover, your business plan should begin with a cover *page*. It does not need to look fancy, but it must look professional. It should include:

- **Title.** Start it with "Business Plan for . . . " so there is no misunderstanding about what the document is all about.
- **Name of business.** Every business needs a name, so don't put "not sure." This may be the factor that forces you to pick a name from those you've been considering.
- **Names of the principals.** Include the names and a brief description of the backgrounds of the owners and any other key personnel who may have an impact on the business.
- **Business address.** If you do not have a physical location yet, use your home address.
- **Contact information.** Always include your phone, fax, and e-mail address.

Table of Contents

Few people read a business plan from cover to cover, so a well-organized table of contents makes it simpler for people to find what they are looking for. The table of contents should list every section with its page number. Chapter headings should be clear and straightforward. "Clever" chapter headings have no place in a business plan.

Mission Statement and Executive Summary

The purpose of this section is to get to the meat of what you want to accomplish so your reader understands the concept without having to read through the entire plan. In fact, the executive summary is often the only section a potential investor will read. Naturally, therefore, it must grab one's attention. And it should generally not exceed two pages.

A good mission statement should capture the big picture, explaining what your company is all about and the reason for its existence. It should describe your business ideas and explain why people will buy from you. It should answer such questions as: Who is the competition? Why is your concept special? What are your advantages?

In more detail, it should cover the following points:

- How are you going to sell the merchandise? This would include "positioning" the store; marketing the products, advertising, and selling to the customer.
- Once you have targeted your market, explain why your plan is well suited to your target audience.
- From your financial plans, explain clearly how much you hope to make, spend, and need to run a profitable business. Prove that the value of your business will increase enough to entice investors.
- Describe who you are and why you can make this business happen. Also, if you have already assembled your team, describe why they are the right people for the job.

Business Description Section

The section directly after the executive summary section should describe the business in more complete detail. It should include:

- Business structure (corporation, partnership, etc.). I describe the possible alternatives later in this chapter.
- Short-term and long-term vision for the business. You have described this briefly before; here is the place to *convince* everyone who reads the document that you know what you're talking about.
- A tag line or slogan. The tag line or slogan (based on the mission statement) should summarize what your business stands for and help your customers, employees, investors, and suppliers understand and remember the essence of your business.
- Location. Include where you plan to locate the business and why that location is especially suited to your business.
- Services and prices. Describe the level of service and prices you will provide and how these compare with competitors.

Business Strategy Section

As the name implies, the business strategy section is where you discuss who or what stands between you and your customer and how you plan to overcome any obstacles you or your investors/partners may foresee. Components of this section include:

- A detailed description of your industry, its current health, and your best estimate of its future. If it is growing, use backup information quoting experts or government or industry reports supporting your claim. If your industry is stable, or even declining, say so. But, at the same time, explain how you plan to buck the trend. In fact, it is quite as important to talk about the problems that may be challenging the industry as it is to talk about the positives. Your investors will believe your optimism far more readily if you temper it with the truth about the hurdles you have to clear. Whatever you say, they know that no business is all honey and roses. They won't believe you if you maintain that yours is.

- Information about the competition:
  - Who they are. It's okay to name names; this document isn't for publication.
  - How long they have been in business.
  - How well they are doing and what plans you suspect they may have for expanding or downsizing in the future.
  - What their strengths and weaknesses are and how you plan to beat their strengths and avoid their weaknesses. How is the competition disappointing its customers, thus providing you with an opening?

Marketing Strategy Section

This section discusses your marketing approach. It gives you the opportunity to explain whether you are self-service, full-service, discount, or regular price. It also talks about your preferred method of reaching customers. It should include:

- **Your market.** Is it local, national, or international? Are customers within walking distance or within five miles? Will you augment your sales—with an Internet site, by telephone selling, with satellite locations (such as ski or beach resorts during the season), etc.?
- **Market share.** Make a reasonable projection of how quickly you can gain a toehold—and then a foothold—into the marketplace. Describe each category of customer and what each is likely to buy, how much of it, and how often. Here's a tip: First make the most conservative estimate of the number of customers you are likely to attract, the amount each is likely to buy, and the minimum frequency with which they seem likely to repeat the purchase. Then calculate what this adds up to in annual sales. Now halve it. If the resulting figure is not enough to make your store a raging success, your business plan is not solid and your business does not have a very good chance of succeeding. Why?

Because of what an old teacher of mine called "The Law of Natural Cussedness," better known as Murphy's Law: If something can go wrong, it will. You'll attract fewer customers than you expect and they'll buy few items less frequently than you expect. Countless problems will conspire to make things worse than you expect. Don't worry—if you've estimated realistically and have forecasted half of what you expect, you'll weather every storm. Then, if you go over forecast, everyone will cheer. Remember, if you forecast one hundred and sell ninety, you're a schmuck; if you forecast fifty and sell the same ninety, you're a genius!

- **Positioning.** How will you stand out from the crowd? How are you going to be perceived by the customers, the community, and the industry at large? What are you going to do to influence this perception? Here is where you describe what your store will look like, including the signage inside and outside the store. Be specific here, not abstract. This rule should apply to the entire document in general.

- **Selling.** How will you entice your customers to buy your merchandise? Describe the actual methods you will use. Are you going to rely purely on storefront retailing? If you plan on using the Internet or a mail-order catalog, provide the details of how this is going to work. This is particularly important if you are forecasting above average success for any particular approach. For example, most catalogs generate purchases from only 1-3% of the catalogs sent out. But some do far better than that, occasionally enjoying returns of 20% or even 25%. If your plan calls for a return of above 3%, you have to be especially persuasive with your investors—and with yourself—about why your forecast is reasonable.

- **Service.** In context with your description of your plan to sell (whatever the channel), describe the levels of service you will provide. Include the status of your selling staff (hourly, salaried, or on commission).

- **Pricing.** Obviously, pricing is one of the most important aspects of retailing. Thus, you must be very clear about your pricing strategy before you start. If you're opening a 99-cent store, your pricing strategy is obvious. If you plan to open a clothing store, do you intend to be high priced, "everyday" priced, or bargain basement? Whatever you chose, be consistent and know why you made the decision you did.

The great cosmetic pioneer, Helena Rubinstein, a screamer when she was crossed, once brought the roof down when she heard that Elizabeth Arden, her arch rival, had not only launched a face cream to compete with Existence, Rubinstein's most revered product, but had actually had the temerity to sell it for *more!*

- **Marketing plan.** What is your message, who will receive it, and how do you plan to communicate this message to others? Advertising is just one part of this process. Discuss all aspects of your marketing plan: public relations, promotions, your marketing calendar, and why your plan will appeal so effectively to your ideal customer.

- **Advertising.** How will you let the customers know about your great business? Discuss the size of your advertising budget and how often and where you plan to spend it. Give a list of the advertising vehicles you plan to use (newspapers, radio, television, magazines, direct mail, Web advertising, etc.). Also, if you plan to recoup some of these funds from co-op advertising offered by vendors, detail that information here.

Financial Plan Section

This is where you show the figures proving that, if you do all the things you said you can do, you *will* be profitable. If there is one section of the business plan that you should always keep close to you, it is the financial plan. It should be updated as often as circumstances change and contain the following vital statistics:

- **Cash flow projection.** In starting your business, your cash flow projection is of the utmost importance. It shows you how much cash you take in each month (including any extra you borrow), and how much you spend (including any debt you repay). If you run out of cash, you're out of business. Thus, you should pore over these figures with the greatest of care. Remember, the amount of cash you have available is stretched by the amount of time your suppliers will let you delay before you pay them. It is shrunk by the amount of inventory you have to buy and by how long you have to hold it. Thus, to maximize your cash flow, you need to keep your inventory for the shortest time possible—"turn" it as rapidly as you can—but pay your suppliers as slowly as they will permit before cutting you off or charging you too much. (Don't worry, all retailers from Wal-Mart to Barnes and Noble pay slowly.)

- **Profit and loss statement.** Called *P & L* for short, this is a summary of the financial activity over a period of time, usually a year. The difference between a cash flow and profit and loss statement is that the P & L reflects non-cash items such as depreciation, but also accounts for the cash you have to lay out for capital items (such as buying a delivery van or a new cash register) that do not lower your profit. Your P&L should correctly reflect your store's profitability. However, even after you start making a profit, you may continue to have a negative cash flow for some time.

    For example, if your sales double from $100,000 to $200,000, your profit may go from $5,000 to $12,000, but you may need $50,000 of extra inventory. You have improved your cash flow but you're running short on cash. So, plan in advance, and when you decide on how much money your new venture will need, it's your cash flow, not your P&L, that is determinant.

- **Balance sheet.** This crucial document shows how much of the business is your own and how much belongs to your financiers. This is important if you are seeking funding because potential investors want to know how committed you are to your business. In the simplest terms, your balance sheet shows assets minus liabilities, with the difference being the business's equals equity or net worth. Assets, the things you own, include cash, inventories, receivables (money or credit owed to the company), equipment, land and buildings, and any trademarks, patents, or copyrights. The assets of the business may also include intangible items called goodwill. If you buy a business for more than the value of its assets minus its liabilities, the difference is goodwill. Liabilities are the monies you owe. Equity, the net worth of your business, is the difference. But of course, it doesn't reflect the real value of your enterprise which, if it is doing well, may actually be worth many times its net worth.

When reviewing your anticipated future balance sheet, a useful rule of thumb is that if your short-term liabilities (i.e., what you owe now or shortly) exceed your short-term assets (i.e., your cash plus what your customers owe you plus the value of the inventory you own), then you may be in difficulties. This ratio of short-term assets to liabilities is called the *current ratio.* If it falls below 1:1, you may be in trouble.

- **Monthly income statements.** These statements, in addition to showing how much profit or loss you expect to make each month, and how much cash you expect to generate or consume, should be arranged so they show which products or departments are bringing in the most profits. They also track the overhead and expenses and pinpoint the business' strongest and weakest areas.
- **Breakeven analysis.** You need to know what volume of business you need to turn a profit at the price at which you are selling your products. Only when you know this can you set realistic goals and chart your business course with confidence. By the way, your backers will be keen to know this too!
- **Sources of funding.** Potential investors will be interested in seeing if you already have any other source(s) of funding. Some sources could include your own savings, a mortgage on the house, cash on a credit card, or a loan from a family member. This kind of funding shows your commitment to the business and reassures potential investors. (See Chapter 4 for a more detailed discussion of funding.)
- **Use of funding.** Having funding means nothing if you do not have a plan to use it. Be sure to itemize what you plan to use the funding for.
- **Start-up costs.** These are the one-time expenses new companies incur, such as furniture, equipment, fixtures, etc.

Management Team Section

Generally, investors in your new business are not betting on your business plan (good though it may be) as much as they are betting on *you*. As a friend of mine says, "I never saw a business plan I didn't like." (Of course—he never sees a plan that promises failure.) The real issue is whether investors believe you can pull it off. Therefore, as I have said before, even if you are the only employee, in your business plan describe your key staff, including their biographies and explanations of their roles, experience, and areas of expertise. For each person, including yourself, give the following:

• Full name and title
• Educational background and/or special training
• Current job and relevant past jobs
• Special skills and talents
• How these talents will be put to use in the new company

Your management plan should also list any planned associations with outside professionals such as accountants, lawyers, or consultants. If you have put together a board of directors or advisers, their names and resumes go a long way especially if they are bankers or well-known current or retired business executives.

Problems and Hurdles

Here is where you talk about what could go wrong with your plan. Landlords and bankers like to see a plan that is well thought-out—that describes both the strengths of your business and also the potential challenges and problems. It's natural to want to downplay these negatives, but resist the temptation to soft-pedal this section of the plan. Professionals will recognize right away that you are holding out on them, and that will hurt your long-term credibility. After identifying possible pitfalls, write a short explanation of how you would respond to each problem. Here are some common risks in retailing:

- **Sales goal are not met.** What will happen to the business?
- **Expenses come in higher than projected.** How will you adjust?
- **Too much merchandise is purchased.** What will you do now?
- **A natural disaster destroys your location.** Do you have enough insurance? Will you rebuild somewhere else?
- **Promotions do not work and all advertising monies are spent.** How would you handle this situation?
- **Wrong merchandise is purchased.** Your customers aren't buying it. What do you do?
- **Good employees aren't found.** What are you going to do until you find them?

Summary Section

Here is where you get one last chance to tell your readers what you want them to remember. Summarize all of your financial plans and remember to accentuate the positive. You may add that you are willing to work longer hours and take less pay in order to build your business. Regardless of what you put here, however, remember to keep this section to one or two paragraphs.

Choosing a Business Structure

Your business structure is the second foundation of your retail model. When starting a business, you need to give it a legal framework. The business structure you choose will affect your taxes, legal liability, profits, and more. Remember that you always have the right to change your business structure at a later date, but for our purposes it is important that you know what those business structures are.

Sole Proprietorship

This is the quickest and easiest route when you are in business for yourself. However, we strongly urge you not to choose this route. For all intents and purposes, the individual owner *is* the business in a sole proprietorship. Thus, *you* pay the taxes incurred by your business. This means that when you pay your federal taxes, your business income will be listed on your individual tax return with a reference to a special form (usually schedule C) that records the profits and losses from your business. If your profits exceed your cash flow, you may owe more than you have cash to pay. Alternatively, if you elect cash accounting (which means you only count cash in versus cash out as "profit"), you'll have the cash available, but if your profit is less than your cash flow, you'll be paying more tax than required.

This discrepancy is what distinguishes a sole proprietorship. However, the main disadvantage with this structure is that you are exposing *all* of your assets to judgments or other debts that may be incurred by the business if something should go amiss. You should never take that level of risk. It's bad enough if your business should go awry. How much worse if you lose your house in the process?

Moreover, it is so simple to incorporate and, done right, you have all the advantages of a sole proprietorship with none of the disadvantages. Your lawyer can incorporate a company for only hundreds of dollars (unless you have an expensive lawyer in which case it will cost a few thousand). On the other hand, if you don't incorporate, here are the risks you run:

- **Personal liability.** The biggest drawback is the "unlimited liability," which means that, as the sole owner, you have sole responsibility for any liability that exceeds your insurance coverage. For example, if someone wins a judgment against you for more than your insurance coverage (or for something for which you are not insured) they can go after your personal assets.
- **Personal credit rating.** If your business goes bad and you pay the bills

late, your personal credit rating is compromised.

- **Taxation.** All income from the business is taxed at personal levels that are higher than corporate levels.

Partnerships

Similar to a sole proprietorship, a partnership is when two or more parties share the responsibilities including decision making, the profits, and the liabilities. Business partners can range from the silent, to the inactive, to the limited, to the very involved. As with sole proprietorships, partnerships are strongly discouraged. If something goes wrong, *both* partners are personally on the hook for the whole loss. Why take that risk when it's easy to set up a corporation owned by your partner and yourself? That way, you have all the advantages of a partnership without the risk of losing everything you own.

There are, of course, considerable potential advantages in having a partner, including:

- **Shared financial responsibilities.** If you do not have enough capital, then bringing in the right partner brings in additional resources.
- **Two heads are better than one.** Assuming that the partner you have brought in is a complement and not a clone of yourself, using the talents of both of you usually results in better decisions.
- **Moral support.** Sometimes you need a partner to bounce ideas off or to raise your spirits. Two people after the same goal push each other to greater heights.

On the flip side, there is one potentially major problem with taking a partner. Like a marriage that blooms in the beginning but ends in acrimony, partners can grow apart or can get on each other's nerves. One partner may not work as hard as the other or not to the same high standards. The partners may disagree over spending or the distribution of profits—one partner preferring to put the profits back into advertising with the other wanting to take out an extra bonus. One partner may decide to sell his part of the business to an outsider the other partner does not approve of. Also, the timing of when to sell the business could cause a major conflict farther down the road.

Even if you have chosen a corporate structure as I recommend, to avoid the potential problems involved in taking a partner, you should both agree on at least the following points:

- What exactly is each partner's role in the company?
- Who is the ultimate decision maker? In my experience, 51/49 ownership deals generally work out better than 50/50 ones.
- What happens if irreconcilable differences arise? The best solution here is to enter into a buy/sell agreement right at the outset. In general, it states that, after a certain amount of time has passed (or a certain level of business is achieved), either party may offer to buy the other out. However, if one partner makes a formal offer, then the other partner may turn the tables and buy out the offering partner at the quoted price (with a reasonable time in which to pay). That insures that the offering partner does not try to pay too little. If he does, he may lose his share for that price.

Corporations

A corporation is a separate legal entity that separates you personally from the business. This means that the corporation enters into agreements, signs contracts, signs leases, and is responsible for the outcome. All liabilities and risks belong to the corporation. Officers and shareholders can come and go, but the incorporated business can continue.

I strongly recommend that your start your business in the form of a corporation, not as a sole proprietorship or partnership. There are almost no disadvantages in doing so, and there are many advantages, including the following:

- A corporation protects you from personal liability. Your individual assets and liabilities are not at risk if the business goes south.

- Transferring ownership by selling, buying, or issuing stock is easy. If an owner dies, the incorporated business is not affected.
- It is easier to raise money for the business because you can sell shares.
- Corporate taxes are lower than personal taxes. Thus, if you want to leave money you earn in the business, you don't have to pay as much tax on it. Of course, if you take out a salary, you still pay personal taxes on that money. But then, as we all know, only death and taxes are inevitable.
- If you prefer, you can organize your business as a Chapter S corporation, or an LLC. These are described in the following sections. It's important that you consult your accountant or a tax attorney before you decide how to incorporate your business.
- The way you run an incorporated business is exactly the same as you would run the business if you were not incorporated. The only difference is that you are supposed to keep certain corporate minutes. However, these can be very limited and take almost no time to prepare. (It's only when you become large and go public that bookkeeping becomes problematic. But, by that time, you'll have a bunch of experts on hand to take care of it.)
- Setting up a corporation and registering it with the state is not expensive. You can even handle it yourself with a kit you can buy at most office supply stores for a few hundred dollars. In either case, this is money very well spent.

Publicly held corporations are traded on the various public stock exchanges like the New York Stock Exchange, the American Stock Exchange, and NASDAQ. The shareholders are typically large numbers of people who have not come in direct contact with each other. Privately held or close corporations are the most common in retailing. In this case, the shares are held by you alone or by you and your investors, partner(s), and key employees. Shareholders may (or may not) sit on your board or participate as officers. These shares are not offered to the general public.

In listing the disadvantages of incorporating your business, I come up blank. There are none.

Chapter S Corporations

This form of corporation is limited to companies with fewer than seventy-five shareholders. The main difference between an S corporation and a regular corporation, known as a *C corporation,* is that an S corporation avoids the risk of double taxation. Double taxation occurs when your corporation makes so much profit that, even after it pays you the maximum salary you can justify (which reduces its profits and therefore its taxes), it still has profits left over. These are taxed at corporate levels and stay in the company. Now, if you want to take out those extra profits, they count as dividends and you pay taxes on them again. (You should be very happy, of course, if you are making that much profit.) However, income from an S corporation is taxed only once as personal income not corporate profits.

For the starting business owner, a major benefit of an S corporation is the ability to take business losses on reductions in personal income. Many businesses experience tax losses in the early years and those losses flow right into the shareholders' personal income, reducing the taxes they pay on other earned income—even on future income.

Limited Liability Corporations

Known as LLC, this is the newest type of corporation, established in the U.S. tax codes in 1988 and adopted in all 50 states. The LLC has the protective benefits of a regular corporation, but works almost the same as an S corporation. The number of members is unlimited and may be individuals, corporations, or any other LLCs.

An LLC can select any form they want for the distribution of profits. Whereas corporations are required to keep at least a minimum of formal minutes, the LLC business structure requires no corporate minutes or resolutions so it is easier to operate by those running the day-to-day business. All your business losses, profits, and expenses flow through the company to the individual members. Thus, you avoid the double taxation of paying corporate tax and individual tax.

Summary

Writing a business plan does not take as long as you might think. Whether you write one or not, you must take the time to research the business, your market, and the competition. The business plan should only be an extension of your research. If you have trouble writing part of it, it is probably because that there is a gap in your research or your thinking. It's better for you to discover such a gap before it's too late to correct.

There are several sources on line that can help you through this whole process. The government small business site at www.sba.gov has all kinds of help to get you focused. The *Wall Street Journal* has a great site for business start ups at www.startupjournal.com, and if you want to see what other business plans look like, go to www.bplans.com. This site helps with business plan writing.

As for business structures, your specific situation will help determine which one is right for you. Depending on the one you choose, be sure to research locally which options apply and have a trusted legal representative do the paperwork for you, or at least have one look over the paperwork you've done yourself.

Retail Detail

According to the May 2004 *American Demographics*, Baby Boomers, born between 1946 and 1964, will account for 50% of the total U.S. consumer spending, which is $2.1 trillion.

Chapter 4

How to Finance Your Business:
You *Can* Do It

If you would know the value of money,
go and try to borrow some.
--Benjamin Franklin

OPENING YOUR OWN STORE may be a dream come true. Paying for this dream may be an entirely different story.

How you structure the finances for your business will have long term effects on your entire life. If it were as easy to get started as digging through your couch to find the change you lost, everyone would be opening stores! It isn't! Unless you are wealthy enough to finance your new store with no financial strain, raising the money you'll need may prove to be one of the toughest challenges you'll ever face.

So, a word of warning: whatever you do, make sure you leave

yourself a few thousand dollars in the bank to pay your living expenses as you grow a business and cover emergencies. Do *not* put every penny you own into this business. You need to get a good night's sleep every night because each morning you need to awake refreshed and ready to conquer the world of retailing.

Self Funding

Lets assume that, by working overtime, perhaps at a couple of jobs, you've been able to stash away a few bucks. If these are funds you've set aside for your retirement or your kids' education, don't touch the money to fund the business. Pulling these funds out may incur hefty penalties, and if you borrow against them, you may have to start paying them back before your business can afford it.

If you have funds from money market accounts, stocks, bonds, and other investments that are not set aside for a specific purpose, they may be enough to get you going. But again, think carefully so you can be sure you keep enough to live on while you are building the business—even if it grows more slowly than you hoped. Remember this: It's always tough to raise money, but when you are desperate for it, it's almost impossible.

Insurance policies may give you the opportunity to cash them out, or if there is cash value accumulated with the policies, you may be able to borrow against them. Make sure there is enough insurance coverage left before you make this decision, because you do not want to leave your family vulnerable if something were to happen to you.

Take a close look at your assets and list the items you own but really do not need. An auction (we Internet junkies love selling stuff on www.ebay.com and several other auction sites), a garage sale, or newspaper ads can turn these items into much needed cash. Big ticket items like extra cars, boats, vacation property, jewelry, art, furniture, and collectibles can raise substantial working capital. With the big ticket items, make sure an appraiser works with you to get the most money for these goods.

Assets you take for granted could be turned into rental income to help with cash flow. Parking spots, garages, basements, storage areas, or even a spare bedroom can produce income to help you start your business or defray living expenses.

Credit Cards

It is very tempting to look at your personal credit cards as a source of money. Don't make this mistake. You need to keep your personal credit and business credit separate no matter how tempting it is to use one for the other. However, you may want to apply for a business credit card. Because they are easier to get than bank loans, this may be helpful. However, two words of warning:

- Make sure you study the interest rate and penalty clauses before you even think of opening a business credit card account.
- Your business credit card should be only a supplement to your financing. If the card is the only way you have found to finance your business, walk away from this dream—at least for a while.

Friends and Family

Most new businesses are financed by entrepreneurs themselves, or by one or more members of their family. Most of us are lucky enough to have a rich parent, sibling, uncle, or cousins! And that's fine, up to a point. After all, where better to get funding than from people you already know and trust and who already know and trust you?

The point to keep in mind is that money has a funny way of souring relationships. Tensions about how the investments made by these family and friends are being used can have a serious effect on relationships. It is amazing how involved relatives who have lent you money become in your business. If you are opening a retail store to give yourself independence, think twice if you plan to finance your store with money from your relatives and friends.

If you do decide to involve relatives, make sure you keep the business side of the relationship separate from the personal side. Sign legal agreements just as you would with other investors. Don't fall prey to the temptation to push these formal arrangements onto the back burner "because it's only good ol' Uncle Maury." If you do, you just might find yourself meeting Uncle Maury in court. And, unless one of your financing relatives is truly an experienced entrepreneur in your industry whose opinion you value, don't invite your relatives onto your board of directors. Nothing is more uncomfortable than entrepreneurs having to justify their actions in front of uninformed relatives.

Above all, before you ask for even a penny from your family and friends, search deep into your heart and ask yourself: "If I lose all their money, how much will I hurt them?" If the answer is more than "a little," find the money elsewhere. There are other ways your loved ones can help you—let them prepare meals for you and your staff, take care of your kids, or help out in your office.

If you really do need to obtain funds from your family—and you are convinced they can afford to lose their investment if things go wrong—try to structure the deal as a loan rather than as equity. Rather than making them part owners of the company, borrow the money and pay it back with interest as soon as you can. That helps to keep relatives out of your hair.

Banks

Today's bankers, unlike the bankers of our parents' generation, seldom have the discretionary authority to grant loans based on their own gut feeling that you are a good risk. Rather, they are only allowed to make a loan to you if it fits the bank's impersonal criteria.

A bank is a retailer just like you. It sells money. Like any good retailer, the bank relies on repeat, steady customers. They even run sales like retailers, such as specials on car loans or a toaster when you open a new account. Like retailers, banks need to make a profit to survive. However, with the major bank mergers of today, there is a drive to increase profit and reduce risk. To this end, huge acquiring banks have replaced the personal banking relationship with statistically based systems. Instead of trusting you, the new type of bank manager relies on a microscopic dissection of your life and business.

The first thing he wants to see is your business plan. Assuming that passes muster—in the bank's opinion the plan is workable, protects the bank from losses, and is likely to generate a comfortable profit—the next step is to review your personal financial standing. The banks will almost never lend you money at the start of a new business without either your personal guarantee (which means you are putting up everything you own as collateral for your debt), or a specific piece of collateral such as your house. One way or the other, the bank wants to make sure you have enough money available to repay their loan even if the business fails. Banks today are information collectors, not your friend. Their focus is on the facts and formulas of *their* business, not on the excitement and potential of *yours*. In fact, your friendly bank manager doesn't even have the authority to make a loan. That is up to a bank committee—whose only interest is in the strength of your collateral.

Of course, banks will loan you money; that's how they make theirs. But, in addition to demanding a personal guarantee, they will want you to make an investment. Banks are much more likely to loan you 60% of what you need if you put up 40%. So if you need $100,000 to open a store, the bank is likely to loan you $60,000 if you put up $40,000 and personally guarantee the rest.

Your local bank sees lots of entrepreneurs with dreams. Most do not have a clue about business financing. Set yourself apart by coming across as a capable professional. First, dress the part. Except perhaps in Southern California, business casual does not apply to bankers. Second, make sure your banker understands that your number one priority is your business. Come professionally prepared with your business plan, list of assets, and financial projections.

Here are some rules to follow when dealing with today's banker.

1. Never rely on what the banker tells you in person. Always get everything in writing. If you are ever forced into court, oral agreements will be hard to prove, and, in the absence of proof, they will be disregarded.

2. Don't sign anything without first carefully reading every document. Always have the banker send you the documents you are to sign in advance so you do not get caught up in the pressure of making decisions at the closing.

3. Jury trial waivers, replacing jury trials with binding arbitration, are becoming more common in business loans. Generally, they are desirable for you. Arbitrators generally find a solution that splits the difference between arguing parties. That is usually better than having to spend huge sums on legal fees to fight a bank with deep pockets and to do so in front of a jury. Even if you win, your legal costs will kill you.

4. Try to avoid signing a liability release, a clause that is showing up more and more in bank loan documents. A liability release says if you go out of business after the loan is approved, the bank cannot be held responsible—even if the reason you are broke is that the bank unfairly called the loan.

5. Your banker's allegiance is to the bank, even though you may have grown up with him and you knew him as a friend. Banks are not in the business of lending you money; they are in the business of collecting the bank's money.

SBA Loans

The small business administration is a government agency that, if they like your business prospects, will offer bank loans to small businesses. The basic 7(a) loan guarantee is the SBA's primary business loan program to help qualified small businesses obtain financing that they could not get otherwise. Loan maturity is up to 10 years for working capital and generally up to 25 years for fixed assets. These loans are made through commercial lending institutions (called "participants") and are guaranteed by the government.

Not all banks choose to participate, but most do, and some non-bank lenders will also make loans. However, please note that the SBA will only guarantee a portion of any loan so the lender and SBA share the risk if a borrower cannot repay. Thus, chances are, you will still have to put up some of your own collateral, just not as much.

If the SBA loan is the avenue you take, be prepared for a drawn out affair. Not only do you have to fill out everything the bank needs to know about you, but now you must also fill out all kinds of government forms and meet government investment criteria. I have never met an entrepreneur who enjoyed this process! But through all the pain, you should not forget that this great program has allowed entrepreneurs throughout the country to live a dream that, without the SBA, they could never have financed. For more information, go to www.sba.gov.

Angel Investors

Angel investors are often veteran entrepreneurs who once started, built, and sold their own companies—often in a field akin to yours. Usually they provide the seed money for the first round of business growth in exchange for a share of your company. Most angels look for proof of your own investment in the company, so do not expect an angel to put money in unless you do. Angels are not easy to find; it's usually a question of who you know and lots of networking. However, if you can find one, you have the advantage that he or she knows about your business and will be less impatient about setbacks that are not your fault than will a banker who looks only at the numbers.

Venture Capital

If a bank says no, you might consider contacting a venture capital firm (VC). VCs typically demand a very high percentage of equity for their investment. Ownership at 70 to 80% is not uncommon. Moreover, VCs are a very tough bunch. They are exposed to dozens of business plans and fund only a tiny percentage. They are often frustrating for entrepreneurs because they require a huge return on their investment, often as much as ten times in three to five years. On the other hand, VCs can open doors that you would never be able to open on your own. Their contacts with influential and wealthy individuals and companies can provide you with customers you would never have known. And they can sometimes help you grow faster than you could on your own.

Strategic Investors

Finally, and often very helpfully, there are strategic investors who will lend you money or, occasionally, invest equity in your business because your success also helps them in other ways. They will rarely give you all the money you need; but they will often give you a major backup.

Typical strategic investors are suppliers who may invest by giving you inventory to sell but allowing you six months or even a full year to pay. Obviously, this is a way of providing you with cash flow—you collect the money from the inventory you sell long before you have to pay the suppliers. Similarly, your landlord or the firm that supplies the fixtures for your store may waive the payments in return for a share of the business.

Slightly further removed, advertising agents, insurance brokers, or even temporary help agencies (if they expect that you will be hiring lots of temps) may loan you money on the condition that you use their services.

Summary

The way you finance the business has long-term effects on your wealth. Doing it all yourself (unless you are rich enough to handle it) could leave you so strapped for daily living expenses that you lose the joy of running your own business. Giving too much of the company away could leave you bitter as you slave away to support your investors. So, deciding on the right balance is a matter of the art of the possible and your own gut feel. It's a tough, exciting call. And that is the reason you became an entrepreneur . . . right?

Chapter 5

Basics of Retail Math, Or:
Crunching the Numbers

*Retailing is all about change, because consumers change
and so do their tastes.
If you don't change, you don't grow.*
—MARVIN TRAUB, former CEO of Bloomingdale's

FINANCIAL FREEDOM. Setting your own schedule. Being your own boss. Take your pick: no matter what your collateral reasons for opening a retail store, the numbers are obviously what drive your decision to invest the large and intense amount of time and effort it takes to build a business you can call your own.

If you're anything like me, seeing a lot of numbers all at once can be intimidating. Initially, that is. However, as the saying goes, there is "strength in numbers." In fact, having a basic understanding of how to interpret these numbers makes many decisions that seem gray at first quite black and white.

This chapter touches on the meaning of the basic numbers you'll encounter in the retail business. If you are coming from another industry, such as manufacturing or real estate, the way retailers figure their numbers may look a little strange to you. Most other industries deal with markups, the profit as a percentage of cost; retailers deal in margins, profit as a percentage of retail selling price.

Retailers typically keep a two-column ledger in order to fully understand what is going on with their business. In the left column, they keep a running record of the cost of the merchandise, the landed price including the cost of goods and shipping costs. In the right column, they keep a running record of the retail value of the merchandise, the sum of the retail price tickets on all the items in the store.

This method lets you keep track of the markdowns in the right column so you can see at a glance the profitability of an item, department, and store. Also, this approach shows you the profit or loss in the month it occurs, and resets the margin for the new month, giving you a true month-to-month comparison. Make sure that any accountant you involve with your business fully understands retail accounting. If not, you could truly be at a loss.

Under the retail methodology, the selling price of an item is always 100%. Therefore, both **cost** (the amount you pay for an item) and **markup** (the amount by which you increase the price to cover your expenses and profit) must equal 100%.

For instance, if you paid $0.55 for a spatula and sold it for $1.00, your gross profit *margin* would be $0.45 (45%) and your cost of goods would be $0.55 (55%). (In other industries, the $0.45 profit might be expressed as a percentage of cost, giving you a *markup* of about 82%.)

Health of Your Business

To determine how well or (perish the thought) how badly their business is doing, retailers routinely compare each month with the same month a year prior. This is because, given the large seasonal swings almost all retailers experience, there is little meaning in comparing this month's sales with last month's. So, if this February you did $110,000 in sales and last February you did $100,000, your business would be 10% ahead of last year. And, if this continues for a while, you can be happy with your trend. Of course, if the numbers were reversed and you did $100,000 this year and $110,000 last, you would be 9% behind, and you would have to take prompt remedial action.

In looking at these figures, you must exclude new stores or departments you opened. To determine how healthy your business is, the comparison between years must be apples to apples, that is, same store performance.

Establishing Initial Margin

To discuss the retail concept of margin it is important to have a few definitions under our belts first. For starters:

- **Cost.** *Cost of Goods (COG)* is what you pay the vendor for products.
- **Retail.** *Selling Price of Merchandise* is what your customers pay the store for these goods.
- **Initial Margin $.** *Initial Margin* is the difference between retail and cost (Retail − Cost = IM$), expressed as a percentage of retail.

So, if you buy a shirt for $3 and sell it for $7, your initial margin is $4 or 59.1%. If you (like me) didn't pay attention in ninth grade algebra, let me give you a quick update. (If you, unlike me, were an algebraic whiz kid, please skip this section.)

In retailing there are three ingredients needed to figure out what your margin is and what the margin should be. If you know two out of three, calculate the third. Then, you can decide whether or not what you have to pay fits into your business plan. Let's run through a few examples.

- **When cost and retail are known (and you want to find out what your margin percentage will be):**

  $$\frac{retail - cost}{retail} = \text{ initial margin \%}$$

  Example: If you buy a lamp for $6 and it retails for $10, initial margin % is

  $$\frac{10 - 6}{10} = \frac{4}{10} = 40\%$$

- **When cost and margin percentage are known (and you want to figure out what the retail should be):**

  $$retail = \frac{cost}{100\% - \text{margin \%}*}$$

  If you know you want to maintain a margin of 55% on the children's clothing and a vendor offers you girls' pants for $5, the retail price you need to charge would be

  $$\frac{\$5}{100\% - 55\%} = \frac{\$5}{45\%} = \$11.11$$

- **When retail and margin percentage are known and you want to find out what you can afford to pay the vendor, the calculation is**

  $$\text{Cost} = \text{Retail} \times (100\% - \text{margin \%})$$

  For your white sale event, you need full sheets to retail for $6.88 and you know that you want to work on a 39% margin. What can you afford to pay for each sheet? Cost is

  $$\$6.88 \times (100\% - 39\% = 61\%) = \$4.20$$

Inventory Turn

Turnover of inventory, or **turn**, is the calculation of how many times you sell and replenish the merchandise in your store over the course of a year. To figure out your turn, divide your annual sales by your average inven-

---

*100% − margin percentage is also known as the cost percentage or the **cost complement** because adding this cost percentage to the margin percentage should always equal 100%.

tory (at retail). For instance, if your sales are $400,000 for the year and your average retail is $100,000, your turn is 4. The more times you can turn over your inventory, the better it is because:

• You will have less older merchandise.
• You will have more opportunities to buy, which should lead to better buys.
• The inventory will be more up-to-date.
• Less money will be tied up in inventory.
• You'll make more profit on your invested capital. (If you need $100,000 of inventory—tied up capital—to feed $400,000 worth of sales and profits, you're obviously better off than if you need double that inventory for the same results.)

Stock to sales ratio is the monthly view of turnover. It is the amount of merchandise in the store at the beginning of a given month divided by the amount of sales of merchandise for the month. It provides you with a quick view on how well you manage the inventory. For instance, if you have inventory of $120,000 and $30,000 in sales for the month, then your stock to sales ratio is four to one. This means that it will take four months of selling at your current rate to sell through the average monthly inventory.

Knowing that there are twelve months in a year, this means you are turning your goods at the rate of three times a year (twelve months divided by a four stock-to-sales ratio). However, if your (realistic) goal is to achieve a stock-to-sales ratio of three to one, that is a turn of four—you are overstocking and need to find ways to operate on less inventory or to sell more!

Your ultimate goal should always be to develop the highest level of sales from the smallest possible inventory. But be careful what you wish for. If you try to push your turns too high, you may run out of merchandise that your customers want, and they may go elsewhere.

The number of turns for which you should aim varies by type of retailer. Thus, before you set your target, you should find out what is the industry norm is. Actually, this is another reason to belong to the trade association most related to your type of retail store. Such organizations can give you the average guidelines for turn and stock to sales ratios for different seasons that should help you keep the right amount of inventory on hand, particularly through your first few years in business.

You should review your turnover ratio every week. The higher the turnover, the stronger the retail business will be. With a high turnover, you have less money invested in the inventory at any given time and a lower risk of carrying products your customers do not want to buy. You get higher sales from the same amount of space, have fresher goods in the store, and can always feature new items to tempt your customers. There's nothing more disappointing to a repeat customer than seeing nothing but the same old stuff.

While turn rates are innately different between different categories of retail, within each category there are two basic, and quite different, strategies that you must decide upon when setting your turnover objectives:

1. High margin, high price, and low turnover
2. Low margin, low price, and high turnover

A low turnover item must give you a high margin in order to pay the rent for sitting on your shelf for a long time. In contrast, a high turnover item obviously has to pay less rent, and therefore can make a lower margin. Strategically, you can mix these two turnover concepts as long as one dominates the other so you are giving a clear message to the customers. For instance, in your toy department, you may price Barbie at cost to create a high turn, but price her accessories higher to create more margin, expecting that customers who buy Barbie because of the price will pick up the other items because no little girl can exist without at least three new outfits for her doll!

Obviously, you want to turn all your merchandise as quickly as possible. The trick is to recognize that you may have to stock low turnover items as a service to your customers to induce them to come to your store and buy the more popular items.

For example, a well-known cosmetic company's president was delving through his firm's lipstick sales and discovered that, of the ninety-six shades they marketed, four did 81% of the business, ten did 94% of the business, and fifteen did 98% of the business. His first thought was to discontinue all but the fast-selling four. Fortunately for him, wiser heads prevailed and the company kept fifteen shades and discontinued the rest. "We'll save so much inventory by eliminating eighty-one shades, we'll increase our profits even if we lose the whole two percent of sales that are in the discontinued shades," the president explained. "In any case, most of the women buying those shades will probably switch to the ones we're keeping."

The result? Sales fell to about half. A large majority of women were buying the same fifteen shades, but they wanted to feel they had a huge choice. They were offended to think that the company was, in effect, deciding the shade for them.

The president not only reinstated the missing shades, he increased their number to 125. The result? Sales grew to about 30% more than the original level—but women still almost exclusively bought the same fifteen shades!

Yes, providing a good selection is often part of pleasing your customers. But it has a cost. **Slow Turn** causes:

- Slow-moving merchandise to clog your shelves and make it harder for customers to find the goods they want
- Excessive accumulation of old styles, odd sizes, and extreme colors
- Increased expenses
- Deeper markdowns and the need to run them more often

The challenge is to balance the inventory level against the service level you want to provide your customers. As I said, it's a balancing act. Too high a turn will produce too many out-of-stock situations and hence lost sales and disgruntled, often non-returning, customers. Too low a turnover could put you out of business.

Determining How Much Margin to Go After

Remember the retailer's creed: Always strive to squeeze as much margin as possible. The more margin you can extract from one item, the more money you have to cut prices (and margins) on the products and deals that drive traffic through your store. However, when trying to raise margins, you must bear in mind what the consumer is willing to pay *in your store environment*. If you are a discount store, you cannot expect to make the same margin the department store down the street makes on the same item. In your store, your customers are only in the mood for bargains.

In general, margin decisions should be based on:

- **Competitors' retail.** If an item is carried throughout your trading area and it's an item you cannot do without, you must decide if you are going to be parity priced with everyone else or have the lowest price in town. Having the lowest price will hurt your overall margin, but it may increase turn and build customer traffic.

- **Last year's sales on this item or a similar product.** Once you have a history of an item, you can determine how price-sensitive it is and if you have room to get more margin.

- **Planned turnover of an item.** If you expect sales to be limited and you're carrying the item only as a convenience for the customers, take the extra margin. I always thought the president of the cosmetics company I referred to earlier should have up-priced all the colors that hardly sold and called them "premium shades"! Not only would he have improved his margins, but I bet he would have sold more of those shades. Cosmetics buyers are always looking for something "exclusive."

- **Wholesale costs.** Be sure to shop around among wholesalers (if you are not dealing directly with the manufacturer) to see if you can reduce the price you are paying. Even a few pennies saved can accumulate into good margin gains at the end of the year. Most retailers make a pre-tax profit of between 2% and 8% of sales; only in rare cases do their pre-tax profits exceed 10%.

Let's assume that your pre-tax profit is 5% of sales. Now, if you can cut the cost of your purchases so your margin increases by 2%, for example, by paying $6.00 for an item you sell for $10.00 instead of paying $6.25, that extra $0.25 drops to your bottom line. That means that your pre-tax profit increases from $0.50 to $0.75—a whopping 50% increase in your profits!

If you can make a 2.5% improvement on all the cost of all merchandise you sell, and your annual sales are $1,000,000, then your pre-tax profit would rise from $50,000 to $75,000. Not bad! Certainly worth pushing your suppliers to give you some price breaks. Because there are no additional expenses, that extra $0.25 drops to your bottom line and you make $0.50 for every $10.00 of merchandise you sell.

- **Manufacturers suggested retail.** Although this is only a guideline, it gives you a sense of the worth of products. If you are a discounter, this also allows you to prove to your customers how much you have cut your price.

- **Handling and selling costs.** Products can vary dramatically in what they cost to sell. Some products (like glassware) break easily so customers or sales people are likely to damage a certain percentage of the stock. Certain goods have a tendency to disappear because of shoplifting (electronics). Others are extremely heavy or awkward to move from the warehouse to the selling floor, so the freight and handling costs may be high. Some may be shipped from across the street while others may be coming from across the country, so transportation costs need to be considered. Some goods may come in pre-ticketed while others require a lot of handling and ticketing in the store, adding to your cost. Some goods tend to have a high return rate. All these costs need to be factored into the product's retail price. A brittle, faddy, easily stolen article with a 60% margin may actually be less profitable than a solid "evergreen" product with a 40% margin.

- **Nature of the goods.** If you are dealing in fad- or fashion-oriented merchandise (which includes everything from fashions themselves to cosmetics to toys to novelties that come and go—remember the Pet

Rock?), know what an item's likely shelf life is. How will the manufacturer help with markdowns? These, too, are factors you need to consider when thinking through how to price merchandise and how much initial margin to achieve.

- **Correlation among departments.** For instance, infant clothing should not be selling higher than boys and girls clothing.
- **Demand and supply of goods.** If you have the exclusive distribution of a hot item, you can usually squeeze out additional margin. If there is a high demand but short supply, and you find there is little price resistance for an item, you can get additional margin there as well.

How to Increase Your Margin

Obviously, the question here becomes, "How do I increase my margin?" An additional question must be, "How do I increase my margin while still keeping my customers happy and therefore my sales rising?" Relax. There are several different tactics you can use to help increase your margin without changing the customer's experience in the store.

Import Merchandise

It sounds complicated at first glance. However, importing merchandise can take on several different phases as your store grows. You may want to start off small, dealing with an importer using his label on the products. Once you reach a certain volume, however, you may be able to bring in your own private label products at considerably lower cost. In addition to saving money, here are some reasons to look into importing:

1. **No middle man.** If you are dealing with an importer directly or eventually importing your own products, you have eliminated the wholesaler or distributor from whom you were buying the goods. Thus, you have added their margin to your own.

2. **Control.** Once you establish a personal relationship with the overseas manufacturer, you may better control the quality, quantity, and timeliness of the merchandise you are buying.

3. **Exclusivity.** By importing a product featuring your name (and, possibly, your specifications), you can display an item that no competitor carries. That means you can sell it for whatever the market will bear without having to worry too much about what your competitors are doing.

4. **Competitive Retail.** You can bring in a high quality, private label item to compete effectively with a higher-priced, branded product carried by your competitors. In this way, you may be able to enhance your low price reputation while still maintaining a comfortable margin.

Cash Discounts

Vendors are generally forced to extend credit. However, because cash is king to them, they often encourage you to pay before the due date by offering you a cash discount for early payment or a payment in advance of a specific date. Among the more common cash discounts are:

1. **3/10 EOM.** A discount of 3% if the invoice is paid within ten days from the end of the month.

2. **2/10 Net 30.** A discount of 2% if the invoice is paid within ten days from the date it is issued. Ten is the number of days the rate is available. Thirty is the number of days within which the invoice must be paid.

3. **3/10 ROG:** A discount of 3% if the invoice is paid within ten days of receipt of goods.

Delivery Terms

Delivery terms indicate when and where the title of the merchandise passes from the seller to the buyer. That is the time and place at which your risk of ownership begins. From that time and place, you own the goods and you pay for insurance and transportation. Therefore, you can save money by delaying the point at which you actually take possession of the merchandise. Two common delivery terms are:

1. **FOB Factory.** Your store owns the goods as soon as the carrier picks the shipment up at the factory. That means you pay the freight from there.

2. **FOB Warehouse or Store.** In this case, because the seller owns the goods until they arrive at your location, the seller pays freight, insurance, etc.

Dating

Dating extends the time by which you have to pay for merchandise. As the saying goes, "Time is money." Dating is valuable for two reasons. The first reason is the interest you save on the money that you keep under your control for longer. This value depends on the prevailing rate at which you can borrow money. For instance, if interest rates are 12% per annum (as they were some years ago), then adding an additional month before you have to pay is worth 1% of the money you owe. If interest rates are 6%, that translates into a half percent gain each month. Always ask for additional dating.

The second reason, and often the more determinant one, is that you are likely to find that, like most retailers, you are chronically short of cash. This is not necessarily unhealthy (although it is uncomfortable) because there is a good reason for it.

If your business is growing (as you hope and intend that it will), you need more inventory. Even if your turn is a very impressive six times a year, in the short run you are still putting out more cash than you are collecting—six times a year turn means you have to buy two months of extra inventory to service your growth. Typically, you have to pay for the extra inventory in one month. Of course, you'll get your money back in time, plus the profit on the extra volume, but you'll be strapped until then. Dating helps overcome this problem. Fortunately, it also helps your supplier because you can buy, display, and sell more of his merchandise.

Dating is always helpful, but there are occasion when you have a particularly strong argument to ask for it. Two such occasions are:

1. **Opening a new store.** The goods will be sitting in a store with no chance of selling or turning until the store opens, usually for thirty days.

2. **Shipping to a warehouse instead of a store.** The store loses the turn-around time it takes to get goods out of the warehouse. Goods could sit in a warehouse for thirty days or more before moving to the store.

Markdowns

As the name implies, to mark something down means to reduce the original retail price. Markdowns are taken for three rather different sets of reasons:

1. To speed the sale of slow moving products; to clear your inventory of odd sizes, colors, and styles, and to encourage the sale of soiled or damaged goods

2. To maintain price competition with other stores

3. To create the excitement of a special sale (the "happiest" of the three reasons because, while you'll still lower your margins, you'll boost your sales)

Other Retail Practices Used to Change Prices

Since the price you charge your customers will always affect your bottom line, you can never overestimate or underestimate the importance of price. Here are some other retail practices sometimes used to change prices:

- **Additional Markup.** As the name implies, this practice changes the price upward. It is mostly used in one of the following occasions:
  - A special sale is run at a marked down price, then the price is marked up to its previous level after the sale.
  - A vendor increases the price on the next shipment of a certain item. Because the competition will be forced to increase their prices, those items already in your store are marked up.
- **Mark Up Cancellation.** When you introduce a new item into your store, you may initially mark it up in order to establish a high price. Then, once that value is established, you may cancel the additional mark up and reduce the merchandise for a special sale. To some extent, you may be able to use the extra margin you earn when you first bring the item in (and it's still new and exciting enough to attract customers in spite of its higher price) to help finance the lower margin sale you run subsequently.

Open to Buy

The purpose of an Open to Buy, or OTB, system is to tell you exactly how much merchandise you must purchase to satisfy the amount of inventory you have budgeted for a specified period of time, usually one month. The simplified way of looking at OTB is:

Planned end-of-month (EOM) inventory for March	$100,000
Plus planned sales for March	+$40,000
Plus planned Markdowns for March	+$ 2,000
Minus merchandise on order and due to arrive in March	−$15,000
Minus BOM (beginning of month) inventory for March	−$90,000
Open to Buy	$37,000

Before you ever commit to buying product, you must have your OTB plan in front of you. That way, you'll know *when* you need (and can afford) to buy new merchandise. You may not have the money to bring it in during March, but with your plan in front of you, you'll be able to see that there is room during the first week of April. Without your OTB plan, you may inadvertently overextend yourself. You may be the best buyer in the world, but if you do not have the money to pay for goods, you won't last long in retailing.

The only way to stay on top of this crucial facet of the business is to have a plan. The first step in developing this plan is to project your sales *by month* for the first year. Of course, this is a moving target, so you need to re-project them, or make sure your prior projection is still on target, at the start of every month.

The second step in your planning is to establish the turn of your inventory so you know how much inventory you will need at the start of each month to feed your projected sales. Once you know your sales and turn, you can quickly calculate your OTB to see how much to purchase each month. If, during the year, you are trending up or down in sales, OTB can easily be adjusted to meet those specific needs. Like all of the retail math tools we're discussing here, look at this OTB as a tool for success, not something that will get in your way.

Retail Method of Inventory, Or:

Stopping Shrinkage

Shortages, also called *shrinkage of inventory* or just *shrinkage*, can cause a store to go out of business, fast. That is why it is important to have procedures in place to keep track of everything happening in the store, from receipt of goods to final sale. There are two definitions of inventory:

1. **Physical inventory.** This is the counting of the stock that is actually on hand.
2. **Book inventory.** This is the record of what *should* be on hand. To derive the book inventory, begin with the starting inventory (either

from store opening or the results of last year's physical inventory). Add all purchases, all returns that are in saleable condition, and any make-goods the vendor may have provided for substandard merchandise. Subtract all sales and the amount of any markdowns that were below the price you paid for the goods.

Shrinkage, or overage, is the difference between the physical inventory and the book inventory. The only cause for an overage is a booking error that should be avoided by double-checking everything. Some shrinkage is inevitable, and you need to plan for it. It represents the loss of merchandise for reasons that cannot be precisely specified. Those reasons include:

- Vendor mistakes or fraud. Sometimes, containers don't include the full count of goods.
- Employee theft. This includes outright theft for profit (e.g., letting a few cases "fall off the back of a truck"), pilfering merchandise for personal use (taking home a box of detergent), and using store merchandise for legitimate reasons but without paying for it (a store clerk who needs a pencil opens a pack of a dozen and tosses the rest).
- External theft. The most frequent method of external theft is shoplifting. More rarely, theft from your warehouses may occur.
- Clerical mistakes and bookkeeping errors.
- Unrecorded markdowns and allowances. These result in the quantity of product sold for the dollar volume recorded actually being greater than the recorded amount. For example, if you mark down a $10.00 item to $5.00 but fail to note the markdown on your books, selling $100.00 worth of that item will sell twenty items but only show ten as having sold. The missing ten items will show up as inventory shrinkage.
- Unrecorded breakage.

How to Minimize Shrinkage

Some shrinkage may be unavoidable, but a majority of the loss is preventable. Whether the issue is sloppy record-keeping or neighborhood hooligans taking a "five-finger discount," take the following steps to minimize shortages:

- Record merchandise as soon as it arrives.
- Properly mark, price, and identify merchandise before moving it to the selling floor.
- Record all price changes.
- Record each transaction.
- Change records before transferring goods or returning them to the vendor.
- Take precaution against theft, as discussed in the following sections.

Shrinkage from all causes has become a bigger problem than ever, particularly for first-time retail business owners for whom paperwork can easily become an overwhelming chore. In fact, the problem has become so prevalent that a 2% loss in shrinkage is a standard of the industry today. As discussed earlier, a positive change in the cost of goods has a huge impact on your bottom line. Unfortunately, shrinkage has exactly the same effect—in reverse! In addition to keeping careful records, there are several things you can do to curb shrinkage.

Employee Theft

Your employees should be the last people to steal from you. After all, you're the one signing their checks! Unfortunately, the opposite is true: *most* employees steal from their employers.

The incidence of employee theft is high in retailing. Employees have greater access to a wide range of consumer goods that they either desire for themselves or know they can resell on the black market. Moreover, employees often view what they take as trivial and don't consider it stealing. "So, I ate a muffin without paying for it; I was hungry." The office employee's equivalent is taking home some ballpoint pens and pads of paper. However, trivial or not, these thefts add up, and their financial impact goes way beyond the items stolen because it reduces your store's productivity, lowers turnover, inhibits hiring, and makes your store less viable.

In addition to casual pilfering, you may well face planned thievery, the willful theft of merchandise, supplies, or cash. Conspiracy with shoplifters or delivery persons is also common.

Shoplifting

Shoplifting is a major problem, especially of smaller, easily hidden items in general merchandise retailers, and of expensive items in larger stores. While most shoplifters simply try to slip some easily hidden items into their pockets or bags, some shoplifters are more sophisticated.

To give you some idea of how tricky they can be, one of their favorite tricks works like this: The criminal legally purchases an expensive article of clothing or an electronic device, takes it out of the store, removes the tags, leaves the item outside, and returns to the store with the tags and the receipt. Back inside, the thief picks out an identical item, takes it to the dressing room or some quiet corner of the store, and removes the tags. Next, he or she takes the item, without the tags, to the return desk, hands it and the receipt and tags from the legitimately purchased item to the harried clerk, and receives a refund. Unless a store security person actually catches the thief removing the tags, it's hard to prove that the second item is not the first one. Even if each item is numbered sequentially so the serial number on the item does not match the receipt (something the clerk at the return desk is unlikely to notice) it is difficult to use that as proof of a scam when the thief can claim that the serial number was incorrectly recorded on the item. Some thieves even have the gall to go to another store in the same chain and return the first item, claiming they lost the tags. Others sell the items to a fence.

Strengthening Store Security

A secure store is a store that is experiencing less shrinkage than its competitors. Security may be costly, but so is shrinkage. Often the mere appearance of security, to both your customers and your employees, is enough to do the trick. Here are some timely tips for strengthening your store's security:

1. Equip the store with a security alarm system hooked up to a central service company. Give each employee his or her own code so you can monitor who comes and goes.
2. Use locked trash dumpsters to decrease the risk of merchandise being thrown into the dumpster and retrieved later.
3. Do not permit personnel to park near loading docks or exit doors. A longer walk to stash or transport items can be a real deterrent to employee theft.
4. Strictly enforce inventory control and tracking procedures.
5. Follow up on all references when hiring any new employee.
6. Implement an anonymous tip program that motivates employees to report theft, drug abuse, and other business abuses by both coworkers and outsiders.
7. Keep a close tab on customers who spend a lot of time in your store. The closer you watch, the less likely a shoplifter is to target your store.
8. Place observation cameras at strategic locations. As long as the red lights blink, they can be fake cameras. One fast-food chain I know has three dummy cameras that appear to be hidden but are easily observed by employees when they are peering down at the cash register. They are inexpensive because they don't work! However, the store also has one real camera that is very well hidden. Employees who decide to raid the cash register naturally turn away from the three cameras they think are observing them, shielding their misdeeds with their bodies. What they don't realize is that they have turned directly to face the working, well-hidden camera. They are surprised when, a week or two later, they are laid off without explanation. The company never actu-

ally accuses them of stealing; if it did, it would have to reveal the presence of the hidden camera, and then the game would be over.

Parting Words

As we have seen throughout this chapter, retail is, indeed, a numbers game. Here we have provided you with the basics of retail math. Still, they are only the basics. Along the way, you will encounter nuances of retail numbers that will only add to your experience in this competitive, thriving, and ultimately rewarding field. I hope that, like the rest of the chapters in the book, this chapter was interactive. In other words, don't be a passive reader—take what I'm offering and apply it to your own situation, either today or tomorrow. Or next year.

Knowledge is the key to success. Knowing the numbers before you start your retailing adventure is vital to your success. Certainly there is a lot to learn, but know this: Understanding the basics will help you fine tune the rest and, in the meantime, will keep you alive and well, the latest addition to the thriving retail industry.

Retail Detail

There are 46,336 shopping centers in the United States, 95% of which are strip centers. There are 1,182 enclosed malls in the United States. In a typical month, 201 million adults shop at shopping centers. That's 94% of people over eighteen.

Chapter 6

Searching for the Promised Land,
Or:
Finding the Right Location for Your Store

*African-Americans place a much greater importance on stores being
involved in the community and having black elements or cultural
cures, things that make them feel more comfortable in a store.
For instance, having staff who are African-American,
an environment where other African-Americans shop,
and more products of a particular interest to them.*
—JANICE JONES, Director of Research Food Marketing Institute

W HEN BEGINNING YOUR SEARCH for that perfect store location, always remember the following maxim: Whereas a *good* location may not guarantee success, a *bad* location will almost always guarantee failure.

You can do all the hiring, recruiting, training, and retaining you want, but in the end, one fact holds true—the retail business itself, the actual location of the building, needs to be where the *customers* are. After all, the law of averages says that, all things being equal, the more people who can get to your store, the more chances you have of selling them something.

Traffic is a must; whether it's by foot, bus, train, plane, or car, the more of it, the better. Quantity can't stand alone, however. The store's location must have quality as well. Other factors to consider are a location with a reasonable degree of security, access to public transportation for both your customers and your employees, adequate parking for both your customers and employees, enough room for adequate selling space *and* a stockroom *and* an office, and restrooms (at least for your employees). A break room and restrooms for your customers don't hurt, either, especially if you have a large store.

Where you locate your store will determine the hours you keep, the customers you attract, and the types of promotions you can run. Your location will also impact how quickly you can grow. Therefore, we need to be looking at the location from every angle, starting with how it affects you.

Getting Personal:

The Personal Angle

Retailing is more than just a way to gain financial and professional freedom. When you commit to retailing, the life of clocking in and out is over. Holidays, vacations, and 9-to-5 workdays are over. Now, heart and soul, you are building your dream. You wouldn't have time to look at your watch even if you wanted to! When is it time to call it quits for the day? When the work is done—which seems to be just about never.

The rewards of retailing are great. Your own store—your own store!—is worth fighting for. Once it succeeds, you will be set for life. At first, however, it will be a struggle. Fortunately, you can make it less of a struggle by making good decisions based on quality research.

One of the most important decisions you will ever make is where to put your store and, since you'll be there so much of the time, your personal considerations are a great place to start.

Lifestyle Issues

The reality is that your store could be open twelve to fourteen hours a day. In some locations and types of retail, it could be twenty-four hours. In the beginning and perhaps for some time to come, you will probably want to be there for a good portion of that time. That's only natural. Moreover, keep in mind that if, for example, your night manager quits, it will be up to you to keep the doors open until you can find a replacement. Clearly, this sort of lifestyle has a major impact on your family and your home life, and quite possibly your health. Anyone going into retailing must have an understanding family. Be careful not to overwork or you will not only get burned out, but you will also begin to question why you are in retailing in the first place!

As you look for the right space, make sure you understand the required hours the store needs to be open. Naturally, different locations mean different hours. In an enclosed mall or heavily trafficked strip center, the hours may be dictated to you in the lease. It will generally require you to be open from early in the morning to late at night. In a downtown location or free-standing store, you can be open as long as you want. However, extended business hours are only one factor when choosing a store's location.

Distance from Where You Live

One of the reasons you start your own store is to improve your lifestyle. Sure, you'll have to work hard, but you're fed up with the corporate hustle. You've worked for someone else. You've put up with the politics. Perhaps you've been underappreciated. So now it's time to put your entrepreneurial spirit, creativity, motivation, and resourcefulness to work for someone who really matters: *you.*

If you wind up fighting traffic to and from work, if your drive takes too long, or if you have to spend time in a dangerous part of town, can you really enjoy what you do and has your lifestyle really improved? The closer you are to your business, the more relaxed you are going to feel. You can pop in any time you want to check on your employees and customers. Or, if you're at the store, you can run back home in time for a family meal and, if necessary, return to the store afterwards to resume what you were doing. If you leave something at the store, you can run over and pick it up. Living close to your store may sound like a luxury. Not so; it's close to a necessity! (You will *really* appreciate this when the store alarm goes off at two in the morning and you need to drive there to meet the police!)

Getting Down to Business:

The Business Angle

Obviously, in choosing a location, you cannot decide based exclusively on personal considerations. You may not live in a place with any appropriate retail locations nearby. If so, I'm here to tell you, sooner or later you're going to have to move.

Deciding on a location is a lot like making a witch's brew: you throw in all of the different ingredients and an appropriate location (or at least a description of what you are looking for) rises to the top. Here are some of those key ingredients:

- **Proximity to a large group of potential customers.** Make sure the customers you want to attract either live or work in the area. For instance, if you're opening a store catering to kids or mothers, a location near a school would be ideal.
- **Competition.** In planning to open a car dealership, a jewelry store, an art gallery, a high-end clothing store, an antique dealership, or a restaurant (to name just a few such categories), you may be well advised to go to a district of similar retailers, an area that has become a destination for customers looking for that type of product. It is no coincidence

that, in many cities, there are whole sections of town dedicated to art or antiques, jewelry, or fashion. These streets become known as *the* place for people seeking that particular type of product.

- **Uniqueness of location.** On the other hand, you may want your store to be the proverbial big fish in a small pond. If you are the only store of its type in the area, you will most certainly stand out and possibly become a "destination store" in your own right.

- **Proper fit.** It's important that the neighboring stores blend in well for your type of customers. You don't want to locate an upscale dress store next to a tattoo parlor, or vice versa. Likewise, you wouldn't want to put a store that's attractive to kids, such as a trading card or comic book store, in an a location that will discriminate against them, such as a strip mall catering to seniors.

- **Traffic count.** How many people that fit your customer profile are walking or driving by the location? The landlord, or a local chamber of commerce or economic development board, can give you that information, but it wouldn't hurt to do a little field research of your own. Go to the location and check it out for yourself. Make sure you do so at different times of the day and different days of the week. It would be a shame to locate your store in an area with lots of weekday traffic because of the offices nearby, only to discover too late that it's dead on the weekends.

- **Visibility.** High visibility is free advertising. Bad visibility loses first-time customers who may not know your store is there. Naturally, visibility is also a major factor in rent—lower rent often means lower visibility. It's a trade-off because lower rent resulting from lower visibility may also mean less business. Actually, the question of how important visibility is depends on the type of retail store you want to open. If you have discovered that there is an absence of a store catering to professional (or serious amateur) musicians, and you plan to fill that gap, then visibility is of little importance. Your customers will come to you if you succeed in spreading the word in the musical community by targeted advertising and word-of-mouth. You're hardly going to attract much off-the-street, walk-in traffic other than curious passersby who are hardly likely to pay several thousand dollars for a handmade violin or vintage electric guitar. Conversely, if you are opening a candy store where sight and smell can easily appeal to passing taste buds, and where your product is by its nature an impulse item, visibility may make all the difference between success and failure.

- **Accessibility.** Is the location easy to reach from any major roads in the area? Is there enough parking, and is the parking close to the entrance? Is it an easy walk to the store? These are all valid questions you should ask yourself before making the final decision. The answers will make a big difference to customers considering shopping there.

- **Parking.** Parking is a key part of location, but it is often overlooked for the more obvious aspects of this choice, such as visibility and size. The very rough rule of thumb about parking: You need at least ten customer parking spaces for every 1,000 feet of store space.

- **Financial obligation for rent.** Businesses that fail usually do so because they used their capital unwisely by overspending on their location, and therefore forced their proprietors to skimp on everything else. If this happens, you won't need Donald Trump to tell you "You're Fired!" You'll know by the lack of customers.

Certainly, you'll have to think long-term because the location you choose needs to be good for today *and* tomorrow. After all, you are going to expand and you can't afford to move your business to a larger location every couple of years. On the other hand, too much space is expensive, not only because of the extra rent you have to pay, but also because you need more inventory to fill the space, more utilities to heat and cool it, etc. Once again you have to make gut judgments about this. Balancing prudence with risk is the definition of today's most successful entrepreneurs.

Are You Compatible?

The Compatibility Angle

So, you think you've found the perfect location for your retail store? Think again: Are you compatible with the other retail spaces on either side of you? Having good retail neighbors can make or break your business.

First determine if your potential neighbors are drawing *your* type of customer. If you can attract the traffic already going to other stores around you, then you can either save advertising dollars and cut down on the cost of cold-calling potential customers, or you can make these efforts more productive. On the other hand, if you are a high-end jewelry store, you don't want to be in the middle of a row of discount stores. Few shoppers looking for three-carat diamonds want to shuffle past pawn shops or bail bondsmen in their Chanel suits. Nor are the folks frequenting the ice cream parlor to your left and the fudge factory to your right likely to be the best customers for your diet and health food store.

Here's an interesting piece of trivia that may not be trivial at all. Research shows that people slow down when they see reflective surfaces and they speed up when they see banks. So, don't open your store next to a financial institution because when passersby reach your store, they will be moving too fast to appreciate what you have to offer. If you *have* to locate next to a bank, make sure you have several mirrors on your facade to slow shoppers down.

Here are some specifics to examine:

- **Smells.** Don't underestimate how much smells from next door can irritate your customers. Restaurants are the most common problem; but be careful of beauty salons that do heavy chemical work, or any stores with gas engines running all day. If your store shares its heating and air conditioning system with its neighbors, their smells can be absorbed by your products, and that can put you out of business.
- **Noise.** Given today's flimsy building materials, noise can often go right

through shopping center walls. If you are located next to a music store, or any store that caters to young people and therefore uses loud and raucous music to attract and entertain its customers, beware. If you are located next to a machine shop or the like, noise can continue all day long—a dreadful distraction both to your customers' attention and your employees'. Incidentally, the opposite problem also applies. If your store is going to be the noisy one, ensure that your neighbors are not going to object. You don't want to be the butt of lawsuits charging you with being a public nuisance.

• **Zoning regulations.** You may have found the ideal location, but if the area is not zoned for your type of business, then you can either go before the zoning board to try to change their mind, or find another location. Be sure to consult a lawyer to see exactly which zone you are in and to determine if you can even legally open the type of business you're considering in the place you're considering. Remember, retail business, like all business, involves making compromises. Falling in love with a location only to find that it's not zoned for your intentions might seem like the end of your dream, but don't let it be. Persevere and find somewhere else. It may just be the best thing that could happen.

Making for a Good Fit:

Matching Your Business with the Right Location

From what you have read so far, it should be obvious that finding a location that will allow you to do the maximum amount of *profitable* business is no easy task. You need a location that fits your products, that customers can easily find, where quality employees are available, that has compatible neighbors, and where rental costs allow both you and your landlord to make money (the old "win-win" situation). It is difficult but certainly not impossible; just look at how many successful stores there are in every town, village, and hamlet across America.

Different types of businesses do well in different types of retail settings. Often you can do more business in one location (such as a regional mall) but make more money in another location (such as a strip center). If you are a hair stylist with a loyal following, you do not need to pay a high rent to achieve visibility because your reputation will bring your loyal customers to a "hidden" location that offers you nice neighbors, parking, etc., but at a pleasantly low rent.

As you are choosing your location, there are basically two questions to ask yourself. How far will my customers travel to reach my type of business? How much freedom do I need to set my store hours and decorate my store as I please? Locations can basically be divided into two categories: **street locations,** where merchants can operate with relative independence but generally have to pay more for advertising to attract customers; and **planned shopping centers,** where merchants usually pay more rent and must adhere to the rules of the center, but where the center takes on much of the effort of building traffic. Let's look at the pros and cons of different retail locations.

Downtown Main Street

Long neglected, in many cities downtown areas are on their way back. In most downtowns you can determine the time your store opens and closes. This is a major benefit because you can experiment with opening and closing times and determine when is the best time to catch foot traffic while not wasting man hours on staying open when no customers are there. The major drawback is the lack of parking, a key factor in building your customer base, especially in cities that are largely serviced by private cars (e.g., Los Angeles) rather than by public transportation (e.g., Manhattan). If your customers habitually drive their own cars, they are not going to be keen to pay ten dollars for parking every time they visit your store.

In some cases, you can mitigate the parking problem by validating parking tickets. However, this can be a major expense. Treat it as part of your rent, and decide whether, given the lower rent you may be paying, you can afford to pay the parking.

Neighborhood Stores

These are the stores that are close to where customers live or work. They offer the feel of a village. Because of convenience, shopping in neighborhood stores often becomes part of a customer's routine. "Regulars" are common, thus giving you the advantage of getting to know your customers—their wants, desires, needs, etc.—and responding with appropriate merchandise, services, and shopping hours.

Peak hours in many neighborhood businesses are in the early morning, when you catch people before they go to work; around lunch time, when they make a quick trip during their lunch break; and, in a heady rush (often on Fridays), as they start for home and realize that they have been meaning to stop in all week.

When it comes to setting business hours don't be afraid to learn from others. If the rest of the stores in the neighborhood close at seven, why stay open until nine? They've obviously been around long enough to realize that the added expense of staying open two hours later each day, fourteen more hours per week, isn't worth the few customers who come to visit during those hours.

Strip Shopping Centers

These locations are built to serve a population of ten to twenty-five thousand people living within ten to fifteen minutes of the center itself. By moving your store into a strip center, you give your customers a better parking opportunity and the convenience of shopping several diverse stores. Moreover, working together with the other merchants on the same schedule tends to increase the business for everyone.

There's a price for all that convenience, however. You give up some of your independence when you sign the lease, because the shopping center will dictate the hours you will be open, the type of store sign you can use, and even the type of promotions you can run.

Most strip centers are anchored by a supermarket or discount store that serves as the primary draw of customers to that center. With simple store-front or flyer advertising and an occasional sidewalk promotion, you can quickly, and inexpensively, capitalize on the traffic they draw.

Regional Malls

Regional malls are the big malls with at least two anchor stores and more than one hundred other retail outlets in between. These malls are located in areas where they can pull from at least one hundred thousand customers living within thirty minutes of the mall.

As one might expect, locating in one of these centers is expensive, but the upside is that these malls deliver customers to your door. The rules in regional malls are the strictest of any location. This is a necessity and a benefit because it maintains the image of the mall. Just as you work on branding your store, malls work to establish their image, whether upscale and elegant or blue collar and discount.

The Landlord and Lease

Dealing with landlords is pretty cut and dried. Usually, the larger the facility, the more professional the landlord. Landlords of large facilities have seen just about every trick in the book and have a pretty standard agreement they will sign that protects them from any tricks you may attempt. Communication with the landlord is essential; to be profitable, rental terms must allow for a long-term relationship for both parties.

Whether the landlord is trying to recruit you, because he has space available, or you are trying to persuade him to let you in, because there is great demand for his limited space, to make the right decision, you need the following information before you sign the lease:

- A list of all the tenants and what kinds of merchandise they sell.
- A site plan showing the location of all the tenants and the spaces that remain available.
- A map of the marketing trading area, marked with the primary and secondary customers' travel routes.
- The number of households in the trading area and the average income of those households.
- The projected population growth.
- The age and gender breakdowns of people living in a one-mile, five-mile, and ten-mile radius.
- A fact sheet about the center that includes a general description of the property, the history of the property, any expansion plans, facts about the developer or owner, a list of other centers they own or manage, and estimated expenses beyond the basic rent costs.
- Any newspaper or magazine articles about the owner or property.
- A referral list of other tenants with whom you can check to assure yourself that the property owners will do what they say they will do. Of course, you can approach stores on your own, but it's easier if the landlord gives you contact information for store owners who may not be at the store.
- Reasons why your business would succeed in this location.

Pitching the Right Landlord

You've seen what the right landlord can do for you, now you need to convince your landlord your business will enhance his property. The key here is to be professional. While you should not volunteer that this is your first store, if the landlord asks, you can't lie about it. Being a beginner is a disadvantage in the landlord's eyes. The landlord may suspect a beginner of being nonprofessional, and thus, giving him or her and the mall a hard time. Or the landlord may think of the possibility that your untried business may fail. To offset this disadvantage, you should be as well-prepared as the landlord. He or she will probably have a professional folder about the property (to impress you); you should have a prepared presentation folder, with your logo attached (to impress the landlord). Your folder should contain:

- A complete business plan
- Funding commitments
- Financial statements
- Space requirements and the plans for that space
- Pictures of merchandise and stores like the one you are opening
- Articles and reports about your industry
- Your business card

What Are the *Real* Expenses in a Lease?

When it comes to your lease, the rent is just the beginning. In the good old days, landlords often paid for heat, air conditioning, and electricity. Most of the good old days are gone, however, and you'll be responsible for a whole host of hidden costs. They're only hidden if you're blind to them. Armed with the following information, those hidden costs will no longer be a surprise. Here is what you need to know about your various lease expenses:

- **Base rent.** This is the amount of rent per square foot of space you agree to pay annually. This amount is divided by twelve to give your monthly rent. For instance, if your rent is $10 a square foot and you rent 2,400 square feet, your yearly rent is $24,000 and your monthly rent is $2,000.
- **Percentage rent.** This is the extra rent you pay once you reach an agreed base sales per month. If your base rent is $2,000 a month, the deal with

the landlord may be that the landlord receives 5% of all sales over $50,000 per month. For instance, if you did $60,000 in sales one month, your rent would be your base of $2,000 plus 5% of the difference between $60,000 and $50,000 ($10,000)—$500 in percentage rent. So your total rent this month would be $2,500. Now, if you do *less* than $50,000, the landlord still gets his base rent of $2,000. This is obviously a winning deal for the landlord, and an easy way to squeeze a first-time business owner. However, there is some justification in this approach. After all, a large part of your volume is generated by traffic the landlord builds. If the landlord knows more income will be generated if you are provided with more customers, there is incentive for money to be spent on building consumer traffic. Percentage rent is more common (and higher) in locations such as malls where landlords play an important role in attracting customers; and less prevalent (and lower) in free-standing locations where the landlord can do less to build traffic.

Remember, because everything, including the level of percentage rent, is negotiable, if you can avoid percentage rent, you'll be better off. If you have to live with it, make sure it's not too high. Also, be aware that as soon as rent is tied to sales performance, the landlord has the right to check your books at any time.

- **Common area and maintenance.** Commonly known as *CAM charges,* these cover the cost of cleaning and maintaining the common areas that all tenants use and share including parking lots that always seem to need repair or resurfacing. CAM charges encompass: outdoor and indoor cleaning, snow removal, painting, public bathrooms, gardening and vegetation, electricity, area lighting and security, general maintenance, and the mall owner's overhead. You pay a percentage based on the space you occupy. There is a potential problem hidden here: if costs suddenly rise (for example, if the mall needs a new roof), or the number of tenants drops so there are fewer people to share the costs, your CAM charges could skyrocket. To avoid this difficulty, you should negotiate a cap to the CAM charges that the landlord may impose.
- **Property taxes.** Like CAM charges, you pay your fair share of the taxes

on the facility. Unlike CAM charges, you cannot place a cap on them; they are what they are.

- **Insurance fees.** These could cover the entire building or just the common areas. Like CAM charges, you will get to pay your fair share of these, also.
- **Promotional and marketing costs.** These may take the form of specific merchant dues, negotiated separately, or they may be pro-rated as part of your overall CAM charges. You may or may not have any say in how these funds are spent. They may include holiday decorations, marketing costs, advertising, or parking lot events.
- **Triple net.** In a triple net (NNN) lease, your rent does not include four things: taxes, insurance, maintenance, and repair. These charges will be added by the landlord, usually pro-rated each month and added or subtracted at the end of the year if the estimates were wrong.
- **Miscellaneous expenses.** Leasing fees, which a landlord may try to slip by you, is one expense you should challenge as you negotiate your lease. Elevator or escalator repair, as well as heating and cooling repair and replacement are other charges to watch out for. The one that gets me is the "bad debt expense," where a landlord may charge you additional CAM charges to cover other stores that are not paying their fair share, usually because they have gone out of business. Beware of this clause!

Before Signing Your Lease:

What to Do Before You Sign on the Dotted Line

Okay, fine. You've found the best location, scouted out the neighbors, decided you'd be a good fit, made nice with the landlord, and are ready to negotiate and then sign the lease.

What next? First and most important, never lose sight of the fact that everything, and I do mean *everything,* is negotiable. Both the tenant and the landlord are in business to make money. A good location is a win-win situation for both parties. Therefore, make sure of the following things before signing any lease:

- Have realistic goals. Make sure you understand what the location can produce in sales and that the rent is fair in relationship to those sales. Make yourself a realistic profit and loss statement that shows all your expenses, and figure out the sales level you need to make a profit that satisfies you. Then consider whether that sales level is reasonable. Are stores around you in somewhat comparable lines of business doing at least that well? If your forecast looks unsatisfactory or even questionable, your rent is probably too high.
- Read the lease and understand everything in it. If you have no experience with leases, a wise investment would be to have a lawyer read through it. You are making a five- to ten-year commitment, so you want to make sure you haven't missed anything.
- Realize that everything is negotiable. Not everyone in the building is paying the same rent. Other stores either were better negotiators or the landlord wanted them badly enough (perhaps because they draw a tremendous amount of traffic) to give them a better deal. Always remember, everything is negotiable.
- Ensure you are not paying rent for other vacant stores. If the building has vacancies, make sure you are not stuck paying their fair share of the rent. For example, if five storefronts are empty, some leases will sneak in a clause that states the occupied stores will share their rents. Be wary of such clauses.
- Understand how a dispute will be handled.
- Give real thought to the length of your lease. Don't make it too short or too long. Try to get a renewal clause included with a pre-agreed rent. That way, your landlord cannot hold you up when your original lease ends.
- Know your refund options for failed maintenance. If the landlord does not maintain the property, know what your options are for seeking a refund of monies paid toward that purpose.

- Ensure that you can leave the center if the major anchor leaves.
- Understand escape clauses. Escape clauses give you the ability to get out of your lease under certain circumstances, such as non-performance by the landlord. Make sure you understand what such non-performance entails.
- Understand the possibilities of a "finish out allowance." Landlords usually turn over the shell of the building to you and leave it to you to have contractors build out the interior. However, in many cases you can negotiate a deal whereby the landlord contributes a finish out allowance. This usually applies to two specific circumstances. The first is a new construction situation when the landlord realizes a certain amount of work will need to be done anyway and feels that the walls, floors, ceilings, lighting, electrical hook-ups, plumbing hook-ups, or insulation may as well be finished to your specifications. The second situation is old construction. If a previous tenant has installed very specialized build-outs, the landlord knows they will have to be dismantled and replaced in any case.
- Know that free rent for one to six months, depending on the market conditions, is an attractive and common incentive. You are in an especially strong position to negotiate this if the landlord knows you will have a time-consuming amount of construction to do before you can open.
- Keep your prepaid rent and securities to a minimum. Most landlords require first and last month's rent, plus a security deposit that can be as much as three months' rent. Negotiate it down to no more than one month.
- Ensure that the lease can be transferred without a problem if you sell the business. Landlords try to inhibit you from passing the lease on to anyone of whom they don't approve. Try to avoid this restriction because it gives the landlord the power to stop you from selling, a power he could use to force you to pay an indemnity. If you cannot avoid the clause altogether (because the landlord claims that he cannot be expected to accept a lessee with a poor credit rating), make sure his approval "cannot be unreasonably withheld." This is an often used legal

formula that protects you from the landlord overusing his power of approval.

- Ensure that you can sublet your space, either entirely or a portion of it. Again, the landlord will rightly place restrictions on whom you can sublet to (for example, you cannot sublet to a candy store if there are already two in the mall). Here, the best you can expect is that the landlord's approval will not be unreasonably withheld.

Conclusion

In the end, as in all real estate, a huge amount of your success or failure hinges on location, location, location. So, do your research. Check out the location on Mapquest.com. Read the relevant books and magazines. Talk to everyone you can find who knows the area. Listen to the rumor mill. But never let any of that substitute for the personal: *always* check the site out for yourself. Not once, not twice, but several times. And at different times of day and night. On weekdays and weekends. In rain, shine, sleet, and snow.

Much of what we do in retail has to come from the gut. If your gut tells you that a location is good, chances are it is. If the paperwork, lease, and landlord don't match up to what (in your opinion) the market will bear, either keep negotiating until you get the (reasonable) terms you need or walk away. Conversely, if the terms seem too good, there must be a reason. As a friend of mine explains, "If you sense there's a sucker in the room, but you're not sure who it is, chances are it's you." So, ask around—both customers and merchants—you may just be surprised by what you hear. Then, when you have the location you want on terms you like, sign the lease and don't look back.

Retail Detail

Jupiter Research found that half of consumers use the retailer's Web site for research before buying a product in the physical store. Surveys by Sears showed that $500 million worth of in-store appliance sales were influenced by customers researching online first.

Chapter 7

Window Shopping Revisited, Or:

Luring Customers from the Outside to the Inside

The odds of going to the store for a loaf of bread
and coming out with ONLY a loaf of bread
are three billion to one.

—ERMA BOMBECK

I T'S IMPORTANT TO REMEMBER that our instinct to shop, browse, and buy actually begins before we even get to the store. After all, most shopping trips start with a ride in the car. Or writing a shopping list at home. Or seeing an ad on TV. Always assume that customers have started to shop long before they have gotten to your store.

What that means in practical terms is that your job is to remind them of what they already know (or half-know) they want. And one powerful tool you have is your store window. In fact, window decoration is a science unto itself. So we'll start there.

As customers pull up in front of your store and park, apart from your store name, your windows are the first thing they will see. But exactly what do they see? In too many cases, all they see is a lot of *stuff*—in a display so crowded that nothing stands out. It's like the writing on a billboard as you drive past—too small and you can't begin to read it, too big and you *still* can't read it.

Of course, your customers can stand close to a window full of merchandise. They can browse until they find something that pulls them into the store. So, the first question you consider as you decide how to decorate your windows is, what is its purpose? If your store is the sort that caters to browsers who aren't sure what they want or what the store may carry—gift, antiques, or sundries—then using your window to show a wide selection of your wares seems a good plan. On the other hand, if you own a specialty store, for example a clothing boutique, an art gallery, or a gourmet food outlet, then showing a single, strong product, preferably in a stunning presentation, may be the best way to use your window.

The lesson here is to understand your strategic goal first. If your aim is to make my mouth water, a single box of chocolates, or perhaps someone hand-dipping chocolate in the window, may be a better idea than a window cluttered with a hundred types of candy. But if you're selling coins to collectors, showing a huge selection may best serve your purpose.

How Big Is Your "Landing Strip"?

Moving on through our virtual shopping spree, we've just walked into the store and are trying to make adjustments from sunlight to store light, or from darkness to light, or, occasionally, from rainy to dry. We are narrowing our eyes and adjusting our mindsets from the parking lot to a store full of . . . something. We are moving our heads from side to side to take in all of the action in the store. We are listening to the sounds, judging the smells, unconsciously figuring out whether the store is "hot or cold" for us.

Even though we are standing inside the store's entrance, our heads are not yet in the store. Are we ready to buy anything yet? Not even close. A major retail fallacy states that you should "lead with your headline," that is, move your best merchandise to the front of the store, in case shoppers don't have the time, energy, or motivation to move any further into the store. I contend just the opposite—the entrance to a store is *not* the place to put your best products or message because the majority of customers will walk right by it as they adjust to their new environment. Displays will be missed, signs won't get read, and the friendly clerk asking, "Can I help you?" can seem pushy. Customers need a landing strip in the first ten to twenty feet of the store to get acclimated.

Rather than asking new customers "Can I help you?", the staff can simply say "Hello" and remind them where they are: "Welcome to Mom and Pop's Potpourri." This tactic has an added benefit. Security experts know that the best way to discourage shoplifting is to make sure the salespeople acknowledge *every* shopper who walks in the door.

Of course, you can't waste the first ten or twenty feet of your store. But you can use it productively without trying to make it your main selling area. For example, you can slow customers down and get them more accustomed to the landing strip by offering a coupon, a map of the store, or just a basket to fill. Or you can put up a giant display that is so tall and wide it has to stop them in their tracks. The best advice, though, is positioning a huge bin of merchandise whose price has been dramatically reduced close to the entrance. That will stop shoppers like a red traffic light!

You may also be able to slow down customers before they hit the landing pad (or, better put, you can move the landing pad outside your store) by selling products on the sidewalk or even in the parking lot. Obviously, each venue has its own rules concerning this profitable practice, but if you are allowed to, this approach will slow the customer down and create enough excitement to attract other customers.

You can also do just the opposite. By leaving the front of the store practically empty, you give up selling space, but you let your customers adjust to your landing strip. By allowing some space between the entrance and a featured product, you may give your shoppers the time to fully focus on the one item that, although they didn't realize it before, they now cannot live without!

A Tisket, a Tasket . . .

It should come as no surprise that multiple sales are the key to growing any business and, since customers only have two hands, without help they can only juggle a few items at a time. Worse still, if a customer needs to carry a coat or briefcase in one hand, all that customer can buy is a couple of items.

Obviously, baskets (or shopping carts if there is room) help create multiple sales. Shopping carts are usually stored outside the store entrance, but baskets are somewhere inside. If you have baskets too close to the landing strip, customers may walk right by them and, rather than return for a basket, they may end up carrying out only a couple of items. All employees, therefore, need to be trained to offer baskets when they see a customer without one, especially if that customer has a coat or baby stroller in hand. Baskets should also be stacked strategically throughout the store. They should be piled (or stacked on a stand) no lower than four feet tall so that they are visible to everyone but still easy to reach by customers with their hands full.

Retailers know that the fastest way to increase sales is to sell more goods to your existing customer base. Most stores use hard plastic baskets with hinged steel handles. But please think outside the box. How about having a rack of canvas or nylon tote bags for customers to carry around their purchases? At checkout, the clerk could ask the customer. "Would you like to buy this tote? It's just $4.99." If they say "yes," you have just saved yourself the cost of a plastic bag *and* upped your sale. And why not put your logo on the bag? That way you'll have free advertising walking around town for a long time. If it's cute or clever enough, it may even become a fashion statement.

Signage:

Play by the Rules

Once inside a store, customers are constantly moving up and down the aisles and peering at shelves. Consequently, they typically have only two to three seconds to read any signage you may put up. Therefore, every sign you use must do two things:

1. **Attract customers' attention.** Colors, shapes, and sizes are important factors to consider. People don't want to crane their necks to read an awkward sign, or wait for a salesperson to show them the right direction or explain a simple product.

2. **Tell a clear story.** People absorb information one layer at a time and in logical sequence. If you can't get their attention at first, nothing that follows will matter. If the message is confusing, too clever, hip, or oblique, it will be ignored. Length is also vital. The entire message must take only seconds to be read and understood. Today's shoppers are pressed for time; they do not hang around stores as their parents did only a short generation ago.

Bottom line? Signing is an important strategic decision not to be taken lightly. You can't just willy-nilly fill up the empty spots on the wall with signs. Rather, you should view your store as a collection of mini-stores *within* a store and map out where every sign should be placed. Create the map on paper. Then walk around your store and ask yourself: "What will my customers be doing here? What will they be looking at? Will they be walking fast, so the message must be short and sweet, or dawdling, with time for a longer message?"

With observation, you will discover customer walking patterns in your store. If you own a drugstore with the pharmacy in the back, perhaps many of your customers tend to rush to the pharmacy and then start shopping from the back. If so, your signage has to do double duty—forwards for regular customers; backwards for prescription-buying customers.

Because very few people look up when they're busy shopping, banners hanging overhead are little more than a waste. Remember this rule: Signs should interrupt the shopper's line of vision.

Depending on the type of store you run, window signs may be inappropriate—or not! If you feel you can get away with using signage as a feature in your front windows, be aware that the most effective signs are the ones customers can read in two seconds. They must be big and only contain one to three words: for example, "Sale!," "50% Off!," "Half Price," or "Today Only." A sign that reads "Going out of business sale—All merchandise half price—This week only" will be much less effective than one that reads merely "Half Price." (There is a reason the owner of the store with the long-winded sign is going out of business!)

If you have a waiting area in your store (pharmacy, auto, etc.), these are ideal places to put lots of signs with tons of information. Before long, your customers are going to become bored. They will look for distractions. Of course, the literature you leave about should be interesting—none of those awful health pamphlets doctors leave in their waiting rooms.

When you are laying out signs, make sure they aren't "too late" to get your message across. For example, there's little point in putting up a sign in the front of the store promoting merchandise located in the *back* of the store. By the time customers see them, they're already checking out.

"Teaser signs" have long been my favorite. They break your message into 2 or 3 parts and communicate your message a little at a time as the customer gets further into the store. Here is an example of the series of ten teaser messages (and images) a store could using during what I like to call a Super Sunday Sale:

First Sign: *Super Sunday Sale!*
Second Sign: Pictures of attractive items that have been reduced
Third Sign: *Hottest Prices of the Year!*
Fourth Sign: More pictures
Fifth Sign: *Hundreds of Items!*

Sixth Sign: More pictures
Seventh Sign: *Two Days Only!*
Eighth Sign: More pictures
Ninth Sign: *Starts Sunday from 7-11!*
Tenth Sign: More pictures . . .

Let's not kid ourselves: America is *definitely* on sign overload. After long, tiring days, many store owners stuck in their stockrooms unloading vendors' signs are unmotivated to use them. Worse, once a sign *does* make it to the selling floor, it may never come down. Check how many Halloween signs are still up in November or how many holiday signs still lurk in February! Don't let that happen in your store. When it comes to signage, keep two rules in mind:

Rule #1: Keep it Simple.
Rule #2: Less is More.

Patterns of Movement

Once inside your store, people generally walk toward the right. The "right bias" seems to have to do with which side of the road we drive on because in left-driving countries (e.g., Britain and Australia) customers have a left bias! Because American shoppers tend to walk to the right, the front right space is prime real estate in any type of store. This is where the most important products or department should go; this is where you set the tone and feeling for your store.

Most shoppers, being right-handed, also *reach* to the right. It follows that items should be displayed just slightly to the right of where shoppers will be standing. For example, if you have a shampoo assortment, the most popular shampoo brand should go in the middle of the section and a brand you are trying to build, perhaps because it is unique to your store or offers better-than-average margin, should go directly to the *right* of it.

The fact that people face and walk *forward* staring straight down a store aisle (not sideways, like crabs) is a challenge for retailers. It's a real effort to turn your head from side to side, and up and down, to see all the products on the shelves on either side of you. To compensate, displays should be *slanted* to one side so they can more easily be seen from an angle. Of course, this doesn't work if people typically walk down an aisle from both directions. In that case, the display should be slightly V-shaped so it angles towards customers walking from either direction. *Endcaps* are the most effective of all display locations. Because customers approach them head on, they see them plainly and fully, provided, of course, that you build them so the products face front from all directions.

When customers turned to face a shelf, they actually *see* only the merchandise within their "sight zone," an area from slightly above eye level to around knee level. Above or below these site zones, the space is relatively dead for impulse purchasing. Of course, this space remains valuable for large items that cannot be stocked elsewhere. Fortunately, such large, economy sizes are likely to be wanted by loyal consumers who will search for them wherever they are housed.

Another predictable movement is called the *boomerang rate.* Despite its flashy title, it is just the measurement of how many times customers fail to walk completely down an aisle because, finding what they want, they promptly retrace their steps and never pass all the other wonderful things you want to sell them! As a retailer, you want your most popular goods in the *middle* of an aisle so as to minimize the negative effect of boomeranging.

It's Raining Men?

Erma Bombeck once wrote that, "Shopping is a woman thing. It's a contact sport like football. Women enjoy the scrimmage, the noisy crowds, the danger of being trampled to death, and the ecstasy of the purchase . . ." While this may be a *slight* exaggeration, as a group, men *do* shop much differently than women. Prevailing retail dogma is that male shoppers don't *enjoy* shopping, which is why they do it much less than women. This has resulted in the entire shopping experience—from package design to store layouts, to advertising and merchandising, to the music being piped in—being focused on the female shopper. In some cases, and for some types of stores, this dogma should be rethought.

The fact is men are doing more purchasing, and this trend will continue to grow. As men stay single longer and get divorced more often, they have to shop for many things their fathers left to their mothers; because married women work longer hours, their husbands are forced to shoulder more of the shopping responsibilities. As a result, men may not enjoy shopping more than they used to, but they are doing a lot more of it. Here, then, are some things you should know about how men shop:

- Men move faster through stores and spend less time looking around. It's difficult to get them to look at anything they did not intend to buy. To offset that, it helps to offer products that augment what is on the shelf—advertise cookies in the milk section or lighter fluid near the charcoal.

- Men don't like asking where things are. If they can't find a section of the store they are looking for, they will spend a couple of minutes searching and, if they still can't find it, they will often just leave the store without ever asking for help. Make sure you signage is visible and unambiguous.

- Men move through a store to the section they want, pick up the product they are after, and are then ready to pay and leave. No ifs, ands, or impulse sales. Your extra sale promotions need to be even more interruptive for men than for women.

- Obviously, men, like women, want to make sure any clothes they buy fit. But if they can't find the dressing room quickly, they may just decide it is not worth the trouble and leave the store without making a purchase at all. So, position fitting rooms near the men's department and mark them clearly.

- Men do not pay as much attention to price tags as women, which makes them a prime upgrade target. Train your staff to offer a better product or an additional one. Because they are so anxious to get out of the store, men may say "yes" to and buy a more expensive item just to make a quick exit.

To sum up, women may have more experience shopping, but the men are slowly catching up. Just give them a little time.

Shopping:

A Battle of the Sexes?

The ideal situation for retailers is clear: Women shopping with women. Why? Because women don't just "shop"; they suggest, consult, and advise each other, thus spending considerable time in a store. On the flip side, women shopping with kids is tough because their focus is constantly interrupted by keeping the kids entertained, in control, and safe. Even worse than that, are women shopping with men; it's a retailer's nightmare. Long before the woman has decided what to buy, the man makes it plain that he is bored and impatient. Tension pervades the atmosphere. Soon, she will stomp out empty-handed.

Knowing all this, a canny shopkeeper can minimize the adverse effects of children by providing entertainment for them: a television set turned to an appropriate children's program works wonders. And men, too, can be mollified. One well-known, expensive clothing boutique in Los Angeles offers any accompanying men a comfortable chair. Then has a pretty sales girl asks him his opinion about a garment she is wearing. "I'm not sure I look good in this," she exclaims. "What do you think?" ("I think I can keep him busy," she has previously explained to the woman he accompanied.) While the woman tries on clothes, time for the man seems to fly!

Although men are becoming more important as retail customers, women remain the retailer's lifeblood. Here then are some of the things you should know about women as shoppers:

- Today's woman is not like her mother. For example, less than 2% of manufacturers grocery coupons are redeemed today, as opposed to an entire generation raised on "coupon clipping." Not surprisingly, most coupons are clipped by senior citizens or highly budget conscious women who aren't working at jobs all day long.

- From prehistoric times, women have been gatherers (while men were hunters). The trait prevails. In most families, it is Mom who finds the car key Dad misplaced and the shoes Junior kicked under the chair. In a retail environment, appealing to a woman's collecting instincts—by offering sets of products or hinting at the need to keep her pantry fully stocked—can build sales.

- For women, shopping is often a chance to get away from the home or office, a chance to relax. Storekeepers are well advised to keep the shopping experience fun. This is especially important because women have less time to squeeze shopping in between their kids' soccer practice and work. The problem is that the less time women spend in stores, the less they buy. But the longer it takes to make a purchase, the more difficult it is for them to find the time. The solution (insofar as one exists) is to make the *shopping* experience pleasant—plenty of browsing, plenty of mirrors, plenty of unusual goods to examine—and the *paying* activity fast and efficient. No one wants to wait around forever at the check-out line.

- Women often view shopping as a social activity. They enjoy shopping with their friends who can help them find the right items and save them from making a poor buy. Retailers can capitalize on this trait by directed promotions ("bring a friend, get a discount") or just by making sure there are plenty of chairs outside of the fitting rooms to allow for a more informal "try on and kibitz" area.

- Women demand more of the shopping experience than men do. Women shoppers are patient and inquisitive and at ease to shop at their own pace. To make it easy for them to "indulge" in shopping:
  - Try not to display merchandise below waist level
  - Don't crowd; leave enough space in aisles so that customers are not bumped or jostled

- Leave enough maneuvering room for carts, strollers, baskets, and purses
- Leave space for examining the merchandise. For instance, if you are selling greeting cards, make sure there is room for readers to stand in the aisle and read several cards while other customers with baby stroller or shopping carts can pass by comfortably.
- Make sure you have a clean, comfortable ladies room

Women are and will remain your primary customers (even though men are catching up). Cater to them.

Boomtown

Twenty years from now, 20% of the U.S. population will be over sixty-five—an 80% increase over that current market segment. This will change the retail landscape in the coming decades because this baby boomer generation will have more money than any previous generation and, being healthier and more active, will have a greater influence on fashion, style, and purchasable goods and services.

This generation, which is now pushing fifty, is having an immense impact on retailing. Just look at the explosion of "nutraceuticals" intended to counteract aging, or of Viagra or Cialis. Consider the vast dieting industry that tries (and consistently fails) to hold down middle-aged spread. Recognize that anti-aging cosmetology—everything from anti-wrinkle creams to Botox to cosmetic surgery—is a boom industry while brightly colored cosmetics are in relative doldrums.

Unfortunately, in some respects, retailers are lagging. For instance, the typeface on many signs and labels in retail stores is much too small. To add to the problem, as we (yes, I am part of this generation so I have a vested stake in the outcome here) enter our fifties, our retinas receive about one-quarter less light than do kids' eyes. This means that the lighting in stores needs to be much brighter than it is today, if only to let us see the same thing we saw when we were younger!

Older folks, even healthy and active ones, aren't as mobile as the younger set. Vision blurs, bones become more brittle, muscle strength declines, and girth tends to expand. To cater to these inevitables, aisles must be wide, paths must be easier to navigate, and stairs and even escalators (which can be tricky for weakened legs) need to be replaced by more elevator space. A few chairs scattered here and there as resting places might be nice, too.

Since older folks can't bend and stretch as well as in the good old days, products must be easily accessible and preferably at waist level or just above. And older citizens will need more in-store service. Today, only one shopper in five seeks an employee's assistance. But among seniors, the number of those seeking help (reading, directions, finding stuff, etc.) doubles to two in five. For one thing, seniors feel more entitled to be helped than do younger folk. Since staff is expensive, retailers will have to redouble their efforts to provide easily accessible directions and information to customers.

So don't wait around for the baby boomers to catch up to you! There are things you can do right now, today, to stem the tide of dissatisfied, older customers. For instance, if you want your customers to read in-store material, make sure you have reading glasses hanging on chains attached to shelving throughout the store. If you carry clothing with tiny hooks and buttons (especially the inconvenient ones on the back), find forward-thinking manufacturers who will use simpler fasteners or Velcro instead. Though buttons on most phones, remotes, and computers are getting smaller, make sure you also carry a selection of bigger-buttoned items.

The irony behind this is that if you watch how technology is sold through print and TV ads, almost all of the participants pictured are under forty—both those selling the product and those behind the counter ringing it up. Personally, I think they are missing the mark. Don't you?

"These Kids Today..."

On the other end of the age spectrum, kids are richer and more independent than ever. As a result, more than any generation before, they are influencing what is produced, how much of it is produced, and even where we shop.

Because today's parents commonly both work, shopping has become "family time." In other cases, because divorce is so common, single moms and dads have no choice but to drag their kids along on shopping excursions. And, because kids today continue to watch TV but now also spend countless hours in computer chat rooms where they are hugely influenced by peers—and "influencers" who pretend to be peers—they apply even more influence on family purchases than kids of prior generations.

So what should your store do to fit into this shopping lifestyle and beat out the competition? First, if your store does not fully welcome children (even if the message is subtle), parents will quickly understand and stay away. How you lay out your store will quickly tell parents if you are kid friendly or not. Wide aisles, automatic doors, and no steps make it easy on parents pushing strollers or dragging younger children through the store. If you are selling a product that requires a parent's concentration, such as a technical or detailed product, you will be well advised to furnish a kid friendly area of the store—complete with coloring books, crayons, toys, and maybe even a video player stocked with Nickelodeon cartoons—where parents can feel comfortable leaving their children. If your store is large enough, you may even be able to afford babysitting services.

Kids have never been more market savvy. (Just try asking one about the latest video game, trading card, or sour candy!) In order not to alienate this growing consumer segment, make sure you market specifically *to* them by putting the products at a level where the kids can actually reach them. At the same time, you do need to childproof the store to avoid accidents, bad publicity, or even insurance liability.

Teenagers are a puzzling market unto themselves. Most stores loathe having them hang out—the boys looking sloppy and vaguely dangerous, the girls looking far too provocative for adult sensibilities. If you are having problems with teenagers loitering outside your building (if you're not selling teenage product, they are not potential customers), just pump classical music outside your store and they will go away!

On the other hand, if you *do* want teenagers as customers, the trick is to get them involved in purchasing, not just hanging out. To do that, you need to understand the hot new products that are getting their attention. Music, video games, the Internet, and Hollywood all influence teenagers more than any other group, so you need to stay (in the argot of our own generation) "with it." At the same time, to avoid your store becoming a teen meeting ground, you should approach them and ask them, politely but insistently, what they would like to buy. If they have no intention of buying, they will soon leave. Teenagers today may look like delinquents (as, no doubt, we looked to our parents), but they are generally polite and considerate. They won't usually loiter where they are interfering with your business.

Don't be too concerned if you see teenagers shopping in groups (of course, always be on the lookout for shoplifting), because the pattern of teenagers is that they get the approval on goods from their peers and then come back with the parents to make the quick buy.

Teenagers are at the cusp of the spending curve. Maturing younger and younger, this vital market cannot be ignored. Moreover and fortunately, they do grow up fast. And you want to keep them as customers when they do.

Why So Touchy?

We live in a "touch and feel" shopping society. Customers want to feel, smell, and even taste what they are about to purchase. Don't you find yourself opening a box to see a product's actual size, utilizing a cologne mister, or sniffing a bar of soap before you buy it? A product's tactile qualities are very important. That is why a typical customer feels six to eight different towels before they purchase.

There are two reasons stores should keep all their inventory on view and keep little backroom storage space. The first reason is that space costs money so as much of it as possible should be used productively for making sales. The second, and even better, reason is that customers want to see and feel the merchandise. As in the law, possession is nine-tenths of ownership. Once a product is in a shopper's hand, the shopper has begun the process of owning it. This is especially important if you are selling private label brands that work just as effectively but cost much less than the big name brands with ever bigger advertising budgets. For such products, customers are especially keen to touch and see.

There are occasional exceptions to this rule. For example, catalog stores and shoe stores only show samples and keep their inventory in the back. The reason for these particular cases is that the interaction between the buyer and the store is necessary in any case, so having the clerk fetch the merchandise is no problem.

However your store is organized, your primary goal is to create contact between the customer and the merchandise. Once that contact is established, your chances of making the sale are greatly improved. Moreover, by placing better quality items next to poorer ones, you can "up sell" the customer to a higher-end product without using expensive staff time to make the sale. The fact is that customers selling themselves are far better salespeople than you or your staff will ever be!

Is Your Fitting Room *Fitting*?

Dressing rooms are the most overlooked assets of most apparel stores. Typically, they are designed just like the gym lockers in my old high school: small, cramped, sparse, and stuffy. The usual reason is that retailers do not want to waste space on fitting rooms that could be used as selling space. In my view, they are wrong. The dressing room can be the most important selling space of all.

A dressing room is not just a convenience. Properly used, it can also be the vehicle by which you convert a browser into a buyer. Research shows that if a salesperson is able to entice a customer into the dressing room, the chance of selling the garment doubles.

Women spend 25% of their garment shopping time in dressing rooms, but most stores don't understand this. What a shame that so many fitting rooms are poorly lit, seem dirty, have worn rugs, and sport cheap mirrors that distort the body like a funhouse mirror.

As you fit out your store, make sure you have enough dressing rooms, that they are clearly marked so customers can see them from a distance, and that they are near the clothing department. The further away they are, the fewer customers will make the journey to find them. Make sure their mirrors are large, numerous, and first class. And then have someone from your staff inspect them every half hour to make sure they are spotless. Also make sure the lighting is bright and *flattering*.

By the way, there's nothing wrong with using the fitting room walls to advertise some of your more desirable merchandise.

Finally, if there is any space you *can* carve out in front of the fitting room where friends of the shopper (or spouses or even kids) can sit and give their opinions, this will allow the customer to spend more time in the fitting room.

Don't Ignore the "Bare Necessities"

Bathrooms help set the tone of your entire establishment. Since everyone uses them, or has kids who do, a large number of your customers will be exposed to this area of the store at one time or another. Clean, well-lit, easily accessed bathrooms with plenty of towels and toilet paper reflect and reinforce your store's high standards. Small, grungy bathrooms give exactly the opposite impression.

Your bathrooms should be big enough so a line does not form outside it. No sales take place waiting to get into the bathroom. And, of course, cleanliness is vital. I can tell you from personal experience that my wife *refuses* to shop in a store with dirty bathrooms.

Fresh flowers on the toilet tank or sink may be a little much outside a very high-end store. But potpourri in a glass dish puts a pleasant spin on an otherwise bland bathroom.

Don't Shortchange Your Staffing

Retailers traditionally consider their business in three parts. First, store design and layout. Second, merchandising. Third, operations (how a store is run, including employee performance). The relationship between merchandising and operations is often strained because most retailers are looking for ways to save on labor costs. Many stores underpay, and thus *undervalue*, their sales staff so the burden of success falls back on better store layout and stronger merchandise to cause products to "sell themselves." However, merchandising cannot fully compensate for insufficient (or inadequate) staffing. For instance, if employees only have time to cram clothing onto a display or dump cosmetics onto a table, the intent of the effort is lost. Customers won't take the time to sort through an ill-organized or overcrowded product array. Thus, the money saved on staffing is lost on unmade sales.

Staffing is a real "gut check" for any business owner. What is the balance between losing sales and having an excessive payroll? Here are the considerations that will help you make the right decision.

Time = Money

The old adage "time is money" definitely applies to modern retail stores. Customer waiting time is a major influence both on their decisions to buy, and on whether they will come back to the store. A short wait is acceptable; a long wait kills shopping enjoyment.

When customers wait less than ninety seconds, their perception of the length of the wait is accurate. However, when they wait any longer, their sense of time becomes *very* distorted. If you ask a customer who has been in line for ten minutes or even five, how long they've been waiting, you will hear answers like "Forever," "Too long," and "Hours." Because waiting time is so distorted, cutting it to under two minutes is almost mandatory if you want to achieve long-term success; conversely, waiting times of over three minutes are likely to be a serious problem.

Unfortunately, because customer count can vary inexplicably from minute to minute, it is almost impossible to have enough staff to handle all peak periods. If you do, most of your people will be doing nothing (and costing you money) for most of the day. Fortunately, there are several things a retailer can do to make waiting time *seem* to go faster:

- Waiting is less onerous after an employee has initiated contact. Just having an employee acknowledge, early in the wait, that the customer is waiting relieves some of the annoyance.
- Telling the customer how long the wait will be also helps. But be honest. Telling someone it will be "just a moment," and then making them wait five minutes is worse than telling them up front that the wait will be five minutes.
- Orderliness can go a long way in quenching time anxiety. Making people guess about where to stand in line is very frustrating. Theme parks have learned to minimize the annoyance of even very long waits by snaking waiting lines back and forth so customers get a sense of forward movement.
- Diverting customers' attention, for example by playing videos of cartoons while customers are in line, may turn a negative experience into a positive one.
- Positioning impulse items along the cashier line is both smart merchandising and a distraction for customers that makes waiting times seem shorter. Keep in mind that the first person in line does not need diver-

sion; their wait is over. Therefore, try to place merchandising materials, signage, and racks so those waiting further in back are kept entertained.

Checking Out

Where to put the cash register is a question that has long been debated by retailers. The conventional wisdom is that near the entrance door is the logical place because the customer enters the store, chooses what to buy, and then returns to the front to pay and leave. From the staffing angle, too, this makes the most sense because, as long as the register is near the door, a small store can be run at non-peak hours with a single employee. Otherwise, you need two employees, or one employee plus a guard (who can cost more than a regular employee).

It is a mistake, though, to position the check out so that it is the first thing the incoming customer sees. This is especially true if there is a long line waiting to check out. If incoming customers see chaos, they may decide, wisely, to go elsewhere. If that happens more than once, well, you won't be seeing them again.

So place your checkout in the front but positioned on the left where it is not immediately seen by incoming customers. And make sure it is large enough to quickly move customers through the line. Doing so not only helps those already shopping, but also avoids putting off potential customers still trying to decide whether or not to enter your store.

Point of Purchase (POP)

Adjacencies is the term used in retailing to create order in merchandising. Because more than half of all purchases are unplanned, encouraging impulse purchases is of great importance to successful retailing. For instance, in the vitamin supplement section, books about diets and health are a natural adjacency.

In this context, as the storeowner, you must come up with a logical, sensible, sequence of products. Then, once you have decided, you know how to position your point of purchase displays (*POP*, for short).

POP is the general term to describe anything that temporarily advertises or displays a product. Thus, POP includes temporary signage, shelf talkers, posters, display units that fit onto shelves or stand on counters, and free-standing floor displays that can be moved anywhere and are especially useful to generate extra sales by establishing an adjacency. You can puzzle together adjacencies by just standing in an area of your store and asking yourself, "What else would I be thinking about if I were standing here?" POPs are a vital ingredient to a store's success.

No doubt then, POP materials are a boon to merchandising. However, you must be careful not to overload your store with too much POP. Even if you are running an informal business, the sort of "country store" where friendly clutter is an advantage, it must be *controlled* clutter.

Also, when you are considering a freestanding display, you should ask yourself, "What will the display look like when half of the merchandise is gone? Will it still look good, or will it look shopworn and forgotten? And, if I have to take it down, where will I put the unused merchandise?"

A final point on all POP: make sure it can be read from at least twenty feet back. Otherwise, hurried shoppers will walk right past.

Build It, and They Will Come?

Competition in the retail marketplace is fierce, and it will come at you from every conceivable angle. Your competition is not limited to stores in your own category. Retailers compete with every other demand for their customers' time and money. As a result, you must pay attention to how today's modern men and women live, what they want, and what they need. If you don't keep in touch with your potential customer base, you will lose it to your competitors. So, let's review some of the things shoppers want:

• **Tactile first.** As I have said before (but it's worth repeating), customers like to touch the product. We live in a tactile-deprived society. We can't touch what is on TV, in catalogues, or on eBay, Amazon, or anywhere else or the Internet. Thus, we go into stores at least partly (sometimes largely) for the pleasure of touching, hearing, smelling, or tasting something. It is from these sensations that almost *all* unplanned purchases stem. This is why correctly merchandising in a store, giving people the opportunity to interact with the product, can be more powerful than any marketing campaign you could ever develop.

- **Excitement second.** The *hunt* for the right product can be as exciting as the actual *buying* of the product—provided it isn't drawn out too long or made too difficult. Too many signs or point of purchase displays block customers' way to their discovery. Customers love to discover some products for which they have long searched. Your job as a retailer is to *subtly* have them find that product by seducing them into continuing their search through easy-to-maneuver aisles and persuasive, easy-to-read signs.

- **The more the merrier.** Stores that attract couples or friends shopping together usually do well because they create an atmosphere that fosters discussion that sells the merchandise for you. ("Ooo! Look what I found. Don't you just love it?" "Maybe I'll get one, too.")

- **Customer service.** The one battlefield where a small, locally owned store can compete against the chains is in customer service, which in turn creates customer loyalty. Customers want to shop where they feel wanted, appreciated, and even pampered. Any genuine contact initiated by a store employee (not including a mechanical, bored "Can I help you?") increases by 50% the likelihood that a customer will buy. And if you actually greet them by name, then they *will* become your loyal customer. At the same time, rude, slow, uninformed, and lazy service will turn them away from your store in a heartbeat, perhaps forever.

    The problem, of course, is that dedicated employees are not easy to come by or train. I will discuss the techniques of how to do this in Chapter 8.

- **Value-added.** Customers need to feel they are getting *real* value for their money. Sometimes we misunderstand this term. Value goes beyond just having the best price on an item. Customers need to be able to "shop" the item and pull it out of the sales rack. They need enough personal space to evaluate the goods without getting bumped or pushed by other customers. They must feel comfortable that if you advertise the product it will be in stock and that each item advertised is clearly marked. They want to be able to move through the checkout line quickly so they can get on with their lives.

Opening and running a retail shop is fun, rewarding, and often deeply satisfying. But it is a lot more complicated than "build it, and they will come."

Retail Detail

According to Walker Information (an Indianapolis, Indiana research firm), most consumers are not thrilled about where they shop, but don't feel a better choice exists. Out of habit or convenience they stick with a retailer, although they are indifferent to them. Their research found:

- Fifty-five percent of consumers aren't truly loyal to the stores they frequent.
- Another 12% are flight risks who may have already contemplated not returning to a store for yet another unsatisfactory shopping encounter.
- Only 45% are truly loyal to the stores where they most frequently shop, which means they both plan and want to maintain the relationship.
- Consumers are so starved for help that 41% are willing to pay more for qualified sales assistance. These customers consider checkout times too long and products too hard to locate.

Chapter 8

Recruiting and Retaining for Retail, Or:

Finding, Hiring, and Training Good People

Gen Xers come into a retail environment well informed.
They do research on the Internet, especially on bigger ticket items.
They'll come in with price-comparison charts
that they have printed out.
But they still need guidance from a trusted retailer.
Customer service can make or break a retailer.
—JENNIFER GANSHIRT, *American Demographics* (05/04)

YOU MIGHT THINK that finding the right location, stocking your store, and pleasing customers are going to be your most daunting challenges when opening a retail store, but think again. The biggest challenge in retailing today is hiring and training qualified people. No organization is stagnant, and today's employee turnover is higher than ever. Being the best and selling the most means recruiting and retaining the best.

Practices such as carefully screening new hires, thoroughly testing applicants, personally meeting each one, and, of course, ensuring that their services are fairly remunerated, lie at the core of recruiting the best employees. Retaining the best includes treating employees with respect, listening to their suggestions, occasionally weeding out the bad apples, and rewarding good performance.

The commitment to excellence starts with you, but since you can't be everywhere at once, quality must filter down through your valued deputies. Hiring less than the best reflects poorly not only on your organization, but also on you. Here are some things to keep in mind that you can tell and demonstrate to your current staff:

- **Always be hiring.** You always have an opening for someone who is very good. Great people always justify their pay, whether it applies to increasing the average sale, or to running the backroom with greater efficiency and expertise to save money. Also, great people help raise the bar for the entire staff, present and future.

- **Never consider your store fully staffed.** Even if you feel you are fully staffed, you should always be in the recruiting mode—looking for great people. Remember, in retailing, you always have to expect someone to leave. Even if your staff loves you and loves the work, a number are bound to leave for any number of personal reasons over which you have no control. When that happens, having a spare, fully qualified replacement already on hand is a Godsend.

- **Strive for excellence.** Your existing staff needs to know you will always hire a great person. If they know you are on a quest for excellence, employees will feel good about themselves for being on your team and yet know that they need to *keep* producing to stay on the team.

- **Use a reward system.** Recognize and reward your current staff monthly or as events call for it. Do not wait until the end of the year to tell them they did well. Recognize hard work and solid performance as it happens. Don't make rewards just an event; make it a mood that permeates the entire premises.

- **Remain focused.** Don't go overboard in trying to keep employees. A little turnover can sometimes be the best for both parties. Your retail store should be an energizing environment; you do not want people on your staff who make it stale or take it for granted.

- **Recognize your strengths.** Every business has assets that attract employees, enticing them to work there. Make your staff constantly aware of those benefits by creating a colorful brochure that lists all your employee benefits, such as discounts, flexible hours, fun working conditions, ample performance rewards, etc. Have your staff hand out these brochures to all potential hires. Those prospective employees will believe your employees more readily than they will believe you—and your current employees will be reminded how good they have it.

Ask Not What Your Employees Can Do for YOU:

What Can YOU Do for THEM?

A good listener is not only popular everywhere,
but after a while he knows something.
—WILSON MIZNER

Many first-time retailers see the hiring process as little more than a power play. "I'm the boss, you work for me. What can YOU bring to the organization?" While it's important to know that the buck stops with you, it's just as important to know what the person who is sitting across from you is feeling.

People work where they are happy, rewarded, and fulfilled. Will your store foster such feelings? As you are getting ready to hire, keep in mind what job applicants are looking for in today's job market:

- **Above average pay.** When you offer minimum or very low wages, job applicants immediately get the message that you don't really value your employees. Ask yourself, how motivated would you feel if you were applying to work in your store? Of course, it is bad business to overpay, but it is just as bad to underpay.

- **A clean, safe environment.** Because customers want to shop in this type of environment, this is how you need to keep your store. This should be an easy sell.

- **A job close to home.** With the ever-increasing traffic on the roads, escalating cost of gasoline, and added travel time, many prospective hires are willing to work for less money if the job is conveniently located near where they live. Try to recruit from your store's neighborhood. However, if your store is in a neighborhood where there are few, if any, potential employees (as may happen if you run an expensive boutique in an upscale area), consider hiring employees from a single location further away and then arranging for a car or small bus to pick them up and return them home every day.

- **A job that is fun.** People who like their work may stay in a job even though they know they can make more money elsewhere. Therefore, a fun environment reduces turnover. Feeling part of a team whose members work hard yet enjoy what they do and enjoy each other helps humanize a crazy work place. New employers often think that employees who are having fun are "goofing off" instead of working, but that may not be the truth. Check it out. If your employees are laughing but remain quickly responsive to your customers, you have fostered the atmosphere you want.

- **Respectful management.** Everyone wants to feel like a part of the team. For that reason, let everyone know that you listen and value their opinions. It will make them feel important and an important contributor to the team.

- **Appreciation of employee work.** Good employees are lost and the remaining employees' attitudes become more cynical if they perceive that they are working very hard but "no one cares." As a rule, people like working hard. If we stand around with nothing to do, time drags. However, there is no worse feeling than working extremely hard, getting everything just right, and then having your achievement ignored. Don't expect employees to give 110% if you're not willing to commend them for it.

There are many simple, quick, and inexpensive ways to reward stellar performance. Gift certificates to local merchants or restaurants, an "employee of the week/month" reward, free passes to a movie theater, or just a private conference in which you look them in the eye and say, "Your work matters, good job, and I'm paying attention." All those are wonderful ways to show employees your appreciation.

- **A place where pride matters.** Self-esteem is a driving factor in building long-term employee relationships. If your store—from the way you treat the customers to the merchandise you sell—is one everyone can be proud of, your employees will in turn reward you by staying a long time. Pride in your store starts with you. Don't be above picking up a piece of litter, helping out at the cash registers if the line is too long, or opening the front door for a customer. Leading by example shows not only pride in your store, but pride in yourself and your employees.

Where to Start Looking?

So now you know what you want from an employee and, in turn, what an employee wants from you. But where to start *looking* for them? There are several different ways to find the right people for your store:

- **Employee referrals.** If your employees are happy and admire the high standards you expect, they can quickly become your most effective "recruiting army." This has the benefit that the referral is usually someone you can trust because the employee who refers them won't want to wind up with egg on their face by bringing you someone unqualified or unreliable. Just remember that, if an employee brings in a recruit who works out and thereby saves you the expense of advertising or paying a recruiter's fee, in all fairness you should reward the finder with a "referral fee."

- **Customer referrals.** This is probably the most overlooked type of referral in retailing, perhaps because storeowners are too embarrassed to tell their loyal customers that they need help. However, part of what makes the customer feel connected to the store is the sense of family that comes from an honest exchange of ideas. You may be surprised at how helpful your customers may be. Not only are they keen to continue to receive superior service, but they may well know just the right recruit, perhaps their own high-school-aged child or a friend who's just reentering the work force. So both of you win. Just as your employees are compensated, if a customer brings in a good employee, you should reward that customer in some way. Of course, you shouldn't try to pay them, that's too crass, but a gift of merchandise or a gift certificate would be appropriate. It's a simple gesture, really just a token, but it's sure to be appreciated, and much cheaper than running an ad!

- **Networking with community organizations.** As you grow, you may eventually have to reach beyond your employees and customers to find good help. Contact both community agencies and government or religious groups that help people find work. Leaders of churches also know people looking for work. Your state's unemployment office may have state-sponsored programs available to help you find employees. Many cities and states offer welfare-to-work programs, Job Corps centers, and one-stop career centers. Senior citizen groups may have members who would be grateful for part-time employment. Let all the local, civic-minded groups know that your business is always on the lookout for great employees. Not only is this an excellent way to find staffers, but just look how many organizations will know about your store!

- **Internet job listings.** There are several commercial Web sites that list local employment opportunities. For a quick jump start, check out www.monster.com, www.careerbuilder.com, or www.jobbing.com. Before paying to be listed on these types of sites, however, check to see if your community has some free sites where you can list your opportunities instead. (Unfortunately for thrifty business owners, the best known of these is no longer free.) Nevertheless, www.craigslist.com remains an outstanding resource. This is a general bulletin board that started in the San Francisco Bay area. Their Web address will start you in Northern California, but just click on any of the major cities listed to go to the area of your choice. It is a free general-use bulletin board that runs the gamut from dating to general classified ads to job notices and is especially popular with creative and wired types. While everything on the site was once free for both posters and responders, they have recently begun charging to place help-wanted ads. Nevertheless, it's well worth investigating, particularly if you're located in a major, somewhat edgy city like Los Angeles, New York, or Seattle.

- **Student employment.** Many high schools and most universities have career counseling offices where, depending on the type of employee you are looking for, you can post your job for free. Also, think about taking an ad out in the school newspaper for a minimum cost. They may also have a Web site where you can post your job for free. Around campus there may be bulletin boards where you can post flyers. Again, not only are you conducting a job search, but you are also earning more free advertising.

- **Traditional newspaper ads.** Obviously, your local newspaper would be more than happy to accept your paid classified ad. And, in fact, this is where most people start their job search. Make sure you put the ad under the proper heading. Try to be as specific as possible so you attract the right people and are not drowned in a sea of applications from people whose credential are wide of the mark. If you don't want to be interrupted all day with phone calls, only put a fax number or e-mail address for the contact information.

- **Non-traditional newspaper ads.** Some of your best potential employees may not be looking for a job but, if they see your ad as they read the newspaper in their daily routine, it may trigger a reason to talk with you. Try running an ad in the lifestyle section of the paper or possibly the sports section to attract this reluctant, but potentially worthwhile, group of future employees.

- **Job fairs.** More and more service clubs and chambers of commerce are sponsoring job fairs. They can be excellent vehicles for finding employees. Local schools also may hold job fairs. Even prisons are holding job fairs to help inmates find jobs prior to their release. Rehabilitated prisoners can turn out to be your most loyal employees. (Also, there may be some financial benefits with tax credits in hiring these "higher-risk" people.)

- **Poach from other companies.** Whenever you receive outstanding service from an employee at another store, give them your business card with a note on the back saying, "Thanks for the great service. My company is always looking for outstanding people. If you are ever thinking of changing your job, please call me." If the person is happy with their current job, you've just made his or her day. If not, you've found a new employee. And, even if the person doesn't want the job, he or she may know someone else who does.

What to Start Looking for:

Ten Characteristics of the Ideal Recruit

Remember, it is impossible to *manage* effectively without *hiring* effectively. As I have said, you can't be everywhere, all the time. You can't be in the store at all times. Therefore you *must* hire good people to represent you to your customers.

The goal, then, is to hire individuals with the personality and service-minded disposition necessary to provide excellent customer service. Here are ten qualities you should be looking for and the probing questions to ask yourself before offering anyone a job:

- **Service minded.** Have the individual's past accomplishments shown a positive attitude and reliability?
- **Motivated.** Is he or she in retail for the right reasons (because of a love for the work) or for all the wrong ones (because no other job is easily found or it seems like the best way to get some neat clothes at a discount)?
- **Self-directed.** Is this the sort of person who will provide excellent service even when nobody's watching?

- **Relationship oriented.** Does the individual seem naturally warm, adept at making polite small talk? Or does he or she sound phony, as if just mouthing nice things to say instead of meaning them?
- **Attention to detail.** Does he or she sweat the small stuff? In retail, it's all about the details.
- **Team player.** Do they seem like they will get along with everyone, or are they just out for themselves?
- **Technical knowledge or aptitude for same.** Can he or she master the technical details required to back up that smile, such as working the cash register, locating an item, or learning what it takes to answer customers questions?
- **Approachable and confident.** Is this someone others feel good about confiding in not only about their retail needs, but also about personal needs?
- **Energy.** Does he or she have the physical and mental energy necessary to do the work?
- **Willing to improve—continuously.** Is this someone who will be up to the challenge of continually evolving as your store (hopefully) improves itself year after year?

Q & A for Your New Talent

The most important quality in a retail job candidate is the ability to communicate effectively, not only with your customers but also with you and the entire team. Here are some questions you can ask to help identify the traits that would make the applicant a great employee. Remember to follow up on all of these items with open-ended questions such as "Tell me more about . . . " or "What does that mean?" The idea is to keep applicants talking because the interview is not about you, it is about them:

- **What did you like most about your last job?** You're in trouble if they shrug and answer "breaks" or "paid vacations."
- **What did you like least about your last job?** Here is where you pick

up any negative attitudes. Anything that sounds like "I had to work too hard" or "My boss never lets me relax" spells trouble.

- **Why did you take your last job?** This gives you real insight into why he or she is applying with you now.
- **What do you consider the most important element of your job?** This will tell you what excites them about retail.
- **What do you look for in a supervisor?** This is actually a question that lets you see if you have the traits to manage this person.
- **Where would you like to be in three years?** This is a trick question in that it may reveal if someone is *not* committed to working for you for a long time. For example, you may find out they are moving out of state at the end of the year. The right answer, of course, is "Working right here for you with more responsibility and making more money."
- **What are your goals?** Most candidates can't answer this clearly and/or concisely, so it is designed to give you a chance to see how they react when they do not know the answer—something that often arises on the floor of any retail establishment.
- **If I were to hire you, can you describe your ideal job?** Listen carefully to this answer because, again, it will give you insight into what excites this person. This way you will know where to position him on the staff.

Top Ten Traits of Effective Retail Employees

The top ten traits you need for successful retail employees are listed below. You may or may not exhibit all of these yourself; nobody's perfect. Chances are that the majority will ring true. In any case, never be afraid to hire someone who is smarter or more appropriate to the task than you. You're still the boss! And your company needs great employees to make your business continue to grow. Your ideal employee will possess:

1. **A positive attitude.** Shopping should be fun; so should working in a store. Can your applicant be positive the whole time he or she is on the floor?

2. **Common sense.** You can't train common sense; people either have it or they don't. Common sense is a vital skill in retail, where instincts as much as rules define a busy sales floor.

3. **People skills.** Retail is all about communication and is the ultimate "people business."

4. **Sales ability.** Whether you're paying on commission or a straight hourly wage, retail is sales and sales is retail. You may not want an employee whose "hard sell" approach comes off as too aggressive and alienates customers, but you do want people who can convince customers to buy, without annoying them. Everyone has a different style of selling. For example, one of the best sales people I ever met had a severe stammer, but he used it to his advantage: people were so keen to finish his sentences, they sold themselves.

   "Would you p-p-prefer to p-p-pay by c-c-cash or c-c-credit c-c-ca—"

   "Oh, credit card, certainly. Credit card," the customer would say, determined to bring things to a close, even if they hadn't previously been sure they wanted to buy.

   The point is, however they do it, every employee should have making the sale the overriding goal.

5. **Strong communication skills.** If, during the interview, you sense a lack of communication, this may not be the applicant for you.

6. **High level of motivation.** A good employee must want the job and must be motivated to succeed.

7. **Product knowledge or the ability to pick up this knowledge quickly.** New products are a boon to the retail business, and failed products are its bane. You want someone who treats a dog of an onion slicer with the same enthusiasm as a spiffy new coffee grinder.

8. **Ability to move up in the organization.** You want someone committed to achievement, just as you are, and who isn't above starting at the bottom to get to the top.

9. **Leadership qualities.** Can this applicant supervise underlings, or even peers, without abusing his or her power and sounding demeaning?

10. **The ability to be a self-starter.** This is a term we hear a lot, but what does it really mean? Basically this term describes people who won't let a display sit empty even if you didn't specifically tell them to fill it.

Motivating Your Staff

Once you've assembled your "dream team" of employees, you'll have to create a good work environment to keep them. The following are some strategies to help you motivate your staff:

• **Hold brainstorming sessions.** None of us has all the answers, all the time, and good employees are close to customers and often see issues we may miss. Therefore, whether you are looking for new ideas or seeking solutions to something you sense is not right, don't be afraid to ask for your staff's input. Far from appearing weak, you will show that you trust and value their opinion. Having your employees participate in problem solving or generating ideas gives them a sense of being a valued part of the business, and thus, more connected and are more likely to be loyal.

• **Conduct training, both in-house and outside the business.** With continued training and education, employees become more skilled, efficient, enthusiastic about their job, and even more dependable. In-store training is great, but don't hesitate to send them to an outside seminar or trade show. It may be costly, but good training pays off in the long run.

• **Make the work environment fun.** A job turns into a career only if employees are enjoying themselves and feel like part of a larger team. Bring in lunch every once in awhile or have everyone pitch in for a potluck lunch. Even something as simple as a break room that's always stocked with a full bowl of candy or other snacks can go a long way toward cheering up an otherwise dour workforce. Run group contests where the entire team wins something. Be creative, be unique, most of all—don't afraid to be *fun!*

An acquaintance had a problem with several members of his staff who, while otherwise good employees, were habitually late to work. He tried everything, including bribes and threats. Eventually, he hit upon a stroke of near genius.

"If even one of you is late, you'll have to buy me coffee and donuts in the morning. But if you're all on time, I'll have to buy coffee and donuts for all of you," he challenged. The result: his staff cheered with glee as he ironically feigned sullen reluctance and bought donuts for eighty-seven out of ninety days. Naturally, the reluctance was all a show to entertain his crew—he couldn't have been happier to buy the donuts. His total cost, he told me, was about a quarter of what the unsuccessful on-time bonus he had offered would have cost him.

- **Treat everyone as individuals.** Everyone is different, with different needs and different strengths. People are motivated in different ways: security, money, prestige, friendship, stimulation, etc. Therefore, you may well have to treat everyone differently, although always with fairness. Never lose sight of the fact that teamwork is what ultimately makes a retail business successful. When you care about your people, they will care about you, your customers, *and* your business.

- **Establish standards of operation.** Chaos reigns where rules are unclear or invisible. Many times employees make mistakes because they do not know which boundaries apply. How much of a discount can they offer on a damaged good? When is a customer's harassment too much? Rules need to be established that are workable and consistent so employees can feel independent and free to succeed (within controlled limits) at what they do best—selling.

- **Make to-do lists for everyone.** Daily and weekly task lists are one of the best tools retailers have to increase both productivity and profitability. These lists should itemize both selling tasks and those non-selling tasks on which employees can work when not dealing with customers. Remember, working hard is more fun than standing around idle. Prioritize the lists so the most important projects are accomplished first. Far from seeing them as a drag, employees will feel a sense of accomplishment when they complete their tasks. Don't forget to check up on these lists because if you don't, employee morale will suffer and even collapse. The worst thing that can happen to morale is that certain employees *always* complete their tasks with no reward, while others *never* complete their tasks with no punishment.

- **Be an effective manager of people.** Supervisors have to wear many hats. They are coaches, mentors, and advisors. Motivation by fear does not work with this generation and a dictatorial style will scare away employees in no time. On the other hand, employees actually want strong leadership. You're not a dictator; you are the boss. Let your staff know that you do not have all the answers, that you want to tap into their knowledge and experience, but that once you've made a decision, that's it.

- **Assign employee mentors.** Everyone needs someone they can trust who they can go to with questions, someone to guide them through tough workplace issues when you are not around or when, as the boss, you seem too intimidating to them. Therefore, employee mentors are a wonderful asset to any retail store.

- **Avoid petty rules.** Nothing turns people off more that rules that do not make sense. Get rid of rules that do not have good reasoning behind them, but keep and explain the reasons for the rules that help employees perform better.

- **Praise good employees.** There are several ways to praise your workers. Face to face is obviously the easiest technique. A personal thank you note goes a long way as well, especially if you make it public by posting it on your bulletin board. Public praise at an employee meeting works well. An official letter to a college or to a potential future employer extolling a student employee is always much appreciated. If your letter gets the student the job, other students will line up around the block to work for your organization! In all of this, remember that praise should be immediate. The longer you wait, the less effective it will be.

Motivating Yourself:

The Eight Principles of Continuous Improvement

Continuously improving the production of your employees requires constant attention and respect. And that starts with you. If you follow the next eight steps, your employees are sure to follow *you*. Here are eight principles of continuous self-improvement:

- **Stress teamwork.** You can't do it all yourself, nor should you try. Work as a team at improving and share the duties, as well as the successes, of your store.

- **Focus on the customers.** When the customer is the focus, the focus is on target. Always.

- **Acknowledge problems openly.** A problem won't go away just because you cover it up. Don't blame, hide, or lie. Admit the problem and move on with full determination to solve it.

- **Always make improvements.** Never stop improving. Learn from your mistakes, learn from customers, learn from seminars, learn from classes, learn from books, learn from tapes—just never stop learning to improve.

- **Inform every staff member.** Through meetings, memos, e-mails, and informal discussions, inform your staff members of steps you're taking for continuous improvement, both personally and professionally.

- **Develop self-discipline.** Start with yourself. Continuously improve, and demand the same from your co-workers and staff.

- **Recruit the right individuals.** Develop a winning team and, as appropriate, add to that winning team with more winners. Don't be afraid to terminate those who are dragging the store down.

- **Enable every staff member.** Don't just tell your staff what to do, give them the tools to do it by establishing rules and leading by example.

Selling Success

Don't doubt for a minute that retailing is a business of *selling*. Contrary to popular opinion, great salespeople do not have a certain look, a certain style, or certain dress code. They don't drive a certain car or live in a certain part of town. But what they all *do* have in common is the desire to serve the customer.

There are no universal traits of a great salesperson. They come in all shapes and sizes. Some are impeccably dressed, some relatively sloppy. But, in your store, you want not only someone who can sell, but also a person who can fit with your team and add to your store's solid reputation. Thus, your sales people should:

- **Look professional.** The image of the salespeople is vital to your store's own image. Whether it's a store uniform, apron, three-piece suit, or the clothes the store sells, you should specify the dress code.
- **Never ignore customers.** A great salesperson is always selling, but selling doesn't mean pressuring. Customers are people, and selling is a people business. So why would a great salesperson ever ignore a customer?
- **Greet customers by name where possible.** Depending on the amount of traffic you see, this could be impossible or easy. Either way, salespeople always try to establish relationships with their customers.
- **Be friendly and willing to listen to customers.** They understand the importance of serving the customer, and know that to best serve a customer they must first listen to that customer.
- **Suggest another item if the product the customer wants is not available.** This is where knowing your inventory is important. Employees should be familiar with all of the store's products, new and old, and where to find them.
- **Help the customer buy multiple items by suggesting related goods.** Any employee can sell a tarp to someone who comes in to buy a tarp, but it takes a salesperson to find out why the person is buying a tarp

and then sell them the brushes, rollers, paint, and all the rest of the stuff they need for their home improvement project.

- **Always thank the customer.** No one should ever take a customer for granted. Without customers, even Wal-Mart would have to close up shop. Customers are always to be thanked, even after a complaint is resolved.
- **Follow up with the customers to make sure they were satisfied.** It's not enough to send a customer on his way with a bag of goods. Great salespeople want to know what they're doing right and especially what they're doing wrong. A phone call to that tarp buyer asking how his or her home improvement is going would work wonders.

Getting Customers in the Mood to Buy

Training salespeople is as much an art as a science. The salesperson's challenge is to turn "lookers" into "buyers." Customers are in the store because the merchandising concept attracted them. But whether or not they actually buy something is still up to your sales staff.

The days of the pushy salesperson are gone. Customers want easy, no-hassle service from people who are non-threatening and non-aggressive. To convert people from looking to buying, that is, to first get the customers into the mood to buy and then to close the sale, good salespeople:

- Talk about what the customer wants to talk about.
- Focus on what the customer wants, not necessarily on what they need.
- Never try to prove they are better or know more than the customer.
- Treat people the way *they* would like to be treated.

The Likeability Factor

Customers often have problems. They complain. They are dissatisfied.

Whether this is really the store's problem or the emotional baggage customers brought with them is not always easy to understand. One thing is sure, those problems will be easier to solve if the customer likes the salesperson. Salespeople can get customers to like them by:

- **Leaving their ego at the door.** Customers don't like arrogant or know-it-all salespeople. It's not their job to make your salespeople feel better about themselves. Instead, it's the other way around. Your staff must be easily approachable.

- **Paying attention to details.** Whether or not they verbalize it, customers really do appreciate the little things. Notifying them of new merchandise that may interest them, remembering their birthdays, sharing good news about something you have in common—all of this goes a long way toward closing the current sale and the next one as well.

- **Extending sincere compliments.** People like doing business with happy, bubbly personalities, and they enjoy sincere compliments. Sincerity is a rare commodity. If customers can find it in your store, they'll find a reason to come back. Beware of salespeople who flatter insincerely; few of us like a sycophant.

- **Using laughter, the great social lubricant.** Have fun with the customers. People love to do business with people who laugh and have a good time. And remember, when you're having fun, time really does fly.

- **Making a good impression right away.** The goal with new customers is to get them talking so you can find out their wants and needs. Never treat a new customer with any less enthusiasm than you would your best customer. Customers *do* judge a book by its cover, so never miss the opportunity to make a great impression.

- **Using the "feel good" factor.** Customers buy with their emotions, and the most successful salespeople are the ones who make customers *feel* good about doing business with their company.

- **Maintaining self-control.** Salespeople must be very careful not to take their frustration out on the next customer if the previous one has caused a major heartache. This is called "last customer residue." So, for the moment, forget what went wrong with the last customer and move quickly on to the new customer with an added portion of charm—just to make sure none of your prior annoyance accidentally bleeds through.

What NOT to Say to Customers

There's a TV show called *What NOT to Wear.* My version is What NOT to Say to a Customer. Knowing what not to say is as important as knowing what to say. Here is a list of comments that drive customers away and should never come out of a salesperson's mouth:

- "You could never afford this."
- "I only work here . . . "
- "Everything we have is out on the shelves."
- "It's over there."
- "We would need cash from you."
- *They* instead of *we.* For example: "Do you sell these in blue?" "No, *they* don't." (The store is every employee's responsibility—and property. *We* should always be the term.)

The Five Steps of the Selling Process

It may seem confusing, but, in fact, the retail selling process is made up of five steps: the greeting, bonding and asking questions, making suggestions, overcoming objections, and closing the sale. Here we discuss each of these five in more detail:

- **Greeting customers.** When customers walk through the door, be sure to express gratitude for their coming in. If the store is extremely busy, acknowledge them with a wave or quick "hello." At the very least, smile! Let them know someone will be right with them. Customers understand if you are busy, they just don't want to be ignored.
- **Creating a bond and asking questions.** To sell something you need to

know something about the customer and what they need. Remember that the customers may walk out with products completely different from what they came in for. The more you know the more you can help them select which product is right for them. Without getting pushy, you need to know who the item is for and the needs of the buyer. Make sure the customer does most of the talking. There's nothing worse than a retail salesperson who takes a customer's well-meaning, "How are you?" and turns it into a five-minute discussion of his or her personal life. That's a sure way to kill a sale.

- **Making suggestions based on what you learn from the customer.** Show the merchandise with style and enthusiasm. Demonstrate product knowledge and personalize your presentation to the customer based on what he or she says, not on what you assume.

- **Overcoming objections.** If the objection is that the price is lower in another store, match it if you can verify it. If the customer objects to the product's quality, recognize that some customers need a choice—that items may look better to them when compared to something similar. The key is not to give up when other options exist.

- **Closing the sale.** This is the most difficult and important part of selling. Most people are actually afraid to close because, like most of us, they fear rejection. As long as they keep the customer talking, they feel as if the sale may yet happen. Of course, they are wrong. If they let the customer vacillate too long, premature buyers remorse sets in (especially if the item was being bought on impulse), and the customer walks away.

  The vital thing to remember when asking for the order (closing the sale), is not to ask a question to which a plausible answer is "no." Do not ask, "Would you like to buy this product?" If you do, you are encouraging a "no" answer just as much as a "yes" answer. Rather, ask a question to which either response is the one you want to hear. "Would you prefer to pay by cash or credit card?" is a classic. "Should I wrap up the red or the blue?", "Would you like this gift wrapped or as is?", "After we make the alterations, should I send it home or would you like to pick it up here?" These are all "closers" because they assume the sale has already been made and now we're only dealing with the post-purchase details.

Of course, there are other ways to nudge the teetering buyer forward, especially when it is too early to use the either/or closer. "Let's just do this" you might say, or "Everyone's buying it" or "Will you be using it during the day or at night?" And then, whatever the answer, "Well, great. Then would you prefer to pay by cash or credit card?"

When Customers Complain:

Five Strategies of Complaint Management

In the wondrous world of retail there is really only one sure truth: customers *will* complain. It may be for a variety of reasons, and not always due to anything you have done. It could be something from their personal lives, or what side of the bed they got up on, a late shipment causing a product delay, a rainy day. No matter the cause, when customers complain, the following five strategies of complaint management will go a long way toward resolving the problem and making sure it never happens again:

- **Accept personal responsibility.** First and foremost, you are the agent responsible for solving the problem. Passing the buck only aggravates the issue; personal accountability solves it.
- **Listen.** Learning to listen is critical to soothing the ego or dealing with the issues of an aggravated or unhappy customer. Try to listen not only to what the customer is saying, but also to what's behind what they are saying. It's a learned skill, but a vital one to your continued success.
- **Apologize.** No matter how hard it is, or whose fault it was, or the circumstances surrounding the complaint, or the time of day, or how hungry you are, or how close to the end of your shift it is, *always* apologize to the customer for any inconvenience.
- **Fix it, and then some.** Unfortunately, apologizing is never enough. Fixing the problem is the only solution a customer will accept.

- **Avoid it the next time.** Complaint management means handling the problem so effectively that it doesn't happen again. Learn from mistakes, and you'll have to deal with complaint management less often and satisfied customers more often.

The Exit Interview

No matter how well you find, hire, and train good people, inevitably you *will* lose staff to illness, family issues, relocation, and even to other businesses. The trick is not to fight it. Instead, embrace it. One of the best tools you have for people who leave your store is the all-important exit interview. Here you can learn some valuable lessons. The leaver is no longer inhibited from telling you the truth. "I'm leaving because I can't stand the assistant manager, Suzy. Whenever you're away, she spends all her time talking to her boyfriend." This is information you wouldn't get nearly as easily from a current employee. Of course, you'll want to check this charge out before accusing Suzy; the leaver may have been vindictive and untruthful. The point is, what you could learn from a departing employee may help you keep other valuable employees.

Don't be afraid to ask for, and hear, the truth. It may be unpleasant, but knowing there are problems you haven't observed, employee resentment, or other issues, could lead to improvements that will save your business in the long run. Provided you solve the problems, that is.

Retail Detail

The Asian population today is about twelve million people and represents 15% of total population growth. Half live in the West with the heaviest concentration in California. It is a young population, 30% younger than eighteen years and only 7% sixty-five years or older. As with the Hispanic market, if a store is located in an area with a large Asian population such as San Francisco (31% of the total population is Asian) or Seattle (13%), signage and products aimed at this group may be extremely helpful.

Chapter 9

Dealing with Vendors, Or:

Vendors Can Be Your Best Friends or Your Worst Nightmares

In our free enterprise system, companies and industries
develop and improve through competition, and a key requirement
for competition is knowledge about the operations of
all major competitors in the market.
Such knowledge inspires one competitor to gain or protect
an edge over another and motivates lesser competitors in a market
to emulate the operations of the market leaders.

—JACK LOVE, Publisher of *Internet Retailer*

L ET'S FACE IT, you want to open your own retail store to be more independent, to be your own boss, to set your own hours, to make your own rules. But, as we continue our journey through the ups and downs of this world called retail, I have a feeling that you're learning, as I did, that in retailing, as in every business, compromises must be made.

One of those compromises is that, although you are your own boss, you still serve many masters. Your store hours may be set by the district, shopping center, or strip mall where your store is located.

Employees need insurance, break times, and benefits both seen and unseen. Customers may ignore your lavish window display, forcing you to change it. Fads come and fads go, and your merchandise, so carefully chosen and researched, loses value. Most telling of all, your customers demand certain products, services, and goods. And, although their demands change, to become successful you must supply them with what they want.

The question is, how can you keep up? This is where yet another contributor to your retail domain comes into play: the vendor.

Working with vendors has dramatically changed over the last decade. At one time you could count on vendors and manufacturers' reps stopping into your store with the latest and greatest items. That was before company mergers, rising gas prices, and the decline in company expense accounts.

Now, especially if your business is outside a major metropolitan area, except for your local suppliers, you hardly ever see a vendor's face. As a result, store owners need to be creative about how they find the right items at the right time at the right price.

Before we start dealing with vendors, let's talk about what makes a good buyer. Great buyers:

- **Understand that buying is an art, not a science.** Much as I would like to write the perfect book on how to buy, it simply can't be done. Not by me and, no matter what they tell you, not by anyone else. Buying is not black and white. It is an ever-changing, market-driven skill, forever in a state of flux.

    Of course, some things are basic accounting, such as, "I sold one thousand packs of batteries last Christmas so there is a good chance that, with the same customer base, I will sell another one thousand packs this Christmas. And if my customers are growing at 10% a year, there is a good chance that this Christmas I will sell an additional 10% of batteries, so I should buy enough for 1,100 sales!"

    However, the majority of what you buy is based on pulling together all of the information you have gathered from your research, readings, and interaction with customers and employees; adding a dose of "gut feelings"; mixing it all up in your brain; and then making an educated guess. So take heart—even if this is your first store, you're up to speed with the best store owners in the world!

- **Understand that buying is actually selling.** You are selling your store as well as yourself to vendors to get what you want. These personal and business assets reflect your advantages and your strengths. A great buyer makes a vendor understand that having their merchandise in your store will be an asset for the vendor. Vendors understand that new businesses and outstanding retailers are the lifeblood of their business. They understand that featuring their products in advertising and in-store displays helps build confidence in their brand. Vendors also understand that you may have an impressive database of customers who would be natural buyers of their products. A great buyer conveys all of these messages in a concise, quick conversation. As a result, the vendor, instead of pushing his merchandise on the buyer, *helps* the buyer, providing concessions, adding merchandising support, etc. You've turned a sales call into a buying call.

- **Understand that vendors need to get as much for their money as possible.** An old retailing saying is: "Money is made in the buy." If you buy a product at the right price and under the right terms, you can sell it for a price that guarantees it will move quickly and make money. If you overpay for goods, you are going to end up trying to sell them for a higher price than they are really worth and, lo and behold, your customers will get to know this. They may not know it right away, but over time they will sense that you are overpriced. Today's customers are savvy, and comparison shopping is the name of the game. One thing you want to avoid is the reputation of being pricey. Therefore, always negotiate with the following in mind: to serve your customers well, to make sure that they will be getting the most for *their* money, you have to get the most for yours.

Pricing Your Product

Before you even talk to your first vendor, be prepared. You need a plan. In your head, or better still, written down in your business plan, you need to have a solid, consistent philosophy on how you are going to price the products you sell.

The problem in setting the right price is that, on the one hand, to please your customers, beat your competitors, and then maximize sales, you want low prices. On the other hand, to maximize your profit margins, improve the quality of your store, provide better service, and ultimately take more money home, you want high prices. As the king in *The King and I* put it, it's "a puzzlement"!

Unfortunately, there are no clear or easy answers to the pricing question. Like so much else in retailing, it comes down to a matter of your judgment. However, your judgment should be informed by a number of considerations that, taken together (and proven in the crucible of trial and error), will lead you to the right answer.

As you think about pricing, remember that while very important, price is not the only criterion you customers consider when they shop. They are also influenced by, and pay extra for, branded products, convenience, hard-to-find merchandise, status products, prestige, elegant surroundings, confidence in the merchandise, and much more. If you buy a diamond at Tiffany's, you pay a lot more than if you buy an identical stone on Forty-seventh Street, Manhattan's jewelry district. Therefore, you're better off buying from Forty-seventh Street, *if* you know a lot about diamonds. If you don't, you may well be cheated in the jewelry district and wind up paying far too much. So, if you are a diamond neophyte, you're well advised to buy at Tiffany's because of the safety factor. You are paying more, you could say, as insurance. And, of course, for the pretty blue box!

Do not make the mistake of thinking there is a set formula to pricing goods. Remember, it is against the law for a manufacturer to dictate what a product is sold for. This is part of the Sherman Antitrust Act, which was written long ago to protect customers from price gouging. These days a manufacturer may choose not to do business with you for any number of reasons, but although they can recommend prices, they may not dictate the price for which you sell the merchandise.

There are several factors to noodle around in your head as you are thinking of what products you want to sell, and at what price. The goal here is to balance maximum sales (i.e., turnover) with maximum margins on every item you sell. Well, not quite every item. You will make mistakes when you buy. Some items won't move. So, when you set your overall pricing policy, remember that you will have to mark down or adjust your pricing on slow-moving goods.

Here is a story I particularly like that sums up a prevailing attitude about pricing: Two butchers are located across the street from one another. One day a lady walks into one of the stores and sees that New York steaks are priced at $9 a pound. She says to the butcher, "You know, across the street, steaks are $8 a pound."

"So why don't you buy them there?" asks the butcher.

"Because," she says, "they are out of stock."

"Oh, well," he replies, deadpan, "when I'm out of stock, mine are $7 a pound."

As this anecdote implies, prices shouldn't be written in stone. Along those lines, here are some critical factors to consider when pricing the merchandise:

• **Price comparisons.** Just as your customers compare prices and quality between you and your competitors, so you should compare these qualities between your vendors. Don't be fooled by the charming salesperson or the impressive sell sheet. Really investigate competitive products and decide which ones will give your customers the best value. "Sell" your vendors by convincing them they *need* their merchandise in your store—and that they should give you a price break to get it in there! Remember, there are always other vendors out there; perhaps one of them will give you a better deal. Keep searching. Effective buying is a never-ending task.

- **Brand value.** Does the brand you are thinking of buying justify a prestige price? Look at the complete value of the item, including quality, durability, and function, not just at the name on the package. Does adding the name to the package make it worth more than another name? Don't forget to keep up with the latest trends. Some brands have less value in the marketplace than others. This is often due to customers' perceptions. If you don't know which brands are hot and which ones are not, it will be hard to price them correctly.

- **Perceived value.** How does the item look compared to its price? If customers worry that there must be something wrong with a product because it is too cheap for the way it looks, then you have under-priced the item. On the other hand, if you overhear customers complaining that a price is too high, that message is clear as well.

- **Competition.** If the item you are selling is carried in a lot of stores, then you will need to price it at or below the going retail rate. As we've already discussed, customers comparison shop, and so should you. Know your competitors' prices for similar items. On the other hand, if your item is unique, or at least can't be found in stores close to yours, then you can grab some extra markup.

- **The fine art of loss leadership.** If you are running a store where low prices are a major factor, then one of your goals is to give customers the impression that you are very low priced— lower than your competitors. The problem is if you price everything below your competition, chances are you won't make enough profit to stay in business. After all, even though you're a good buyer, you can't pay *that* much less for your merchandise.

So, how do you demonstrate to your customers that you are the lowest-priced store in town? The answer is to keep most of your merchandise at competitive levels, that is, at the same price as your competitors, or sometimes at slightly more. You accumulate all these small extra profits into a war chest. Then, you choose a popular item whose price is well known to most of your customers, and you offer it at a drastically low price. You may even lose money on it. But that's okay because you've covered your loss with your war chest.

And what do your customers think? "My, did you see that his store's selling steaks at two bucks less per pound than anyone else? Boy, does that store have hot prices!"

- **Merchandise department.** Every merchandise category has different parameters defining what customers are willing to pay. And every type of store engenders a different pricing mindset in its customers. A woman willing to pay $100 for a treatment cream at Neiman Marcus, would balk at paying $19.95 for a jar of cream at her supermarket. Thus, you need to understand your customers' price limits by type of store and by each product category.

  My wife and I were just in Nordstrom Rack, which is where Nordstrom moves their markdowns when they are done with them in their main stores. We were there to find my wife a dress for a wedding. We walked into the designer room and in a mere five minutes she walked right back out. When I asked her why, she said the dresses were too expensive even though they were only 25% of the original selling price. So I went back in to check it out in more detail. Dresses that were originally $1,000 were now selling for $250. What a deal, I thought. But my wife was not about to buy a $250 dress from a markdown store. At *that* location, they were outside her category comfort level. Customers know what something *should* cost in a specific type of store and in a specific merchandise category. So should you.

- **Store ambiance.** The way your store looks will also influence your pricing. Does your store feel like a warehouse, where only bare-bones pricing is expected? Does it look like a luxury store, where customers expect to pay more because the perception of the goods' value will be higher? Prices that don't reflect the décor, and vice versa, will give customers mixed feelings as to your sincerity as a merchant. Not a good feeling!

- **Employee input.** Don't be ashamed to ask your employees (or even some of the customers you trust) what an item should sell for. Don't tell them what you are paying for it, of course; just ask what they *think* it should sell for. You may be surprised that they feel you can sell it for more than you thought. A side effect of this exercise is that they really do appreciate your asking them for their opinion. You may also recruit certain employees (especially one from a generation different than yours) to shop the competition, keeping their eyes, in addition to your own, on those trends, fads, brands, and prices that are so important for your staying at the cutting edge.

- **Merchandise look and feel.** We've already discussed how customers treat shopping as a tactile experience. This should go for retailers as well. Case in point: sometimes you should not price a product until it actually arrives at your store. Samples or pictures you buy from are sometimes better, and sometimes worse, than the actual merchandise.

- **Market value.** The cliché, "Get what the market will bear," always applies. Of course, you should consider what you paid for the merchandise but the real decision on pricing doesn't depend on cost. If what you paid determined what you can sell it for, I wouldn't be sitting here with a bunch of worthless dot-com stocks! The decision whether to buy an item at the best price at which it is offered depends on the price at which you believe you can sell it. On some items you can take a large margin; on others your margin will be small.

    The problem, of course, arises when your competitor is "low-balling" a must-have item. Competitors know about loss leaders just as you do! One answer is to take a deep breath, match your competitor, and take your loss with the best grace you can muster. Another is to keep the item in stock at a reasonable price, but deemphasize it. Feature and display something else, ideally something your competitor is selling at a slightly elevated price.

A Few Words about Margin

There are several different ways to make money in the retail business. The first and most obvious, of course, is to sell a ton of merchandise at small margins. The second is to sell fewer products with a higher margin. The third is to sell a lot of merchandise at decent margins.

I have always believed in the third option, but to make it work, each product and category must be analyzed to maximize the difference between cost and retail without putting your retail price out of the reach or expectations of your customers.

Preparing for the Buy

The most crucial, yet most difficult aspect of retailing is managing the type and amount of merchandise in the store at any given time. Why? This is difficult because of three factors:

1. **Temptation.** As you begin dealing with several vendors in several different settings, whether in their beautiful showrooms or at booth after booth at a trade show, the temptation is always there to buy a lot more than can actually fit into your store—or your budget. Trust me, vendors know this. Always remember that you will be dealing with polished sales reps with smooth presentations and goods that scream out "choose me for your store." Knowledge (and a firm grip on your Open to Buy) is your best weapon against temptation. Be sure you know exactly what you need and what you can afford. And remember, each time you buy something, be sure that you reduce your remaining Open to Buy. When you've used it up, *stop buying.*

2. **Timing.** The timing of product coming in to your store is crucial. The problem is if you give an order to a vendor today, he may ship tomorrow or, if his delivery is delayed from overseas, in a month. In that case, the shelf where the goods normally sit in the store may be empty. In retail, as in just about everything else you do in life, timing is crucial.

3. **Planning:** Paperwork can be a comfort or a nuisance, depending on your point of view, but planning and keeping the paperwork organized is vital to your long-term buying success. Never, and I repeat *never,*

make a buying decision until you are sure it fits within your financial buying plans. It is okay to substitute one product buy for another; it is *not* okay to buy more than your Open to Buy permits. Many major chains have gone broke simply by bringing in more products than they could afford. The vendor community shares information on retailers who pay on time and those that do not. You can afford to be *somewhat* slow; however, you never want to be relegated to the "slow pay" category. It is always better to pass on a deal than to buy something you cannot afford.

Basic Steps to a Successful Negotiation

Real communication is an attitude, an environment.
It's the most interactive of all processes.
It requires countless hours of eyeball-to-eyeball back and forth.
It involves more listening than talking.
It is a constant interactive process aimed at creating consensus.
—JACK WELCH, Former CEO of General Electric

Like buying or selling, negotiating is another skill that can't be consigned to some black and white category. Often unpleasant, occasionally emotional, and *always* challenging, the art of negotiation is just that—an art.

Each vendor and each deal may be handled differently, depending on what is at stake. Some buyers think negotiating is the highlight of their job, while others dread this aspect of the retail world.

Don't get too hung up about negotiating. The more you do it, the better you'll get at it. Until then, however, if you keep the following negotiating skills and tips in the back of your mind at all times, you should fare well with all your vendors.

Be Prepared

You know your store, your customers, and your niche intimately. Your vendors, however, sell throughout your region or even across the nation. They probably don't know what is exactly right for your community or your store.

Moreover, however helpful and friendly vendors may be, remember that just like you and me, they are looking out for themselves first. As such, most vendors will try to push what is right for their business, not necessarily for yours. To counterbalance their enthusiasm for their products, you must be prepared to evaluate their products and decide, as objectively as possible, what is right for your business. Always remember, *you* are the customer. You are in the driver's seat. You *know* how much you can spend; the vendors don't. Here are six risks you face if you are *not prepared* when you sit down with a vendor who is, of course, prepared for you:

1. **Being shortsighted in evaluating issues and products.** If you are not prepared, you can't compare one vendor or product to another, thus putting yourself at the vendor's mercy.

2. **Succumbing to pressure to close the negotiation.** Without knowledge, you have no ammunition to counter a vendor's claims, inflated or not, about a particular product. Therefore, you may agree because you are in no position to disagree.

3. **Giving up too much too soon.** Whether it is price or quantity or timeliness of delivery, if you don't know where you should be, you don't know what to ask for or what you are missing.

4. **Forgetting key details.** "Retail is detail." It's not just a catchy slogan; it's a truism. Every aspect of a successful retail business blends together when the details are known; and quite often falls apart because some detail is unknown. If you forget to document why an item did not sell last year, you may buy it again this year. Errors like this will eventually kill your business.

5. **Not considering all alternatives.** Don't be rushed into making a decision. Remember, no matter what the vendor tells you or how quickly

a product is moving, the manufacturer can always make more of the product and the vendor can always get more of the product.

6. **Losing control of the negotiating process.** If you do not know what you are talking about, the other party will grab the upper hand, possibly without your even realizing. You don't have to be louder, bigger, stronger, or more successful to stay on top of a negotiation, just more knowledgeable.

Maximize the Alternatives

In most negotiations, several paths can lead to the right solution. If you have some creative ways you would like to work with your vendors, be polite but persistent in pushing your ideas. Remember, vendors are there to do business, not waste their time. They wouldn't be seeing you if they didn't need your business.

Don't let minor setbacks stop you from getting the product or product line you think is right for your store. As you explore alternative ways to work with vendors, always keep in mind that the best ways to reach your goals is to help them reach *their* goals. It's important that you don't go into the negotiation seeing the vendor as your adversary. Of course, both of you want different things; accept that and work together to get what you both want.

Negotiate with the Right Person

When buying a car, you don't want to waste your time dealing with someone who has to keep running to someone else to make a decision. As quickly as you can, make sure you are dealing with a decision maker for this vendor, not just an order taker or gatekeeper. You may be small, but you're going to grow. Convince the vendor that you are someone to watch—that it's worth the boss's while to meet you.

Give Yourself Room to Maneuver

Without appearing to be too coy, don't back yourself into a corner by being too black and white in dealing with people. Always have a back-up plan if you really want a certain product but you cannot get it at the right price or for the right deal. If one approach does not work, be ready to try others.

Don't Give Away Too Much Too Soon

Vendors can sense when a buyer is overanxious for a product. When this happens, buyers lose the leverage they had when they started negotiating. As successful gamblers maintain their "poker faces," the retail buyer's "game face" has to be on in all dealings with vendors. Of course, that doesn't mean you have to be stern or dour; by all means, be warm and pleasant. It never hurts to have a good laugh. Vendors who like you are more prone to give you a break. Just don't let them see what you are really feeling behind that smile.

Be Prepared to Say No

Saying no is the hardest, and yet most essential, skill for a buyer to learn. You should come prepared; you know what will work in your store and you are determined to find it. But if the price isn't right, and you can't make enough money to warrant the outlay, you have to be prepared to say no and walk away. Often the vendor will come back to you with the right deal. I call this "buyer chicken." Who will blink first?

Know Your "Walk Away" Point

Saying no and "buyer chicken" only work if you're prepared to back these tactics up by walking away. If the vendor calls your bluff by refusing to come down in price and you come crawling back to accept their existing deal, you lose all credibility and have a lot of trouble winning any future negotiations.

So my message is clear: when you decide on the highest price you can afford, you must be willing to stick by it. As the form of the offer changes and as the negotiation process continues, you must weigh the pros and cons to see where you stand compared to your internal maximum. Use a calculator if that helps, and don't be afraid to slow vendors down if they go too fast (a common vendor tactic).

Make Your Word Your Bond

In retailing, as in life, ethics make the man or woman. Your word is your bond. If you commit and give your word, make sure you follow up and execute what you say you are going to do. If you say no, stick to it. If you say yes, don't deviate. Such reliability and honesty will pay dividends. Vendors, knowing they can count on you, will help you in many unexpected ways.

Negotiating Tactics Used by Vendors

Vendor negotiating tactics all have one thing in common: they rely on some form of pressure—on you!

However, there is a big difference in how that pressure is applied. Some vendors still base their philosophies on the old-school style of high pressure, we-win/you-lose selling. If possible, avoid them. You're not there to be hustled; you're there to do business.

Fortunately, most modern vendors prefer to pressure you in more pleasant, refined ways. Keep in mind that pressure derives from one, or all, of the following: position, power, knowledge, or time. Not even the most refined vendor is above explaining that, if you do not buy at once, the stock may run out, the price may rise, or some other disaster is likely to occur. If you would prefer not to buy right away, but you know you need the product, your job will be to determine whether or not the vendor is bluffing. To be prepared to successfully negotiate, watch out for the following vendor tactics.

I Want It All

This type of negotiator starts high and then gives away a series of small concessions to persuade you to buy more than you need. The idea is that you will be so relieved not to have to buy a carload, that you are happy to buy two-thirds of a load—when you really needed only a half. If you fall for this play, you participated in a clear win-lose situation. You will wake up in the morning realizing that you have been had, that the agreement is inherently unfair. Probably, there's no way out. The vendor has erred, however—any chance for a long-term relationship has been jeopardized. The approach is often effective in the short run, but hard-sell vendors eventually go out of business. The most effective counter to this technique is to have a very clear understanding of your goals and objectives. Know when to walk away.

Good Cop, Bad Cop

Vendors often use this tactic to save on freight, advertising, etc. Usually a senior executive will talk about how they lost money on your account because sales were so low. Then the executive closer to your account will try to calm down the situation by making a compromise offer "so we can continue to work with you." The offer is never as good. If you need the vendor, this tactic is hard to resist.

The best strategy against this tactic is knowledge: know what the competition is doing, know your store, know what sells, know what doesn't, know what your employees can push, and what they can't. That way, you can't overpay or over-promise.

Team Tactics

Vendors often negotiate with a team approach, pulling together accounting, marketing, manufacturing, and sales specialists and throwing them all at you at once. When your store is confronted with team tactics, unless you are uncommonly well prepared, it is hard not to be overwhelmed by all the facts and figures at the team's fingertips. However, there are a couple of effective ways to counter this tactic:

- **Form a team of your own.** Pull together people from the different specialties in your organization to aggressively challenge the vendor's team and support the goals you want to achieve. Make sure your team is as prepared as theirs.
- **Face the team alone.** You must be well prepared in all aspects of the negotiation. Take a deliberate and methodical approach and refuse to be stampeded by the team. By being firm, knowledgeable, and able to stand your ground, you will effectively counter the other team's tactics and reach your goals.

Approval Authority

Everyone you deal with in business (from the company who leases you the building to the vendor who supplies the goods) has some limitations on their authority or power. Approval authority, or rather the lack thereof, can be a very effective tool in the negotiation process.

When you are not dealing directly with the owner or president of a company, you leave yourself open for the person you are dealing with to say he or she does not have the authority to make a decision and must get the boss's approval first. Think how many times you have settled for something less than you wanted because the person had limited authority.

Do not assume that when someone says he or she has limited authority, that this is truly the case. Often, the vendor is using these tactics to test if you are willing to make a concession in order to avoid the prolonged process of getting a decision from a superior. So, be patient. If you do not cave in, if you do not allow yourself to be pressured by need or time, you may find your vendor is suddenly able to make a decision after all and conclude the agreement in very short order.

Time Warp

Time may be money, but if you allow yourself to be pressured by a lack of time, the money it costs may be your own! Using time as a weapon is another classic vendor negotiation technique. Time tactics can be used in a couple of different ways:

1. **Limit time.** Time limitations are used by vendors to force a decision. The best way to ensure that you are not taken advantage of by being forced to move faster than you want is to call the bluff. While some time limits *are* real, most are not. When you test the vendor, what seemed like a real deadline suddenly becomes fuzzy and soon seems to evaporate altogether. On the other hand, if you have no good reason to delay, you shouldn't. Always remember that being helpful to a vendor will get you better deals in the long run than being a pain.

2. **Delay time.** This technique is just the opposite because, instead of using deadlines to apply pressure, the negotiator uses delays to achieve the same result. Once you realize the vendor is stalling, you know this method is being deployed. The approach is usually used to get you to commit at a higher price because you are duped into thinking the vendor is about to sell the goods elsewhere. If you know what you want, the maximum you can afford to pay, and when you need the goods, the technique won't work. State what you want, provide a deadline, and

walk away if it passes. Once vendors know you mean what you say, they won't delay you unnecessarily again.

Turn about is fair play. Don't lose sight of the fact that delay may also be a great tactic for you as a buyer. Most vendors have quarterly budgets they need to meet. If you can afford to delay your order until the last minute before the end of a budget period, the vendor, possibly hard pressed to make his numbers, may offer any number of concessions.

Power Plays

In some negotiations between two parties, one reaches a winning conclusion merely by exerting power over the other. People who are sufficiently authoritarian use this technique most frequently and often with success. Perhaps it is simply another way of saying, "I wish to be respected."

Many vendors use this tactic on buyers who are not owners by implying or sometimes boldly stating that they are intimately related to the owner, intimidating the buyer by warning that you'd "better do what I say." A classic old school negotiating style, injecting fear of being fired into the sales pitch, is how this type of vendor tries to secure the order. If anyone in your store ever encounters this tactic, make sure everyone in your organization knows that no vendor will tell you, or them, what to do. Then, take the vendor aside and explain that, if anyone is going to lose their job, it's going to be him!

Money Crunch

Vendors use the "money crunch" excuse when they insist that they cannot accommodate your promotional needs due to financial constraints. The excuses flow thick and fast: the budget won't allow additional expenditures, funds are already committed to other projects, or, worst of all because it's such a weaselly cop-out and rarely true, "any discount I give you comes out of my own pocket."

Don't ever forget that, as the buyer, you have "the power of the pen." The easiest way to tell if someone is using the money crunch ploy is to call their bluff. Communicate your offer, be firm, and stand by it. If necessary, use the walk away tactic. If the other party is bluffing, you'll soon know. If not, you'll lose the purchase. But you shouldn't castigate yourself—the product was simply not available at the price you could afford to pay.

Ultimatums

Ultimatums only work against targets with no options. Therefore, to negotiate a purchase successfully, you must make sure that you have options. The key to avoid having to succumb to ultimatums is to know your alternatives. As always, knowing your store and planning ahead leaves you prepared. There is almost never a circumstance where no option exists. Therefore, as long as you are properly prepared, you will hardly ever have to give in to an ultimatum. And when you resist successfully once or, at most, twice, you'll never face an ultimatum again (at least from that vendor).

Retail is a "trial by fire" business. Good merchants know all of the above, and a hundred more things. After only a few months in business, so will you.

Finding the Right Suppliers

Many manufacturers sell their goods directly to retailers. Most smaller retailers, though, buy from wholesalers for a number of reasons: the wholesaler carries a wider assortment of items, thus making stocking the whole store (a time-consuming chore) easier and faster; the wholesaler gives excellent *local* service and cuts down on the number of vendors the dealer has to buy from; and the wholesaler delivers items in smaller lots. On the other hand, wholesalers charge a lot more than do manufacturers. It's a trade-off.

As you know if you've read my résumé, I am a cofounder, President, and COO of DollarDays International. The reason I helped found this company and now run it is that I saw a need for a wholesaler who can supply the lower quantity you need at manufacturer (not wholesaler) prices. In the old days, this would have been impossible because the cost of contacting you would be too high relative to the amount of product you could afford to buy. However, today, we can contact you via the Internet or an inexpensive phone call and so we can provide a service that never existed before. So (and here comes my shameless plug) check out our DollarDays.com Web site. You'll find that we carry a huge assortment of products (far bigger than your local wholesaler); we FedEx or UPS the goods right to your door; we are always there if something goes wrong; and we're impressively inexpensive compared to what you're paying now.

Whether you use it or not, when you set up your vendor network, here are some points to keep in mind:

1. **Limit the number of vendors in each category.** You want to become important to your vendor and your vendor wants to become important to you. The more volume you do with a resource, the better pricing you will get. You will also participate in more promotional programs. Thus, you don't want to split your purchases among too many vendors.

2. **Comparison shop.** Every manufacturer or wholesaler has their own way of doing business, so compare their benefits to make sure they fit in well with your strategy. We often have to work with vendors or manufacturers with whom we are less than compatible, but the goal is to whittle these vendors and manufacturers out and concentrate on those who are compatible.

3. **Be aware of the distribution solution.** Each supplier needs to be evaluated for their distribution pattern in your marketplace. How common are their goods in your trading area, and, in that context, what margins can you expect to achieve on their products?

4. **Maintain personal standards.** Ultimately, the relationship between you and your vendors is based on how well their products are accepted by your customers. Therefore, you must make sure that your vendors' service, warranty, and return policies reflect the standards your customers expect.

5. **Conduct ongoing evaluation.** Remember, vendors (like all human organizations) change and evolve—and not always for the better. So, even though you are satisfied with the group of vendors you have chosen, never stop evaluating their products, service, and distribution methods. Don't allow them to become complacent. If their services fall below what you need to run a successful business, do not hesitate to eliminate them from your supplier group and go elsewhere.

Ten Basic Questions to Ask Potential Vendors

As we have seen, gathering information is part of making the right buying decision. Don't be afraid to ask your vendor the following questions before you decide whether or not to buy:

1. **Who else does well with your line?** You have a right to know the answer to this question because if these are competitive retailers in your marketplace, you need to decide whether you are going to enter the fray or walk away. Moreover, if there are other stockists, you will want to see how fully they present the line.

2. **What are your order minimums?** This is an important opening question because many companies refuse to open an account if the dollar amount of the order is too small. If you have your heart set on doing business with this vendor but cannot meet their minimums, you can try a couple of tactics. First, write the order for what you really want,

explain to the salesperson that you expect to grow rapidly and, if the company helps you now, you will be a large and loyal customer in the future, and then leave it with the salesperson to try to take care of you. Your order may be close enough, or your future business may be important enough, to secure the order despite the minimum. Second, go ahead and mail the order to the company with a professional letter saying you would like to try this order as a starter and, if it works out, you will be happy to meet their minimums for your next buy. You would be surprised how often this works. As I always say, "The worst they can say is no."

3. **Can I buy any promotional or off-price merchandise to help maintain a good margin on your goods?** This is a question to ask every time you work with a company because, just as you do in your store, vendors frequently mark down their goods. Why not reap the benefits of these discounts? This is an exemplary case of "if you don't ask, you won't get."

4. **Can I reorder these goods?** You also need to know this, and communicate it with your staff so everyone knows how to merchandise the product. If it's a one-time sale and the price and margin is right, go ahead and "blow it out." Most of your business comes from repeat purchases, however, so either make sure you can get more when you need it, or make sure your customers know this is a once-only opportunity!

5. **Do you have a catalog or color photos?** This is helpful if you decide to advertise the vendor's goods in a flyer or in the local paper. It is also good to have them lying around the store to share with employees and possibly even customers. Many companies these days can e-mail you pictures for use around the store, in advertising, or on your store's Web site.

6. **Do you have a Web site?** Many companies are now able to get new information and products up on a Web site quicker than communicating through "snail mail."

7. **Do you offer co-op advertising monies?** Co-op advertising (short for *cooperative*) is advertising for which vendors pay for part or all of the ads you run for their products. Co-op applies to newspaper, magazine,

television, or radio ads and in some cases, even in-store displays. Typically, the advertising schedule and reimbursement are agreed on ahead of time.

The rules with most co-op advertising are very strict. For instance, when I owned a chain of hair salons, one of my major suppliers of shampoos and hair coloring helped pay for local magazine ads that included their line. The details of the program would be agreed on at least three months in advance. The suppliers would send me the latest fashion head shots and, to be reimbursed, I would show that the product name and picture was in at least 65% of the ad. Once, an ad accidentally slipped through in which 50% of the space was used for the supplier's line. They paid nothing!

So, as part of your purchase decision, find out what marketing money the vendor will tap into, and what rules attach to it. Co-op advertising helps stretch your advertising dollar, but read the fine print. If you don't, as happened to me, you may find yourself with a bill to pay. Assuming the deal is fair, you are well advised to run as much advertising as the vendor will pay for, even though the time and paperwork involved can be annoying. Advertising gets your store name known. You're on the map.

8. **Can I exchange goods that are not selling?** If you are dealing with quality vendors who want to develop a long-term business with you and not just make a quick buck from a one-time sale, they will usually help you out if you are stuck with goods. Naturally, you cannot take advantage of this privilege very often. Except in a few categories of product, books being one of the biggest where you can return anything you want any time, returns and exchanges are no substitute for buying right in the first place.

9. **When will the goods be delivered?** You need to know when to expect goods in your store, not just in general, but specifically. Don't let a vendor get away with telling you two to four weeks when you really need them in three weeks. In most cases, you should be able to get a date that is accurate within two to three days. Also, make sure

you have automatic cancellation dates on all your orders. If each order specifies "cancel if not shipped by _____," you won't end up with Christmas goods arriving in January.

10. **What are the terms of payment?** Do I need to pay for goods up front before they even arrive in my store? Am I going to have to pay with my company credit card (which may not be a bad deal since you usually have thirty days to pay off the balance before interest payments kick in—and you might even get airline miles for airfare, hotels, and various products)? Will I get thirty-day dating, meaning that I don't have to pay for thirty days after I receive the vendor's invoice—and I may be able to stretch that to forty-five or even sixty days? If I bring in Christmas goods in August, can I delay payment until November? (Some vendors grant this sort of dating privilege.) Can I take any of the vendor's slower moving goods into my store on consignment, that is, not pay for them until I sell them, and return them if they won't sell? Can I get a guaranteed sale, which means I have to buy the goods (unlike goods I take on consignment), but I can send back everything that doesn't sell?

All of this information is key input into your spending and cash flow plans. Certainly this litany of questions sounds intimidating now, but, trust me, practice makes perfect and you will soon be rattling off these questions by rote!

Ten Guidelines to Buying Wisely

Never lose sight of the fact that when you are making buying decisions, your job is to see the product through your customer's eyes. Don't buy based only on your own personal tastes; you are buying for the hundreds of customers who will be in your store checking out these products. Also, keep in mind that you always have the power of the pen. No order gets written unless you *choose* to write it. So the mind game you need to play with yourself is to really believe that *you* have the power, not the vendor, because he gets nothing until you say okay with your pen.

Knowing that you have that power, you can take all your meetings with a positive mindset, and thus, achieve positive results. You will do even better if you understand that your aim is to create a personal relationship with your vendors and make win-win deals. With this in mind, here are some proven buying guidelines to follow:

1. **Do your buying in your own store whenever possible.** Like a sports team with home field advantage, if you are comfortable and in familiar surroundings it will help reinforce the feeling of power you'll need to buy wisely. If the vendor is in your store, you can show him what you are talking about. Even if you're phoning in an order, being in your own store still gives you the advantage of being totally prepared and placing the call at your convenience.

2. **When going out of town to buy, don't overload your schedule.** Obviously, when you go out of town, you give up your home field advantage. To compensate, make sure you have plenty of time to think, plan, and shop for the right products. If you are going to a show, give yourself plenty of time to see what vendors you don't know are doing. If you are going to a different city, give yourself time to shop in their retail stores to learn what you may be missing.

3. **Never leave home without your Open to Buy.** A profitable retail business is an organized business, and at all times you need to know your inventory position and how much you have to spend. That is especially important when you are out of your element and on the vendor's turf.

4. **Never buy an item the first time you see it.** Take some time to consider not only how the product will fit into your store's goals, its "big picture," but also the price for which the vendor's competitors are selling their products. Remember, the product you are considering isn't going anywhere. It'll be there, along with the vendor, when you get back.

5. **Buy a digital camera and every time you see something you want to buy, take a picture of it.** Pictures help you keep what you have

bought straight in your head. That way you'll avoid buying the same thing twice. The photos are also a great training tool for your salespeople back at the store.

6. **Always be honest and ethical with your suppliers.** This goes a long way in building a long-term, win-win relationship. Keep in mind that your personal reputation as a business owner and as an individual is something you should always protect, defend, and enhance. In this respect, vendors are no different from customers.

7. **Before you sign a purchase order, confirm the agreement with the supplier.** Restate what you are planning to buy, what the terms are, what the vendor is going to do, what you are going do, etc. You do not want any misunderstandings. Far from begrudging this step, vendors worth their salt will appreciate the attention to detail.

8. **Keep a supplier notebook for your top vendors.** This need not be fancy. It is merely a journal to keep track of meetings, phone calls, and deals. Over time, this notebook becomes a valuable resource and you will be surprised how often you refer back to it.

9. **Print your own purchase order instead of using the vendor's.** Purchase orders (PO) are not expensive to print and this gives you the edge of professionalism that vendors rarely see in independent stores. Your purchase order should include your terms and conditions. This will avoid later misunderstandings.

10. **Realize that the terms you negotiate with a supplier can become more important than the price.** We are all focused on the cost of goods, but do not lose sight of how the total package of a deal can drive additional dollars to your bottom line. Remember, "Retail is detail." And details don't get any bigger than the terms you negotiate with a supplier. Terms of a deal may include:
    • Who pays the freight to get goods to your store?
    • The number of days you have to pay for the goods. Can you get additional dating if you accept the goods ahead of the actual selling season?
    • Allowances and rebates tied to the size of your order.

- Money available for co-op advertising.
- Returns policy, including who pays the freight on damaged goods.
- Markdown money if the goods are not moving.
- Fixtures to display the goods, such as a free mannequin or other vendor-supplied fixture like sunglass holders or revolving book racks.
- Selling aids, such as sheets, tags, videos, promotional bag stuffers, etc.
- Samples for demonstrations.
- Product knowledge training for the staff.
- Vendor-paid trip to their showroom.

How to Find the Goods

You are now ready to deal with just about anything a vendor can throw your way. There is still a key question to consider before we wrap up this vital chapter: How do you find the type of merchandise you want to carry? Where do you go to buy it and from whom?

Keep in mind that buying today is completely different than it was just ten years ago, so make sure your research is up to date. The Internet has brought together buyers and sellers who could not have found each other in the past. During the past decade, manufacturers and wholesalers have cut way back on the sales personnel who used to visit stores all over the country. They no longer do so today because the cost is too high, and because business has become more concentrated. If you have to spend half your life visiting Wal-Mart in Bentonville, you don't have time or money left to cover the country.

Of course, this isolation from vendors is even more of a problem for stores not near metropolitan areas. So remember, this is not the buying world of our parents' generation. The following are different ways to find goods and, like most successful entrepreneurs, I am sure you will add your own resources as you continue to learn, grow, and succeed in retail.

Buying from the Manufacturer

The manufacturer is the company that creates the product being sold. However, it may do little more than assemble parts made by subcontractors, often in foreign countries. Where you find this to be the case, you can sometimes discover that the "subs" make the same product under their own name. Since their names are not well known, they sell their products for much less. By stocking both the brand name product and the identical, cheaper "no-name" product, you can offer your customers a great bargain.

If you know the name of the manufacturer you want to do business with, search the Internet for the company's Web site. This should tell you who to contact, what minimum orders are required, and all other information you need to do business.

Even though you have found the manufacturer, you may not be able to buy direct because the minimum orders may be too high, or because the manufacturer is saturated with accounts in your area. In that case, the manufacturer will put you in touch with the appropriate wholesaler. If you can buy direct, you can do so in several locations:

- **In their showroom.** Many manufacturers have permanent showrooms, either at their district offices or in major cities.
- **In your store.** If the manufacturer has a sales person in your area, you can get them to stop into the store. These "direct manufacturers' salespeople" work exclusively for one vendor and are generally paid a salary augmented with a performance-based commission or bonus. They usually have company cars and benefits. Their interest, of course, is to sell you their products whether you need them or not.
- **At a trade show.** All industries have trade shows where you can meet most vendors.
- **On their Web site.** More and more buying is being conducted over the Internet because of the convenience that this new distribution method offers both the vendor and the store. That is how most customers buy from DollarDays. Don't ignore this new outlet. You can often get better deals via the Internet than in any other venue. And it's not hard.

However old-fashioned you may consider yourself, after just a few hours of practice you'll have no trouble navigating the Net.

Buying from Independent Reps

These are independent contractors working for more than one vendor strictly on commission. They can meet with you the same way a manufacturer does: in your store, at a permanent showroom, or at a trade show. The advantage of dealing with them as compared to dealing with a direct salesperson is that they usually carry several different lines appropriate to your business. Thus, they save you time and allow you to exercise more clout. Moreover, because they are independent, these reps are more flexible; they often go to bat for you with a manufacturer by explaining, "This is a good customer for me in my other lines. You are missing the boat if you do not help me build him up. By giving him a price concession now, he'll become as important for you in the future."

Distributors

These are companies that purchase merchandise from manufacturers in large quantities at discounted prices and sell them in smaller quantities at higher prices to smaller businesses. Since they typically carry many lines, they can consolidate shipping so stores receive goods from several manufacturers in one shipment. Unless you can buy in large quantities, the price you will pay the distributor will be about the same as you would pay if you bought direct.

Dealing with distributors can fill a major void because of the one-stop shopping they provide. Distributors work hard at developing a consistent and long-term relationship with the stores they service. They have to, because small retailers are the lifeblood of their business. Networking with other retailers usually helps find the best distributors in your area.

Jobbers

They are often called *wagon jobbers* because they go from store to store with their products in the back of their van ready to be bought on the spot. Whereas such jobbers are usually much smaller than distributors, they nonetheless fill the same role and usually have routes they work every week. Dealing with jobbers can be a great convenience. However, convenience is not free; generally the jobbers' prices are on the high side.

Buying Groups

These are associations of retailers who have joined together to buy as a unit in order to get better deals directly from manufacturers. "All for one" is a good slogan to describe these buying groups.

You must pay dues to belong to such a group, but the savings could be huge even considering the initial price of joining. Before you join, however, estimate how much you can expect to buy through the group. If you don't expect to buy very much, the dues may not be worthwhile.

Belonging to a group gives you the added advantage of having an inside track on what is happening in your industry. There is power in working with a group of like-minded individuals. As they say, two heads are better than one.

Buying Services

These services function in a similar way to buying groups. Rather than being owned by its members, however, buying services are independently owned and need to make a profit. You pay a monthly fee and, in return, the buying service tells you about hot deals, helps find specific items you may want, shares vital industry trends with you, and often helps negotiate group discounts. If they have a good reputation, your association with them may also enhance your credibility.

Trade Shows

Your first buying experience should be at a trade show. This is where all the players in your industry come together. You can go online to find out where the trade shows for your industry are located, or just contact a large manufacturer who will clue you in on the upcoming schedule.

Fair warning: Be prepared to be overwhelmed. Many of these shows are huge and confusing. After walking around one all day, a friend of mine complained that his feet hurt so much he was sure he was two inches shorter.

To get a sense of what is going on, you should spend the first day just looking around. Figure out who is selling what and for how much. Find the busiest booths and try to figure out why they are so busy. Don't buy anything yet. I trust we have hit home throughout this chapter that knowledge is power and the more you have before you actually visit a booth to buy, the better off you will be.

To become a respected buyer in the vendor's eyes, you need to know what is going on in your own marketplace. When you can tell a vendor what your competition is doing and at what price, you immediately gain their respect and give them a focal point around which to build your individual order.

Keep in mind that you will be exhausted from walking around the huge exhibit rooms on this first day, so don't make any major evening plans. On the second day, you are ready to start work with a few of the key vendors you scoped out the day before. Remember not to leave home without your buying plan.

Introduce yourself to these key vendors and don't pretend you know more than you really do or are a bigger buyer than you really are. Then start to put into place all of the information from this chapter to build the order you need.

Buying from Catalogs

Many companies print a complimentary catalog showing the merchandise they will gladly sell you. Without even talking with a rep, thus avoiding the uncertainty of a negotiation if you still find yourself uncomfortable with this hard-earned skill, you can place an order over the phone with a customer service person or just fax or mail in an order. But beware: the catalogue you are looking at was printed a while ago. You never know what is in stock and what is out. Moreover, the prices in the catalogue are fixed. It is hard to negotiate lower prices when buying directly from a company catalog.

Over the Internet

Before we begin, you must realize that I am very biased in favor of this newest method of wholesale distribution because www.dollardays.com is the largest business-to-business wholesale Web site selling products to independent businesses. Do check us out! Just like you, my job is selling!

That being said, the Internet truly is an efficient way to communicate and conduct wholesale buying. First, it is convenient. After a long hard day at the store, you can come home and relax in front of your computer with no salesperson telling you what to do. All by yourself, you can find what you think is the best product for your store, in the best quantity, at the best price.

Second, you can be pretty sure that the prices you are paying when you buy on the Internet are the lowest going. That is because you can so quickly compare various companies' products, prices, and attributes. Within minutes, you can compare every product there is. Of course, you'll only buy the ones that offer you, and your customers, the best deal. Only a few years ago, it would have taken days to do this kind of comparison shopping.

Third, communicating via the Internet is so much more efficient than the downtime experienced while playing "phone tag" with live sales reps. You can send an informed, well-thought-out, and explanatory e-mail and you never get an answering machine, or a busy signal. And you're never put on hold.

Fourth, in today's world, buying over the Internet is as secure as placing an order over the phone. Particularly with the more advanced sites, you do not need to worry about fraud.

And, finally, you can use the Internet to keep yourself informed about the latest news affecting your business by subscribing to various trusted retail newsletters, e-zines, and newsgroups.

Summary

Buying goods from the right resources is the very heartbeat of retailing. No matter how dynamic you make the store look, or how good the location of your store, if you have the wrong goods at the wrong price, you just won't make it in the highly competitive world of retailing.

There are plenty of resources out there to make your store successful. Because buying is both an art and a science, throw all the information available in this chapter together and find your niche. After all, you are an entrepreneur and that is what entrepreneurs do!

Retail Detail

According to the National Association of Resale and Thrift Shops (NARTS), there are more than 15,000 resale shops across the country. Sales have increased almost twice as fast in these stores over traditional retailing and Americans spend $12 billion in merchandise purchased at these stores.

Chapter 10

Marketing Your Business, Or:
Spreading the Word

Baby Boomers have changed every market we entered,
from disposable diaper market to
the stock market to the job market.
We like to be marketed to.
—LYNN LANCASTER, author, *When Generations Collide*

WHAT IF YOU OPENED A STORE and nobody came? It's a nightmare all retailers have in the days, weeks, and even months before they open their doors. And for good reason: How can customers find your store if they don't even know it exists? That's where marketing comes in.

In retail, we have a saying: "Good ideas are a dime a dozen. Great ideas are slightly less plentiful." It's simple, but true. We have another saying: "If it works, even if you didn't come up with it, use it." Retailers steal each other's ideas all the time! So, if we're all using the same ideas, why are some stores successful and others not? The difference between a successful retail store with a great idea and an unsuccessful store with exactly the same idea boils down to how well the idea is implemented.

In the end, it's not great ideas that make the difference, but great *implementation*. My favorite saying, and the theme I've had running through this book, is: "Retail is detail." It applies not only to how well the store is run, but also to how efficiently, creatively, and energetically your marketing ideas and campaigns are carried out.

The successful retailer must be an expert in just about all phases of the business, and marketing is no exception. You must know at all times what you, your staff, your customers, and even your competitors are doing. So, comparison shop, read competitors' ads, study the trade magazines that cover your area, go to trade shows, read relevant books, listen to lectures by experts, pick manufacturers' brains—be and remain a true expert in your chosen field. Before any marketing campaign is launched, make sure you know the answers to the following questions:

• Who is your audience?
• What does your audience want?
• How do you reach your audience?
• How can you expand the base of this audience?
• How can you get your audience to frequent your store more often?
• How can you get your audience to spend more money every time they are in your store?
• Why have you previously lost customers?

Marketing:

Timing Is Everything

There has never been a better time to be an independent retailer. Rather than having to deal with rigid policies dictated from a home office that may be halfway around the country (and well out of the loop), as an independent retailer you have total flexibility to address local marketing and promotional opportunities, to develop personalized customer service policies based on the needs of your customers, and to participate in and take advantage of the events, feelings, and traditions of your local community.

More than ever, a local storeowner can gain a huge advantage over ever-larger and more impersonal megastores by being a known quantity to his customers, by building a personal reputation for integrity and service, and by becoming a leading citizen of his community. Customers know the difference between a true community leader and a hired gun who pulls dollars out of the area and sends them off to some home office to line the pockets of greedy executives and stockholders. The local retailer can attract local loyalty by making a significant economic impact on the community. He is keeping the money he collects from the community in the community where it belongs.

Nevertheless, local retailers do not all succeed, some fail. The reason for this often lies in the local retailer's unwillingness or inability to change. To succeed, retailers must be forever vigilant for the next great marketing idea to promote their business. The storeowner must be ready, willing, and able to make any changes necessary to keep his store competitive. Resistance to change and the fear of failure are the greatest inhibitors to business success.

Above all, to succeed, you must banish the fear of failure. You will fail only if you do *not* change. Like any winning sports team, you have to make constant adjustments to stay ahead. You must closely follow all the trends and changes taking place both in your local community and nationally.

Independence:

How Much Is Too Much?

No matter how good you are, it is not wise for you to market your business totally alone. There are going to be times when you would be well advised to market with fellow businesses. Sometimes, you may even want to cooperate with your competition to develop strategies and programs that will ensure a vibrant, pro-small business environment in your trading area.

Unfortunately, independent retailers have frequently failed to work together in the past to create a unified front. And, because of this failure, municipal, county, and state governments have bowed to pressure from big box and national retailers, granting them all sorts of concessions such as tax breaks, improvements in traffic flow, new streets, and better access to major highways—all because the independents were too independent to organize and fight off the well-financed public relations and lobbying efforts of the chains.

But it's never too late. So don't ignore the power of banding your businesses together for the good of all. Certainly you want to run your own store, be your own boss, but sometimes cooperation with others, even with your competitors, is for the good of the whole group, including you.

This leads to the first great promotion I'm going to discuss, namely one in which all the small businesses in town get together and hold a small business (retail) day or week. By pulling together, independent retailers can get free support from local media, free PR. For example, the mayor can proclaim the importance of small retailers to the community. Participants run their own specials in context with the promotion, but they share the cost of promotional flyers and possibly radio or television advertising. And, of course, they all place signage throughout their stores announcing that they are proud members of the local retailer community. The beauty of this promotion is that it kills two birds with one stone. On the one hand, the power of a large number of stores offering specials is bound to attract more buyers than any single store could, thus providing a business boost to all; on the other hand, the community will realize the value of keeping small retailers in business—and perhaps of keeping the huge stores away—and that is of immense importance to the survival and growth of every independent in the area.

Competitors:

Friend or Foe?

No doubt you've heard the adage famously uttered by the young Al Pacino in *The Godfather: Part II,* "Keep your friends close, and your enemies closer." It certainly rings true for retailing. By knowing what your competitors are up to, you will be able to better choose your products, establish your margins, and please your customers.

Of course, your competent competitors are just as interested in you as you are in them. And, since ideas are easy to duplicate, you want to keep the competition at arm's length and share as little of what you are doing with them as possible. So, keep your eyes open and your mouth shut!

Here are some techniques to help you keep on top of what your competitors are doing (and to keep them from finding out too much about you):

- Have a relative, friend, or professional shopper shop the competitors' stores. Let them try to make friends with one or more salespeople there. By doing this, they may learn of upcoming sales or gather other advance information that will help you in planning your promotions. They may have to buy some items from your competitors, a marketing expense likely to pay dividends in the future. At the same time, warn everyone on your staff not to talk about your future plans and to keep their eyes open for competitors' shoppers. If they suspect someone, they should remain perfectly polite, even welcoming, but give out no information.
- Have your shopper get onto your competitors' mailing lists and any special clubs or programs they may offer. Be discreet about this. You should try to use someone with a different last name than yours.
- Closely monitor your competitors' advertising program and estimate their expenses. Chart the pattern of their advertising so you can predict, and possibly counter, their advertising waves.

Promotions

When beginning a marketing campaign, remember that no promotion can replace the basics: good merchandise, fair pricing, convenience, service, and a caring sales staff. Now, as you start developing your promotional campaign, you should consider the following:

- Make sure your promotional dates do not coincide with religious holidays celebrated by a good number of your customers.
- Don't schedule a promotion when people will be on vacation. If major local plants shutdown for vacations, make sure you know the dates. If you are in a college town, make sure you are in sync with the school calendar.
- Be flexible and factor in snow or storm days.
- Decide whether major local events such as key high school or college games are good or bad times to schedule events. I was in Green Bay during a Packers game once. You could have walked from one end of town to the other without encountering a single soul!

Retail Versus Theater:

One and the Same?

*In the modern world of business it is useless to be
a creative original thinker unless you can also sell what you create.
Management cannot be expected to recognize a good idea
unless it is presented to them by a good salesman.*
—DAVID OGILVY, Former CEO Ogilvy & Mather Worldwide ad agency

When I ran a major department store branch, I used to pretend every morning that the curtain was going up on a brand new show and that everything in the store had to be perfect so the audience would give us a standing ovation.

Retailing is like theater in that people like to be entertained when they enter your store. If they find your store exciting and your competitors' merely routine, you will gain their loyalty. You can generate this sense of entertainment through many touches, including, but not limited to:

- Lively in-store promotions such as demonstrations or sampling (which your suppliers are often willing to pay for), gift-with-purchase events, or other promotions appropriate to your store such as:
  –Author signings at bookstores
  –In-store performances at music stores
  –Tastings at food or beverage stores
  –Fashion models at clothing stores
  –Play demonstrations at toy stores
  –Perfume testers at drug stores (but make sure they don't spray unwilling customers, especially men who will have to explain why they smell of perfume to their colleagues or their wives)
- Show-stopping displays, especially ones that show a little whimsy and originality. A horn of plenty with candy spilling out of it may be more fun than a basket of candy. A huge display of soap packages in front of a washtub that actually bubbles can make people laugh—and buy.
- Theme-related sales and special events. By all means, have your staff, and your store, celebrate Valentine's Day, Easter, Mothers' Day, and Fathers' Day. (One storekeeper had all his predominantly female staff wear men's clothing and painted-on moustaches on Fathers' Day!)
- Warm, friendly customer service atmosphere. This includes music that is appropriate to the preferences of your audience, bright but warm lighting, and a pleasant temperature (remember that in cold weather people wear warm clothes while the opposite applies in the summer, so keep your store *cooler* in winter than in summer). In some cases, such as in upscale clothing boutiques, a subtle fragrance may enhance the atmosphere. And never let unpleasant smells intrude.

Holi*daze*:

Minding the Calendar for Marketing

When it comes to marketing, the calendar is your friend. The holidays that fall throughout the year, the four seasons, and significant local and national events can set the tone for exciting weekend, weeklong, or longer seasonal promotions.

Whenever running a promotion, you need to carry out the theme you have chosen throughout the store, in your advertising, on your Web site, and in all the publicity you generate. In-store decorations should tie the entire store into the event, holiday, celebration, or season. Store windows need to reflect the consistent theme. Salespeople's dress or accessories or buttons should reinforce it. Nothing should go unnoticed in presenting a unified, thematic front. Most important of all, of course, the merchandise you choose to feature must tie into the theme and seem more desirable, and saleable, as a result.

In developing promotional plans, always remember that you need to be thinking at least one quarter and probably six months ahead. The following sections describe some of the major (and minor) themes that may work in your business.

First Quarter

The first quarter of the year is known as "the sale quarter" because stores are selling out leftover Christmas goods and may run White Sales and Presidents' Day sales. Because this is not a big gift-giving quarter, I would recommend taking a conservative approach to how much you spend in promotions. Use that money to mark down and clear out overstocks of leftover Christmas products. Often suppliers will help by providing mark-down allowances.

That being said, here are some great opportunities for unique, inexpensive, and creative ways to celebrate holidays and other special events that occur in the first quarter:

- **Happy New Year.** This is a great theme to run from the day after Christmas through the first week in January. You can build it around a New Year's Eve party or New Year's resolutions or New Year's predictions. This is an ideal time to give away calendars or notebooks with the store's name on them. You can actually have a New Year's Eve party in the store all week with hats, refreshments, etc., to really get people in the mood. The buying mood, that is.

- **Elvis Presley's Birthday.** "The King" was born on January 8 and this is a one-day promotion from which you can get great publicity. You could hold an Elvis look-alike contest, plug in a karaoke machine full of Elvis tunes and run a sing-a-long, or even have the shopper with the best 50's or 60's outfit win a prize. This would be a great co-sponsored event with an oldies radio station.

- **Martin Luther King, Jr. Day.** There should be no commercialism attached to this celebration—only respect. Ideas for celebrating it include using window displays or giving a percentage of the day's sales to a local civil rights group.

- **The Super Bowl.** The most publicized sports event in the United States gives retailers a chance to say goodbye to the football season. The name is licensed by the NFL so you must be careful how you present your promotion. It can also be called "The Big Game," which does not violate the NFL license. No matter what name you use, however, be creative because this really gives you an event that will exude excitement, especially if your favorite team is involved.

- **Chinese New Year.** Even if you do not have a large base of Chinese-American customers, there are all kinds of promotional events you can tie in with the Lunar New Year. Giving the store an Asian theme featuring made-in-China products could work well. Passing out fortune cookies or giving away dinner coupons to local Chinese restaurants can create a buzz.

- **African-American History Month.** Like the Dr. King event, this celebration would call for a non-commercial tribute or display. Working with local African-American leaders and educators in your community during this event can be fine public relations.
- **Valentine's Day.** This is the second busiest greeting card holiday (Christmas is the first). It is also an important gift-giving day, although gift purchases fall in a limited range of categories, primarily candy, flowers, jewelry, and lingerie. It is also a very close buying holiday, which means that the buying activity centers on the three days before Valentine's Day. Nevertheless, these promotions should start a week to ten days before Valentine's Day and then end on Valentine's Day. If you have the kind of retail store that doesn't carry traditional Valentine's products, you can still get into the spirit by running a "red sale" where everything red carries a discount. You can take pictures of customers in a red, heart-shaped background and insert them into a special Valentine or gift certificate. In-store drawings may offer boxes of candy or dinner at a local restaurant. You can also tie in a promotion with the local American Heart Association. Here's a little trick I learned: if you have left-over Christmas gift items in January that are "gifty" (e.g., perfume sets) but not too tied into Christmas (no Santas, Christmas trees, snow scenes, etc.), buy some self-adhesive paper hearts, stick them prominently on the gifts and, voilà, an early Valentine's gift (which is much better than a leftover Christmas item)!
- **Presidents' Day.** Celebrated as the third Monday in February, this is historically a huge sale day. It can be a one-day event, a three-day weekend event, or run from Lincoln's Birthday on February 12 through Washington's Birthday on February 22. You can tie in with a local bakery to offer cherry pies as a snack in the store. The timing on this holiday sale is ideal for "blowing out" all of your remaining Christmas overstocks at significant savings. Since most types of retailers use this holiday to scream "sale," it takes on many of the advantages of a community sale, without the trouble of tying all the businesses together. Themes could include "We Are Chopping Our

Prices," "Stretch Your Washington Dollar," "President's Day Values," "One-Cent Sale," etc.

- **Mardi Gras.** This is the natural time to give the store a New Orleans feel. Costume parties or contests along with giving away beads or having beads on sale make sense. Getting a jazz or rhythm and blues band to play in the store can create excitement that gets your customers in the mood to buy.

- **St. Patrick's Day.** This has become an "event holiday" (whether or not you have a large Irish-American population in your trading area) because it is another excuse for everyone to have a party. Start the promotion a week before March 17 and end it on St. Patrick's Day. Green or Irish-made products should be featured throughout the store. Irish coffee is a great refreshment to serve if liquor laws in your area permit. Irish hats, music, or even a local bagpipe player could create a spirit of fun. Maybe a local talent agency could supply a leprechaun.

- **Winter Festival.** This festivity can be held during any of the three months of January, February, or March. Great sale themes to move winter merchandise include "It's Snowing Savings," "The Thermometer and Our Prices Are Dropping," "We've Thawed Our Prices," "Hot Bargains on a Cold Day," "Meltdown to Spring Savings," etc. Don't let the first quarter end without taking advantage of winter's great last gasp—at sales!

Second Quarter

This is the second strongest gift giving quarter (after the Christmas quarter, of course) because it includes Mother's Day, Graduation, and Father's Day. Those aren't the only causes to celebrate during the second quarter. Here is a list of sales-inspiring festivities for this quarter:

- **Spring Sale.** Spring is a season of renewal. Not only are new leaves emerging, but so are shoppers. So, run seasonal events such as "Spring into Savings" or "Spring Ahead to Bigger Bargains" to spotlight your new spring merchandise and get the customers who were too cold to shop last quarter back into your store and into the mood for some great spring shopping.

- **Easter.** Easter displays are a must for most retailers because Easter not only represents an important holiday, but also ushers in the change of season. Easter egg hunts for kids drive traffic into the store as parents enjoy a brief respite from keeping the kids occupied and also use the time to do some shopping.

- **Cinco de Mayo.** In the many cities with a large and growing Hispanic-American population, this May fifth Mexican national holiday is another opportunity for an exciting in-store event. Cinco de Mayo celebrates the Battle of Puebla in 1862 when greatly outnumbered Mexican troops defeated the French. Tie in with a local Mexican restaurant or feature products from Mexico to provide authentic flair.

- **Mother's Day.** Promotions for this no-brainer should run from the prior weekend through Mother's Day. A special "kids' shopping time" may be set aside for kids to buy their moms' gifts.

- **Armed Forces Day.** Celebrating our armed forces is always right. Armed Forces Day is celebrated on the third Saturday of May and there are all kinds of patriotic themes you can develop, including tying in to a local veteran's association or giving away American flag pins or even miniature lawn flags. This is also the perfect time to promote products that are "made in the USA." You may want to offer a discount to all members and retirees of the Armed Forces and their families.

- **Memorial Day.** This festive time ushers in barbecues and summer sales. Make sure you show the same respect you gave Armed Forces Day earlier in the month.

- **Graduation.** May and June are both graduation months. Themes and products around graduation tying in with the local high schools and colleges can be a great way to push products for the younger generation. Honoring graduates with prizes or discounts may also work to entice this new group of buyers into your store, not only to spend some of that graduation money, but also to become future regular customers.

- **Weddings.** May and June are also big wedding months, so don't forget those with upcoming nuptials by offering special promotions to newly-weds or newly betrotheds.

- **Father's Day.** Father of the year contests always work well. Since male-oriented products normally sell at a slower pace than female-focused goods, this is the time of the year when you can reverse the norm and gain strong sales on such traditionally male goods as golf products, knit shirts, ties, tools, and gag gifts.

Third Quarter

This is a tough promotional quarter because of summer vacations and summer activities that tend to lure customers away from your store. Consequently, you'll need to reach deep into your bag of special events to drive traffic into your store. Here are some great places to start:

- **Independence Day/Summer Promo.** Set up your Fourth of July and summer displays beginning at the end of June. Once Independence Day has passed, don't fret: You can still have a good summer promotion after taking off the July Fourth products. Sale themes for July Fourth could include "Star Spangled Savings," "Firecracker of a Sale," or "Fourth of July Sparklers." Summer themes could be "Beach Bargains," "Sun & Fun Sale," etc. Remember to reach out to where your audience is spending time. If you're near a beach, hire kids to place flyers advertising beachwear or toys under windshield wipers.

- **Christmas in July or August.** This is the ideal time to drag out any old Christmas goods you have left over from previous years. Take your lumps and mark them down to traffic-building prices. Maybe have Santa arrive at the store amid a flurry of fake snow, which will likely generate local media coverage. To get reluctant shoppers into the Christmas spirit, you may want to structure this sale so they get a coupon for a Christmas item in the fall if they buy some type of Christmas item now.

- **Back to School.** This promotion is starting earlier and earlier each year.

Most stores are ready for Back-to-School promotions to begin right after July 4. Tying in with your local schools by giving a percentage of your Back to School sales is another way to get attention. Tying in with the Teacher of the Year could get some publicity as well.

- **End of Summer Sale.** This is the perfect time to mark down summer goods and introduce fall products such as sweaters, footballs, and blankets, as you entice customers to "stock up early" and "beat the fall rush."
- **Labor Day.** This is a second bite at the end of the summer season—a good way to take your final markdowns on summer goods and a fine opportunity to start the fall rush into your store. You may even give discount coupons for future sale merchandise.

Fourth Quarter

Ready, set, hut! This is the quarter when retailers make most of their profits, so pull out all the stops for your biggest selling season of the year as you gear up:

- **Fall promotions.** Football season, leaves changing, new and heavier clothing coming back—these all give you an excuse to create fall promotions any time sales start lagging.
- **Columbus Day.** This national holiday is another great excuse for a weekend sale. Themes could be "Discover a New World of Values" or products on sale for $14.92.
- **Halloween.** This month-long October celebration has now turned into the second most active holiday for retailers. Themes could include "Trick or Treat Sale," "Broomstick Bargains," "Orange & Black Sale," "*Falling* Prices," etc. A good way to promote your store is to give out empty bags with your name on them for kids to use when they go trick or treating. All kinds of contests can be held around the Halloween theme—everything from pumpkin decorating to costume contests.
- **Veteran's Day.** This is a traditional sale day as we honor the veterans of all wars. The themes here are similar to all of the other military holidays.

- **Thanksgiving.** With the Christmas selling season starting earlier every year, it has unfortunately sapped the importance of the Thanksgiving holiday selling season. Don't let that stop you. If nothing else, Thanksgiving promotions get more customers to do their Christmas shopping earlier. Remember, if they buy early from you, they won't buy later from your competitors.

- **Christmas/Holiday Season.** We usually call it the Christmas season but, depending on the ethnic makeup of the area in which you operate, there are actually three different holidays involved: Christmas on December 25; the eight-day observation of Chanukah, the starting date of which varies from year to year; and Kwanzaa, the seven-day festival that begins on December 26. This is when you pull out all the stops. Turn Santa into a profit center by selling portraits of kids with jolly St. Nick. Tie in a philanthropic event to benefit the needy. Offer a discount coupon on new toys for every used toy a customer brings in to be given to charity.

  Christmas is a natural promotion time, and you know as well as I do the type of promotions all stores, including yours, will run at this time of year. Don't forget to try some unorthodox ideas, too. Give out "charity coupons" that let consumers donate to a designated charity every time they make a purchase of the couponed item. Build a Christmas attraction in the parking lot outside your store. (One sporting goods store I know gave an ice-skating demo on a tiny artificial rink—and sold a ton of skates!)

  The holidays are a warm, family-oriented, and fun time. Make sure your store fully reflects this spirit.

In-Store Special Events

Customers love to be entertained while they shop. The promotions mentioned above provided an energizing "what will they think of next?" beat to your business. In doing so, they attract new customers and keep your

existing customers coming back. However, before you go to all the extra
time and effort needed to create special events, you must first ask yourself this critical question: "What promotions will actually appeal to my
current and potential customers?"

If most of your shoppers are harried and pressed for time (for
instance, if they are office workers out during their lunch breaks), you
should avoid special events that slow them down. Ask yourself: "Will my
event take up too much floor space or hide merchandise so that I lose
more sales than I gain?" Or: "Will the event create too much noise and
distract too many shoppers from their appointed task of buying my
goods?" And the most important question that sums it all up: "Will this
special event bring in enough additional revenue to cover its cost?"

I could spend the rest of this book listing every special event I
have run or witnessed. Instead, I am just going to list a number of events
that I have seen work especially well. I hope they spark your creativity
and help you develop the right events for your business:

• **Anniversary Sale.** Whether you have been in business for one year or
  twenty years, celebrating your anniversary gives you unlimited marketing opportunities. By focusing attention on your anniversary, you are
  showing the community that you have a successful operation that has
  been part of the community and, perhaps even more importantly, will
  continue to grow with the community. The celebration can run anywhere from a weekend to a week to a month. The theme is to thank
  your customers for making your store a success. All of your advertising, windows, and in-store signs should contain the phrase "Thank
  You." This will make your customers feel they are part of "the family."
  Special tributes to customers and employees should be part of this
  anniversary celebration. You can get the customers involved by having
  them nominate candidates for Employee of the Year. Offer "thank you"
  door prizes. This is the ideal time to present employee awards based on
  years of service. Hold special receptions for your best customers by
  serving birthday cake.

      Your anniversary promotion is also the perfect time to make

significant announcements regarding your business, such as introducing a new merchandise program, new policies, or new store hours. You might want to start a tradition of (temporarily) "rolling back your prices to the year of the business founding."

- **Costumed Characters.** You can either rent a costume, have your local team mascots from the high school or college show up, or check with your suppliers to see if they have any licensing agreements and access to use cartoon characters for a day or a weekend. Make sure that, if you hire someone or use an employee to become that character, the person can relate well to people and has a (not so) hidden desire to become a star. Position the character near the front to greet customers and attract the attention of passersby. Have cameras ready to take pictures of the character with customers. Also, encourage the character to sign autographs. One of the key functions of this character can be to entertain the children while the parents shop. You could also offer to have the character appear at a birthday party for either kids or adults. If there are too many requests, you can choose which ones to attend by holding a public drawing.

- **Live Music.** When deciding to use live music in or around your store, make sure you are confident it will enhance your business and not divert attention away from the selling floor. You can have music scheduled at the same time each week (for example, every Friday night or Saturday afternoon) or just for special occasions. Tie in with a local school to showcase their best musicians, or tie in with a local radio station to feature local talent. Make sure the talent you present is sufficiently skilled to avoid embarrassment. Of course, little kids doing their best, even if they aren't all that good, can be a charming family event.

- **Magicians.** You can use magicians to draw people to a certain product or area of the store, or just to fascinate people. Remember, however, that this performance needs to be choreographed so the customers are forced to move around the store and are given enough time to shop. Make sure the performance is no longer than ten minutes and each performance is scheduled with different tricks. A schedule of performances should be posted (and the time of the next show announced at the end of the prior one) so customers may hang around the store longer to see the next act.

- **Caricaturist.** People love to be the subject of a drawing and usually display them proudly in their homes. So if you have a caricaturist sketching your customers, make sure they work the name of your store into the picture so that it becomes part of the customer's home décor. Pick a slow day to offer this service because it may help build traffic. You may want to offer this as a gift with purchase.

- **Psychic Readings.** If you have a large female clientele, this is a clever promotion for slow days. You can also use this promo as a gift with purchase. To get publicity outside the store, have the psychic predict what is going to happen during the year or forecast the results of local sporting events or the local economy. Newspapers typically eat up this type of story.

- **Other Artists.** Entertainers can create all kinds of excitement in your store. Balloon sculptors can entertain the children; mimes hold people spellbound and can quietly advertise a product you want to feature; puppeteers can baby-sit both kids *and* husbands; clowns appeal to all ages; origami artists give you an opportunity to have customers take a novelty item home. These are just some of many artists and performers who can make yours a "destination store."

- **Pets Are a Customer's Best Friend.** Almost every man, woman, and child loves pets. Have your local humane society (www.american humane.org) or pet rescue group bring in puppies and kittens for adoption. A local pet store may cooperate by putting on a display of reptiles or parrots or miniature piglets. You may want to stage a dog or cat show and let your customers bring in their pets to win ribbons. With enough creative categories like "Biggest Smile," "Least Obedient," "Slowest Eater," "Fastest Scratcher," etc., *every* pet can be a winner. You can also hold a pet photography show and have your customers bring in pictures of their pets. Here everyone can also win a ribbon with categories such as "Best Costume on a Pet," "Most Unusual Pose," "Biggest Eyes," etc. Any way you slice it, pets really are a customer's best friend. And a retailer's, too!

- **Celebrities.** Celebrities always create excitement, but make sure the additional cost is worthwhile—as you would expect, celebrity appearances cost money. Check with your suppliers to see if they have any celebrities under contract for personal appearances. Find out if any celebrities are coming to your town to perform. If they are not too famous, they may welcome the opportunity to appear in your store to promote their show, especially if you carry anything in the store that relates to them such as a book or any of the products they endorse. If that is the case, you can give this product away, choosing the winner by a drawing that the celebrity will pick. Alternatively, you might buy tickets to the celebrity's show (or get them as comps) and give them away with great fanfare at another drawing. Some local charities have relationships with celebrities who may come to your store if you donate a percentage of generated sales to their charity. Local celebrities, such as news anchors, radio personalities, sports reporters, authors, coaches, local chefs, and retired athletes may appear for small fees, or no fees at all, if you have an event that also benefits their organization. Whenever you get a celebrity, try to get the media to do interviews from the store.

- **Designers and Presidents.** Designers of all kinds—fashion, beauty, interior design, automotive—often make store appearances and, even if not well known, can create a buzz in your community when you promote their appearances correctly. Make sure the appropriate editor from the local paper and the radio and television bookers know about the appearance. The president of a company whose products you carry can also be used as a valuable "celebrity." Few know his name; but the title carries cachet. You can capitalize on the visit by running a "President's Day" promotion, provided it is a major firm. Make sure the local business-oriented media know when the person will be at your store. This is an ideal event to introduce new products from the manufacturer.

- **Private Shopping Night.** Special nights can be set aside for groups such as senior citizens, Kiwanis, unions, armed services members, teachers, working women, singles, husbands or wives (before Valentine's Day), and so on.

- **Welcome Back Party.** This would be a great event for inviting customers who have not shopped with you for at least six months back to the store for a party or special discounts. This is also a great way to find out why customers left you, especially if you offer incentives like discounts or prizes after they complete an in-store survey or comment card.

- **Fashion Shows.** If you sell fashion goods, putting together a show of them does drive traffic into your store, especially if you can get the local media to cover the event. It is easiest to use professional models. However, as an alternative, you might use customers and make it a charitable event by donating part of the day's sales to a not-for-profit organization. Customers, even those who pretend to be unimpressed, will often be elated to be asked to model. And naturally they will invite oodles of their friends and family to witness their modeling debut!

- **Product Promos from Around the Country and Around the World.** Special events featuring products from a certain country or a certain region of the United States offer all kinds of promotional opportunities. Examples include a Southwest promotion featuring goods from Arizona and New Mexico, an English promotion featuring goods from the United Kingdom, an Australian promotion featuring goods from Down Under, etc. Often you can get help by asking the relevant tourist board for literature or display material. Be creative and the costs will be minimal.

- **Children's Story Hour.** This could be a monthly, weekly, or even daily event, especially if you have a large number of customers with small children.

- **Supply a Meeting Place.** Many organizations don't like to meet at restaurants because they have to pay for a meal. Offer your store as an alternative meeting place. They can meet before the store opens, after it closes, in your stockroom, or in an area on the selling floor you prepare for them. Not only will you be showing your civic pride, but there is a good chance that people who would never have come to your store otherwise will become customers.

- **Parking Lot Promotions.** If local ordinances and lease agreements permit, running truckload sales in your parking lot, perhaps featuring products you do not normally carry, will generate extra sales and lure customers into the store. Alternatively (or additionally) setting up a petting zoo or pony rides will attract families with young children. Offering a tethered balloon ride (it is tied down so it only goes so high) with a minimum purchase adds a feeling of adventure. Holding an arts and handicraft show for a local group brings all kinds of notice. Exhibiting memorabilia or antique cars creates a crowd.

- **Health Screenings.** Free health screenings in the store can create a buzz. It is usually easy to tie in with a local hospital or medical group because they too will get good public relations and exposure for this event. February is National Heart Month, so this is a good hook to sponsor cholesterol and blood pressure screenings as well as to promote nutritional products you offer for sale. Making your store available as a blood bank site or for flu shots and other inoculations where customers pay a minimal fee is a good way to grab traffic and further increase your status as a civic leader.

Sales That Drive Traffic

The easiest sale to run is putting everything in your store on sale, but easiest is rarely best. The *smartest* sale is to focus on one theme and make it meaningful to create excitement and traffic, not only for that product but also for the entire store. That way, you will be cutting your margins on only part of your inventory, but selling a lot of your other merchandise at full profit.

For instance, if you are overstocked in one category, say, housewares or junior miss, that is what you put on sale. Or, if you want to promote a department you feel has more potential than it is realizing, that is what you feature. You can even turn a sale into a treasure hunt by giving a percentage off everything of a specific color or with an identifying label. Here are just some more ideas of sales that will build traffic:

- **Opening a New Store:** There are two key reasons to run a Grand Opening sale: taking in cash and building awareness. When you first open, you want to expose your business to as many people as possible. "The stronger the opening the stronger the store" has long been a retailing axiom. To make your store opening a success, you'll need to pull out all the stops. It's never true that "money is no object," but your opening is as close as it gets. Here are some of the ingredients that go into a strong new store opening:

  - Make sure you choose a date that doesn't conflict with other crowd-attracting events (unless they happen to be taking place at your front door), or with days when you have to be off doing something else.
  - Run as much advertising in local media as you can possibly afford.
  - Offer spectacular specials: "*Free* pound of coffee with every order over $10.00." "Everything half price." This is one of the rare times you are justified in running a storewide sale.
  - Decorate the outside of your store with as many flags and banners as city ordinances allow.
  - Post notices about the opening around local colleges, factories, health clubs—anywhere your potential customers are likely to gather.
  - Attract a celebrity if you can.
  - Run a parking lot event (like having elephant rides for kids).
  - Of course, notify the media and make as much noise as you can.

- **Making Room for New Merchandise Sale.** Keep your merchandise fresh. Your store should be big enough to house all the merchandise you need, but no larger than that. If you have space you don't need, you may find yourself hiding slow-moving, problem merchandise for years, instead of promptly marking down older goods to make space for the latest items. The first markdowns you take should always be deep enough to get rid of the merchandise and build traffic. As the retailing adage goes, "If you can't make money, at least make friends."

- **Happy Hours.** Happy hours build traffic at restaurants and bars, so why not try them at your store? Happy hour can be the theme at any time of day, but the promotion is most effective when your store is at its slowest. Limit happy hours to no more than two hours, be specific about products that are on sale, and don't continue to offer the discounts once the happy hour is over. You don't want to "train" your customers to think they can get a deal out of you whenever they want. You may want to serve refreshments during your happy hour or even champagne if that's your sort of audience and local laws permit. Promote your happy hour to local organizations such as senior citizen groups and PTAs. You may be cutting down on profits during this slow time, but at least it will help cover the overhead you would be paying anyway.

- **Birthday Sale for Customers.** Make each customer's birthday a special occasion by offering them a special deal during their birthday week. Invitations for this birthday discount should be sent to customers two weeks prior to their birthdays.

- **Temperature of the Day.** Depending on your location, this sale kicks in when the temperature either dips below a low number (such as 15 degrees) or above a high number (such as 100 degrees). This will bring people into the store in bad weather when they would otherwise stay at home. Themes for this sale could be "Warm Up to our Cold Day Deals," "Cool Prices on a Hot Day," or "Our Prices Drop with the Temperature."

- **Rainy/Snowy Day Sale.** Since business is usually much worse during inclement weather, you may have a policy that prices drop when it is raining or snowing outside. The deals could kick in after 1 inch of snow or after it has been raining for an hour. Promoting this policy with the local weather reports helps drive customers into the store during what otherwise may be dead selling periods. In these type of promotions, you should be a bit loose in your interpretation of the weather. If someone has ventured out to your store in a snowstorm, you can hardly refuse to give them the discount just because the snow is only a tenth of an inch.

- **Weekly Senior Citizen Day.** This is another particularly good event during the slow period of the day or week, and easy to tie in with senior's organizations. Since seniors usually have flexible hours, it does not matter when you run this promotion.

- **Late Night Sale.** Occasionally you may want to stay open late and run a special sale for night owls. This is a way to pick up an entirely new customer base. If they are sufficiently impressed with your products, convenience, and service, they will return to the store during normal business hours.

- **Customer Appreciation Sale.** Let your current customers pick the sale items. Give them a ballot listing products you are willing to put on sale and have them vote for their top three choices. Then put the top five to ten winners on sale. Your promotional message should explain, "We asked you what you wanted on sale and here is what you voted for . . . "

- **Let the Dogs Out Sale.** "Dogs," in this case, refers to merchandise that has been hanging around the store that nobody wants to buy at the current price. As the buyer for the store, this is merchandise that you once loved—but nobody else did! At least once a year you need to clear your stock with heavy markdowns known in the industry as a "down and dirty sale." Yes, you will take a loss on these goods. But, the fact is, you have *already* taken the loss because the goods are not worth what you paid for them. By selling them off at rock bottom prices, you are merely recognizing the loss. But at least you are pleasing your customers; salvaging what cash you can; and giving yourself the space and money to buy more stuff that, hopefully, the customers will like as much as you do.

- **Surprise Special of the Week.** Feature a different product at a generously discounted price at the same time each week. Don't advertise the product or price in advance, just promote the concept. The idea is to get the customer to visit the store weekly to see what the promotion will be.

- **Moon Sale.** Based on the positions of the moon, you can run all kinds of themes around a scheduled event like "full moon," "half moon," or "new moon sales." For an added touch, tickets on the sale goods could be in the shape of the moon.

- **Blood Donor Discount.** Blood is often in short supply just about everywhere. Thus, giving a special discount to anyone who donates blood is a great public relations move, builds sales, and helps people— a heady combination!
- **Tax Time Savings.** Run this sale around April 15 to help ease the taxpayers' expenses, or just to give them an excuse to find a bargain to ease their annual tax pain.
- **Private Sale for Private Groups.** Such sales can be directed to non-profit organizations, civic or business organizations, or non-competing firms who may want to offer a special benefit to their employees. You can keep the store open after normal closing hours or open up early for these groups.
- **Welcome to Our Community.** Mailing addresses of new residents can be obtained through your county clerk and some towns even have services that will provide you with this valuable information. Special discount coupons mailed to newcomers have a higher redemption rate of return than normal coupon mailings because new residents are still looking for the right places to shop—you will have helped them decide it's you!
- **February 29 Sale.** Even though leap year only comes every four years, take advantage of it when it does come.
- **Diet Sale.** This is a two-part sale because customers who want to participate have to weigh in when they start the program and weigh out a certain number of days later (twenty days is a good number). Their discount will depend on how much weight they lose, say 1% for every pound. If someone loses fifty pounds and you lose money by having to give them 50% off, don't worry. The money you lose will seem trivial compared to the publicity you gain. You can add further excitement by running a special drawing for a larger prize among everyone who loses more than 15% of their starting weight.
- **Cheaper by the Dozen.** The theme for this one is simple: the more you buy, the less you pay. Quantity discounts are always a favorite for customers and, if you pick the right items, this is a quick way to get the

average sale up.

- **Two for the Price of One.** Before jumping on this one, make sure you pick products on which you make a high margin or on which the supplier is willing to give you goods at a reduced price. Variations of this sale include the "One Cent Sale" and "Buy one and get the second at half price." Personally, I would try this last one first to maximize profits.
- **Grandparents and In-Laws Sale.** Grandparents Day is the first Sunday in September after Labor Day. Mother-in Law Day is the fourth Sunday in October. Father-in-Law Day has never been officially designated, so you can assign any day you want. Each of these days lends itself to heartwarming or funny themes to attract these oft-neglected groups.
- **Next Season Sale.** When a customer buys something from this season, hand them a coupon for a percentage off on specific items for *next* season.
- **Specific Person Sale.** Retailers traditionally hold manager's sales. So if you have a manager named Bill, consider naming your next sale "Bill's Sale." Take it a step further and have your customers register to have a sale named after them and draw a winner. This is a great way to include both employees and customers in your interactive sales promotions.

Contests:

Everyone's a Winner!

Everyone loves a contest and, when it comes to marketing your business, carefully planned contests offering meaningful prizes can build excitement and added store traffic. There are basically two different types of contests:

- Sweepstakes where no skills are required to win; customers only need to enter to win. In this type of contest, you may not legally require a purchase—everyone who fills in a sweepstakes entry form must have an equal chance of winning. One typical example is a scratch off card that is given to everyone who enters the store.

- Contests where the customer has to exhibit some skill to win, for example, writing a slogan for the store. If skill is involved, you may require a purchase as the price of entering the promotion. Please note, however, that the rules governing sweepstakes and contests vary by state, so you need to seek legal advice before proceeding.

When deciding whether to run a sweepstakes or a contest, consider this: sweepstakes attract more entries because they don't require a purchase. However, for exactly that reason they may not build sales. Contests, on the other hand, attract fewer entrants (and maybe not enough to justify your time and expense). However, at least you know each bought something and you have collected their names for your mailing list. Thus, both approaches have advantages and disadvantages. The best thing to do is to experiment with both approaches and repeat the one that works best.

In order to keep costs down, have other merchants or your suppliers provide the prizes free or at least at a favorable price. After all, they are getting a lot of publicity when you make their product your main prize; they should be pleased to supply it for little or nothing. Here are some more great sweepstakes and contest ideas:

- **Rent a Roulette or Carnival Wheel.** Have the customer spin the wheel to determine their percentage off on products. Obviously, you want the odds to weigh in your favor. (Check for legality on this one; it may not be allowed in some states.)
- **Scratch-off Tickets.** These fun, interactive cards can determine either discounts or prizes.
- **Pick from a Container.** You can have capsules inside which are the discounts customers can get (same day only). All the capsules are in a drum from which the customers can pick when they come through the door. You can control the amount of discounts by what you put into the drum.
- **Treasure Chest.** Pass out keys as the customer is leaving the store or via mail. When the customer next comes in, their key will open the treasure chest of discounts.
- **Guess the Number of Items.** This is good almost any month of the

year, from chocolate kisses in February to golf balls in May to candy canes in December. Putting this container in the window will attract the casual passerby.

- **Poetry Contest.** This idea is great PR that attracts media. Have the contestants write an ode (or perhaps a limerick) about your store, a favorite salesperson, a particular product, or the community in general. You can even start the ball rolling by offering your own limerick. Mine used to run like this:

    > *Marc Joseph started out poor*
    > *But thought if he opened a store*
    > *His income would rise*
    > *But to his surprise*
    > *He found charging less gave him more.*

    Okay, so it was pretty blatantly self-serving; but it got my point across. And I was delighted when one of my customers responded:

    > *His customers entered his store*
    > *Fearing they'd have to pay more*
    > *But to their surprise*
    > *Their delight on the rise,*
    > *His prices had dropped to the floor.*

    A panel consisting of educators or media personalities can choose the winning entries.

- **The Bests.** This is a promotion that could cost very little but generate a lot of publicity. The best could be "Best Mother," "Father," "Teacher," "Grandmother," or "Grandfather," etc. And the entrants could be supplied as essays written by elementary-age kids. Contact your local elementary school teachers, who can use this as part of their class assignment. To ensure the kids are doing their own work, accept only entries that are handwritten. As entries come in, post them around the store and in the windows so passersby will stop and read. Judging should be done by people outside the store. Once winners are picked, be sure to notify the local media. A valuable reward should go to the top three.

- **Look-alike Contest.** This one is another great PR ploy, especially if you can get the local media to be the judges.

- **Shopping Spree.** Just as you've seen on TV, this sweepstakes creates real excitement in the store. People come in once to sign up; again to witness the drawing; and a third time to see the "spree-er" in action. The winner's spree can be based on how much they can carry with their bare hands (no carts allowed).

- **Best Tan in Town.** This one is a good sweepstakes to have in July or August, especially if you sell health and beauty care products, sportswear, health foods, or cosmetics.

- **Home Video Contest.** Solicit videos of children, the beach, Thanksgiving dinner, etc, and limit tapes to five minutes. Have a local television station judge the best, possibly even airing it, and give the winner an impressive prize.

- **Sponsor a Walking or Running Race.** If you can tie this event into a non-profit organization that will be using this event to raise money, you can create considerable press coverage.

Building Customer Loyalty

Gaining repeat customers, the essence of retail success, depends on their satisfaction in seven respects: 1) the quality of the products you carry, 2) the selection you offer, 3) your pricing, 4) the treatment they receive from your personnel, 5) the store's ambiance, 6) its location, and 7) the hours you are open. If you cannot satisfy your customers in these respects you won't keep them.

However, if you do satisfy them in all seven respects, you can, and should, still develop ways to accelerate repeat business. The best technique is through a customer rewards program. The customer wins by getting better deals, but the retailer *really* wins because it costs less to keep a customer than to attract a new one. Thus, a business with a core of repeaters will almost always be more successful than one that has to rely on constantly attracting new customers. Of course, every retailer has to do both. But the higher the ratio of old customers to new, the more profitable the store is likely to be. Here are some great options for customer reward programs:

- **Rewards Card.** Also called a savings card, bonus card, or courtesy card, this is a free-of-charge card that lets customers take advantage of discounts offered only to cardholders either in the store or via coupons or deal announcements sent by mail. The cards can be given out to every customer who signs up for one, or it can be a gift with purchase tied to a certain level of purchases, or (as at Barnes & Noble, for example) it can be sold to customers.

- **Frequent Buyer's Club.** This card rewards the customer at the end of a specific period (usually the end of the year) with cash back or a special award. The awards may kick in once customers reach certain total purchase levels for the year. Awards may include (but certainly not be confined to):

  - Store discounts either as cash back or as reductions on future purchases.
  - Free gifts chosen from among designated store merchandise. Instead of actual merchandise, the store may prefer to give out gift certificates that represent another way of attracting customers back into the store.
  - Outside gifts chosen from a catalog, possibly at different values based on the points earned by customers. (The number of points may be tied to the dollar amount the customer buys, or varying points may be awarded on different items base on which products the retailer wishes to emphasize.)
  - Travel awards.
  - Tickets to special events such as the circus, the theater, or sports events.

Using PR to Get Your Message Across

Whether or not you decide to buy advertising, you can (and should) add to your exposure with a creative publicity campaign. The media is always looking for newsworthy story or photo opportunities. You can often get free exposure by providing products for contests sponsored by the media.

Don't limit your thinking about media to only dominant papers and TV stations in your market. By all means, include alternative weekly newspapers, cable television, ethnic and foreign-language media, local magazines, high school and college newspapers, free publications, union publications, tourist publications, and literature from all kinds of business, civic, religious and nonprofit organizations. Each has some readership and, not infrequently, the relatively small number of people who read these local media do so with intensity and are strongly influenced by them. And even a few new customers are important to your business. So, go after every medium, however small.

If you have the budget, you can hire a public relations agency. However, unless you can afford to handle what is usually a pretty hefty fee, you will probably do better handling the publicity yourself. You may develop an internship program with a local college and get a public relations student to help out, but let's assume you need to do everything on your own. Here are some effective, simple ideas for getting local media coverage:

• First, find out who the key people to contact are. This shouldn't take more than a few phone calls. There aren't usually that many media outlets. Make sure you get their e-mail addresses because most editors prefer e-mail to phone calls. This is now your media list. The art of getting your information published is to make it sound like news, not a commercial announcement—even though that is what it is.

So, let's say your purpose is to announce a new line of clothing that has just arrived at your store. "Schmolowitz Fashions proudly announces the arrival of the newest shipment of Thierry Mugler

Blouses, ready-to-wear" won't make the news. But this might: "Julia Roberts to attend Academy Awards in Thierry Mugler blouse announces Joe Schmolowitz of Schmolowitz Fashions, the only store in our area to carry the sought-after designer's fashions."

Of course, what you write in your press release has to be true. However, almost always, when a new product is launched or newly arrives at your store, the manufacturer will know something unique and newsworthy about it. By concentrating on that newsworthy aspect, you can often get your point across—vigorously and for no money. However, be careful not to send the media "non-stories." If you do, they will soon completely ignore you.

- Let your media list know that you are willing to give out prizes for their contests, either as merchandise or as gift certificates. Since prizes are promoted on the air and in the press, this is an excellent way to get free publicity for your store. Entry forms will be available at your store, and filled-in forms may be dropped off there.

- Because you are a retailer and viewed as an expert in trends in your field, push yourself to your media list as a spokesperson who would be glad to do a guest appearance on an interesting topic. The topics you can tell your media list you would be glad to discuss (as applicable) include:
  – Trends in retailing
  – What is new for the season
  – What toys to expect for Christmas
  – What's the latest in cooking and gourmet foods
  – What are the hot colors this season
  – What's hot, what's not
  – What gifts men are buying
  – What gifts women are buying
  – How the small retailer survives against the big chains
  – The importance of product safety
  – What to look for when reading labels

- Use a significant milestone like a twentieth anniversary or Santa coming to town to get your media list interested in doing a remote broadcast from the store. That costs you nothing and is wonderful publicity.

- Volunteer to make your products or your store available for media stories such as trends in women's clothing or having young children test toys for Christmas. Or give some of your products to decorate the Christmas tree in a local homeless shelter or orphanage.

- If you have a newsworthy announcement or an idea for an article, e-mail the announcement or the facts of the story to your media contacts—and hope for the best. Getting a story into the newspaper rarely involves face-to-face meetings, but if you fail to get any "hits" from your e-mail, review why. All media need material and are always looking for prepared information to put into their publications. Therefore, the fact that yours didn't get picked up probably means one of two things: either it wasn't newsworthy enough, or it was too poorly presented to get its point across. So, learn to do better next time.

- If you are confident of your writing abilities and you have something newsworthy to say, by all means, write a full article in the form of a press release. Harried newspaper editors are pleased if they can "lift" a complete article and print it without too much rewriting. If you cannot write well, you might retain a young local writer to do it for you. Starting writers are very inexpensive.

- Be aware that ethnic publications are also good for news placement, but they are only interested in news that affects their *precise* market. Be targeted in what you send them.

- Remember that high school and college newspapers are worthy targets if you want to attract students. They will often run such things as your announcement of an intern program, an interview with a graduate who has worked his way up in your store, teen shopping trends, announcements of special programs, or contests for students.

Parting Words

Marketing is vital for your survival and growth. Fortunately, there are almost as many ways to market your store as there are customers to frequent it. I hope that this sampling of ideas both assists you in keeping your store crowded and inspires you to develop and implement even more successful ideas of your own.

As you grow in experience, you will grow in creativity. As you learn ever more about your customer base, you will come up with more personalized, powerful, and exciting ways to market your store.

Retail Detail

A recent report in the *Journal of the American Medical Association* reported that 30.5% of Americans are obese, up from 22.9% a decade ago. Nearly two-thirds, 64.5%, are classified as overweight. Half of all U. S. women today wear size fourteen or larger. In 1985 the average size was eight. The growth projected for the plus-size customer is more than two-and-half times that of the average population over the next ten years.

Chapter 11

Cheaper by the Dozen:
Opening a Dollar, Discount, or Variety Store

A number of factors are converging to drive the success
of dollar stores. Rapid store count growth is
making the format accessible to more people;
the economy is prompting more people to become bargain shoppers,
and dollar store retailers have made their stores more appealing
by cleaning them up and improving both
the assortment of products they carry and
the quality of those products.
—TODD HALE, VP, ACNielsen

WHEN IT COMES TO COMPETING with Wal-Mart and continuing to grow even in proximity to a Wal-Mart, price plays a crucial role. After all, aside from the debatable convenience of finding motor oil and hair gel in the same store as lawn chairs and Fruit-of-the-Looms, Wal-Mart's real advantage is that its merchandise is priced at significantly less than, well, just about *anywhere* else. So how can you compete? Take heart. Americans have always had a taste for frugal shopping—just check out the crowds in the clearance aisle in any retail store. That desire can play into your hands as well. How? The answer could be as simple as opening your own Dollar Store.

Variety and discount stores can trace their origins in the United States to a little over a century ago when Frank W. Woolworth created his five-and-dime empire and Sebastian S. Kresge created Kresge's, which eventually evolved into Kmart. The Dollar Store concept is the latest evolution of the discount store philosophy and it started on both coasts around the same time in the mid-1980s.

Dave Gold (known as the Father of the Dollar Store Industry), founder of 99 Cents Only Stores based in Los Angeles, California and today a successful New York Stock Exchange company (symbol NDN) began his career running his own liquor store. Now he is on the Forbes 400 richest list. His seminal idea was: "Wines of the World. Your choice: 99 cents."

It was not until 1982, when he was 50 years old, however, that he decided to take the success he had learned from his 99-cent promotions and turn them into the chain he has built today. Dave is a modern-day example of the entrepreneur who got creative and realized the American dream. And he did it for less than a buck!

On the other coast, in Virginia Beach, Virginia, Bo Perry owned and operated a jewelry store on the beach. When he took his jewelry down to $1, lines began forming around the block. Not one to let a good idea lose momentum, Bo quickly began bringing all kinds of goods in to sell for $1. This was the humble beginning of Everything's A Dollar stores, which took the stock market by storm in the early 1990's and eventually grew to 420 stores before going bust because of over expansion.

Macon Brock, Jr. read about Bo's early success on Virginia Beach in the Norfolk, Virginia local newspaper. Excited by the concept, he opened his first Dollar Tree store in 1986. Based out of Chesapeake, Virginia, Dollar Tree (DLTR on the NASDAQ) has over 2,500 stores and a value of over $2.8 billion!

The lesson of Macon's success is always keep your eyes open and feel the pulse of what is going on around you. You probably have a Dollar Tree or a comparable store near where you live. Or two or three. Visit them all. And ask yourself, "What works? What doesn't? How could I do this differently? How could I do this better?"

There is still plenty of room there for you to open your store. But, of course, you have to find ways to improve upon what David Gold and his successful competitors are doing. As Robert Burton wrote more than 380 years ago, "A dwarf standing on the shoulders of a giant may see farther than a giant himself." If you were to investigate what Dave Gold does to achieve such astounding success for his chain, here's what you would find:

- 99 Cents Only Stores move into middle-class neighborhoods, not poor ones. Other chains, such as Family Dollar and Dollar General target low-income areas, but Gold's philosophy is that lower-income people will go into better neighborhoods while middle-class customers also shop for bargains but won't travel to poor neighborhoods. Many of his stores are located on the border between middle- and low-income neighborhoods. In fact, one of his best performing stores is on Wilshire Boulevard in Los Angeles, right on the border of mega-rich Beverly Hills!

- Whenever Gold's managers are in contact with a working-class person, whether the waitress, busboy, or maître d' at lunch or salespeople at other stores or the guy who fixes the plumbing, they hand out vouchers for a free item at any of their stores. Since their average store item costs about $0.60, attracting a new customer at that price is a bargain.

- An average store carries around 6,000 different items, of which 40% are closeouts.

- Gold's buyers are always open to new products and new vendors. To make sure they miss nothing, they have weekly open buyer meetings where any vendor can pitch any product, whether the chain currently buys from them or not.

- All stores open fifteen minutes earlier and stay open fifteen minutes later than the posted hours. This harks back to Gold's entrepreneurial roots—he just can't stand to lose any kind of sale.

- Negative signs such as "No shirt, no shoes, no service" or "We don't make change" are not allowed anywhere in the store. Only positive signs such as "Come as you are" or "We gladly make change" are permitted.

- All promotional pictures of employees show them in action. Pictures with employees with their hands in their pockets don't work for this chain.

- When opening a store, this chain blankets its trading area with ads offering TV's and other unbelievable items for 99 cents for the first few people in line. This always creates free publicity because the grand openings have lines around the block and the media always jumps on this. Taking the loss on an absurdly low price pays off several times over in free media coverage.

Why the Dollar Store Business?

Some people assume the dollar store business is based on selling a bunch of cheap items no one else wanted. But if dollar stores, called *specialty discount stores* by the investment community, projected nothing but this cheap image, they wouldn't have been around for long. In fact, the successful ones (and most are successful) create an exciting place to shop with real bargains on every aisle.

Successful dollar stores focus on two general categories of products: those with known brand names or non-branded products. Brand name products are usually available because the manufacturers have overstocked products and are prepared to sell their excess inventory at below cost. Non-branded products are often those produced overseas and are as good (or very nearly so) as the branded items and are available at remarkably lower prices.

The specialty discount market is estimated to be a $40 billion industry and is growing at around 7% a year. This growth is more than triple the growth for department stores. The larger, publicly traded dollar stores such as Dollar Tree and 99 Cents Only Stores all average over $250 in sales per square foot and have an annual store-level return on investment from 55% to 100%. In comparison to almost any other kind of business, these numbers are impressive.

In addition to high growth and high return on investment, the dollar store business benefits from several other trends affecting retailing, including:

- The quality of imported goods, now available in most categories, has increased dramatically, so customers feel they are not only getting a lower price but also better value. However, although customers are paying less, retailers are making more because overseas labor and raw materials are often much lower. Because of the breadth and rapid pace on new product introductions from overseas, imports bring that elusive sense that every day is a treasure hunt. In a well-run dollar store, there is always the excitement of a newly arrived shipment, full of potential treasures. No wonder customers keep coming back!

- Tied to the growth of imports is the emergence of private label brands as a way for dollar stores to build their own customer loyalty while generating higher gross margins. Customers are willing to try private label brands if they have confidence in the store offering them.

- Another supply trend benefiting dollar stores is the increasing availability of national brands. Many of the larger consumer goods companies have decided "if you can't beat 'em, join 'em" and are dedicating sales teams to service the discount, closeout, and dollar store industry. They provide national brands (often in less expensive formats, for example without outer packaging) at impressive discounts for the store. The availability of such "branded" goods raises its image and attracts more customers.

- Customers like the convenience of a local dollar store where they can get low prices and good merchandise without the hassle of shopping at an enormous Super Wal-Mart.

- According to the U. S. Census Bureau, incomes for the bottom 40% of families have not increased at the same pace as for the middle class, putting additional pressures on this 40% of our population to stretch their shopping dollar.
- As the population continues to age, ever more consumers on fixed incomes are faced with tightening budgets. They are prime targets for the local dollar store.

When you add up all of these factors—a growing customer base, strong gains in customer purchase rates, above average sales per square foot, and higher than standard return on investment—it is easy to see why this retail concept is fast becoming one of the most exciting and enjoyable businesses to be in.

As more and more customers from all income levels are telling their friends how pleasant it is to shop in a dollar store, business continues to get better. Industry experts judge that the market can absorb another 15,000 dollar stores before it becomes saturated. You could be one (or several) of them!

One very interesting opportunity is a chain called Big Lots, Inc. Currently there are 35 operators of closeout chains with Big Lots, Inc. The largest of these is based out of Columbus, Ohio and does $4 billion with over 1400 stores averaging $2.9 million a store. Big Lots combines closeouts of clothing with standard home products. The combination keeps customers coming backing to see what new deals have arrived. Though they may not find a deal they want, while they are in the store, customers pick up staple household needs at prices they enjoy. Thus, they rarely leave empty-handed.

The success of dollar stores has grabbed the attention of many retail chains. Kroger is testing Kroger Dollar Stores, featuring 500 square feet of space devoted to dollar store merchandise in a section of their test stores. Wal-Mart is experimenting with a Pennies 'n Cents shop. Target is testing One Spot departments. And Mervyn's has introduced $1 to $5 shops into its stores. These new departments are usually located in the front of the store and are designed to build traffic by replicating the treasure hunt appeal that has made the dollar stores so much fun. For you, the independent entrepreneur, this trend has the disadvantage of adding to the competition. On the other hand, it has the advantage of building consumer awareness of this great retailing concept. More and more consumers are realizing that they can buy the same product at a dollar store that they would normally purchase at a traditional retailer, but at a far lower price.

Here are some statistics that A. C. Nielsen found about dollar stores:

- Blue-collar households account for more than one-third of sales volume.
- Households with five or more members or children under the age of eighteen are heavily represented in this customer base.
- The following percentages of shoppers in various income groups are dollar-store customers:
  - Less than $20,000   74%
  - $20,000-$39,999   70%
  - $40,000-$49,999   64%
  - $50,000-$69,999   58%
  - $70,000 and over   45%

At www.dollardays.com, we help entrepreneurs like you open dollar stores they can be proud of. In this context, one service we provide is a series of charts that you will find useful as guidelines. The first chart (Figure 1) gives you an idea of the financial commitment it takes to open a store. Obviously, the money needed is based on the size of the store. The second chart (Figure 2a) shows what sales per day will do on an annual basis. The third chart (Figure 2b) gives you a guideline of the money it takes once the store is up and running. Feel free to call my office or e-mail me (contact information can be found at the end of this book) if you have any questions about the numbers.

Figure 1

www.dollardays.com
D.E.A.L.
DollarDays Economic Analysis List

DOLLAR STORE COST TO OPEN

SQUARE FEET	MERCHANDISE	FIXTURES	EXTERIOR SIGN	INTERIOR SIGNS	TOTAL
1000	$15,000	$6,000	$3,000	$500	$24,500
1500	$22,500	$7,500	$3,000	$500	$33,500
2000	$30,000	$10,000	$3,000	$500	$43,500
2500	$37,500	$12,500	$3,000	$500	$53,500
3000	$45,000	$15,000	$3,000	$500	$63,500
3500	$52,500	$17,500	$3,000	$750	$73,750
4000	$60,000	$20,000	$3,000	$750	$83,750
4500	$67,500	$22,500	$3,000	$750	$93,750
5000	$75,000	$25,000	$5,000	$1,000	$106,000
5500	$82,500	$27,500	$5,000	$1,000	$116,000
6000	$90,000	$30,000	$5,000	$1,000	$126,000
6500	$97,500	$32,500	$5,000	$1,000	$136,000
7000	$105,000	$35,000	$5,000	$1,000	$146,000
7500	$112,500	$37,500	$5,000	$1,000	$156,000
8000	$120,000	$40,000	$5,000	$1,200	$166,200
8500	$127,500	$42,500	$5,000	$1,200	$176,200
9000	$135,000	$45,000	$5,000	$1,200	$186,200
9500	$142,500	$47,500	$5,000	$1,200	$196,200
10000	$150,000	$50,000	$7,000	$1,500	$208,500
12000	$180,000	$62,500	$7,000	$1,500	$251,000
15000	$225,000	$75,000	$7,000	$1,500	$308,500

Figure 2a

www.dollardays.com
D.E.A.L.
DollarDays Economic Analysis List

OPERATING PLAN

	DAILY	WEEKLY	MONTHLY	YEARLY
Sales	$1,500	$10,500	$45,000	$540,000
Operating Hours	12	84	360	4320
Employee Hours	24	168	720	8640
Sales	$2,000	$14,000	$60,000	$720,000
Operating Hours	12	84	360	4320
Employee Hours	24	168	720	8640
Sales	$3,000	$21,000	$90,000	$1,080,000
Operating Hours	12	84	360	4320
Employee Hours	36	252	1080	12960

Figure 2b

www.dollardays.com
D.E.A.L.
DollarDays Economic Analysis List

YEAR PLAN	$1500 DAY	$2000 DAY	$3000 DAY
Sales	$540,000	$720,000	$1,080,000
Cost of Goods	$297,000	$396,000	$594,000
Gross Profit	$243,000	$324,000	$486,000
OPERATING EXPENSES			
Wages	$86,400	$86,400	$129,600
Payroll Tax	$26,784	$26,784	$40,176
Workers Comp	$1,728	$1,728	$2,592
Rent	$40,000	$40,000	$40,000
Electricity	$4,000	$4,000	$4,000
Telephone	$1,200	$1,200	$1,200
Insurance	$4,000	$4,000	$4,000
Supplies	$1,000	$1,000	$1,000
Advertising	$4,000	$4,000	$4,000
Freight	$54,000	$72,000	$108,000
Total Op Expenses	$223,112	$241,112	$334,568
Gross Profit	$243,000	$324,000	$486,000
Total Op Expenses	$223,112	$241,112	$334,568
Net Income Before Taxes	$19,888	$82,888	$151,432

Opening a Discount or Variety Store:

Where to Get Your Merchandise

How do you stock the store once it's set up? After all, offering products for a dollar is a great come on, but how can it last? Closeout retailers and wholesalers provide a valuable service to manufacturers by purchasing their excess merchandise. There is a lot of it around, due to the following:

- Consolidation of retail chains (with some of them going out of business) has created merchandise that was manufactured but never shipped to the stores or was shipped, never paid for, and returned. Manufacturers need to move this inventory.

- Large retailers' insistence on buying just-in-time has shifted the inventory risk from the retailers to the manufacturers. In the past, inventory excesses were spread over many retail stores. They marked them down, took a small loss, and the goods never surfaced. Now, the retailers don't buy excess inventory and if excess production occurs, the manufacturer is left with the problem. What was a minor excess for such individual stores becomes thousands of cases in the manufacturer's warehouses that have to be closed out, often below cost.

- The trend toward shorter product cycles especially for products related to a movie, a personality, or a fashion fad generate more left-over inventory.

- Manufacturers have increased the number of new products they launch in an attempt to build market share. Naturally, therefore, they also have more failures, with excess inventory the result.

- Manufacturers' salespeople are the ultimate optimists. They habitually estimate that they can sell more than they do. The left over inventory is grist for dollar stores' mills.

Closeout Retailing

Closeout retailing is one of the fastest growing segments of the retailing industry with store owners and managers very focused on buying at rock bottom prices, so they can offer their customers impressive bargains. Such discount and closeout stores need to be located in low rent, high visibility areas with easy access to major thoroughfares.

A Note about Point of Sale Registers (POS)

Point of Sale Registers (commonly known as POS) are the modern retailer's way of keeping track of what comes into the store and what is sold. Most of today's POS software gives the retailer the ability to analyze just about anything going on in the store from sales of individual items, to sales by category, to stock level of items on the shelf. You can even track the performance of any of the employees. Today's basic POS systems include:

- POS-register unit (computer)
- POS-store manager retail software
- Cash drawer
- Impact receipt printer
- Barcode scanner
- Barcode and label printers
- Keyboard and optical mouse
- Rolls of receipt paper
- CRT monitor
- PC charge credit card payment software
- Credit card reader
- Pole display for customer to follow the transaction
- Cables
- One-year hardware/software support

When you are starting up a retail store, don't overbuy the technical systems you will need. Most POS providers have the ability to add on to a basic system, so just start out with a basic system and then build onto it as necessary.

Ever since the dawn of the computer era, the expression "garbage in, garbage out" has been a popular slogan; if you input inaccurate information, the information you get out will be meaningless. So, take those extra few minutes to make sure you and your staff are scrupulous about entering the correct information.

Summary

All things considered, the time has never been better for you to open a dollar store. A convergence of plentiful products at reasonable prices means great opportunities for both retailers and customers. Economic and demographic trends are making consumers more open to the idea of shopping at dollar stores and doing so regularly. Thus, by opening a dollar store today and offering consumers both good prices and the convenience and personal service they cannot get at the big box stores, you could be in a prime position to compete successfully with Wal-Mart in this thriving new subset of the retail industry.

Retail Detail

African Americans are the most fashion-conscious group, with 34% likely to keep up with changes in trends versus 28% of Asians, 27% of Hispanics, and 25% of whites. Blacks are also the most likely to travel an hour or more to shop at their favorite store and almost twice as likely as the average consumer to go out of their way to find new stores, especially for a bargain. To shop at a factory outlet store, 33% will travel an hour or more, compared to 27% of all consumers. Once they get there, they prefer conquering the sales racks alone rather than with friends.

Chapter 12

Opening a Clothing Store:
Clothes Make the Entrepreneur!

Independent businesses have discovered ways to compete.
Almost all provide superior service.
Their sales staffs know their products and customers well
and stock what the locals want.
They emphasize convenience and make things easy to find.
Some choose specialties in which they can excel,
whether it's children's books or saltwater fish.
And many now employ more sophisticated pricing strategies.
—TIME MAGAZINE (10/21/03)

NO MATTER WHAT KIND OF STORE YOU OPEN, you should always strive to make it a "destination store." One of the biggest mistakes apparel store owners make is buying primarily, or sometimes exclusively, for their personal tastes. Certainly you should not ignore your gut instincts, nor should you try to cater to everyone (if you do, your store will look like a hodgepodge that has no fashion sense and therefore caters to no one). However, you do need to look beyond your own closet to encompass the views, tastes, and "gut instincts" of the cadre of customers to whom you plan to cater.

In setting the fashion tone for your store, you need to define (in your mind and by the example of what you buy) the store's point of view. The Gap doesn't look like Ralph Lauren. But within the broad parameters you set, you can never be certain how a particular garment or set of garments will sell. Believe me, both Gap and Lauren often end up with garments they thought were terrific, and often that the stores advertised nationally at great expense, but which consumers flatly rejected.

That is why experimenting is so crucial. For example, occasionally have one of your assistants dress one of your store dummies in her version of your store's fashion so you can observe how your public reacts to her version as compared to your own. The point is, there is no *one* resource to tell you what to do when it comes to stocking your retail clothing shop. But then, the fun of the clothing business is being able to anticipate a trend and capitalize on it before your competition does. That is why being a keen observer of real life is a main key to success. You need to soak up information from all kinds of resources, digest it, and then make your buys based on your head and your heart. The kind of information you need comes from several different sources:

- Watch television. Of all the nerve! Can you believe I am telling you to spend your spare time watching TV? This is not just entertainment—it's research: While you're watching, pay attention to the hip shows. Not the plots, mind you, but the fashions. Designers use what they refer to as "the TV platform" as a way to test and get free advertising for their creations. Think Oscar night or sweeps week.

- Go to movies that aim to be hip or contemporary. (Neither Westerns, nor historicals, nor sci-fi will do. Nor will anything set in Russia, where, as far as I am concerned, no fashion emanates at all.) Again, look beyond the plot and watch the fashion. How high are the skirts? What kind of tops are the men and women wearing? Of course, only new releases will do. By the time the movie is out on DVD, its fashions are long since passé.

- Observe what fashionable people on the street, the expensive street in your town, of course, are wearing. It's true that people spend the bulk of their clothing budget on boring necessities and mere comfort. However, you'll soon recognize that special pullover shape, that new pastel shade. Don't miss the boots. But don't wait until "everyone" is wearing something; by then, you're too late.

- Read trade publications such as *Women's Wear Daily* or *Daily News Record*. These time-honored periodicals give you an early insight into the industry trends.

- Read the same magazines that your customers read, such as *Glamour, Vogue, Seventeen, Young Miss,* or *GQ*. This way you can see if you are missing a look that is consistent in all the major publications.

- Visit clothing manufacturers at one of the merchandise marts located in major cities. Most items on display lead the season by about six months, so you can get a feel for upcoming fashions.

- Go to the major shows like the MAGIC (Men's Apparel Guild in California) to see hundreds of booths filled with timely goods. If you are frequently seeing the same new look, there is a good chance it will show up on TV, in the magazines, and then on your customers' wish lists. By then, it should be in your store!

- Use your reps as resources. All reps, and certainly all apparel reps, want to sell you on their merchandise. However, the best of them realize that they can sell you more if they help you to build the business. Once you have found such reps, use them as a resource. Pick their brains, not only about their own lines, but also about what their competitors are selling. Experienced reps visit so many stores, they know what is moving and what is not.

- Build a network with other stores. Other independent apparel retailers are an important source. By building a network with stores in different parts of your city and in other towns, you form a non-threatening environment where sharing information helps all stores. One store may pick up on a hot trend you missed or note that a trend is on the wane before you notice it, especially if you are in a smaller town and your correspondent is in either New York, Miami, or Los Angeles, where trends (upwards or downwards) usually start.

Your Store Image:

In Clothing, It Really IS Everything!

More than in any other segment of retailing image, is what distinguishes your store from everyone else on the block. But what exactly is image? Image is the composite impression made on your customers by the types of fixtures you have in the store, how the employees dress, the look of your ads, the music you play and, of course, your merchandise. One important part of your image depends on the second thing you decided (the first was to go into the apparel retailing business in the first place). It was the name of your store. This holds true for naming *any* kind of retail store, of course, but holds especially true for the apparel industry.

From an advertising and customer recall standpoint, a simple name is generally the best. Although Abercrombie & Fitch, Yves Saint Laurent, Bergdorf Goodman, Sears Roebuck and many others attest to the fact that a complicated name can do pretty well, I still feel you should strive for a name that at least hints at what you sell. On the other hand, names that are too cute is a pet peeve of mine. Unless you are selling novelties, using a pun or other word play as your store's name lacks dignity.

You want customers to be able to identify at a glance what sort of merchandise you are selling. If you are a plus size store, why hide it? Rather, let the world know what you're selling. "Plus Sizes on Main" might be a good name. Or, if you sell to men (and your name is Michael), "Michael's Big and Tall" might fill the bill. Eventually, once you are widely known, the name makes little difference. While I wouldn't recommend starting out with "Neiman Marcus" as your name today, now that it's an established, universally known, prestigious name, no retailer would dream of changing it.

Regardless of your store name, your image should be consistent with everything in, out, and around the store. For instance, if your image is folksy and friendly, you don't want hard edges or modern art all around the store. Likewise, if you're going for urban hip, you won't be plastering chickens and cows all over the cash register. Image may be everything, but consistency is key.

Women's Apparel Store

In order to run a successful women's apparel store, you must really, *really*, really love clothes. This is an exciting business because women love change and *always* like to try new styles. Knowing that you cannot be all things to all women, you need to decide at the very outset of your retail adventure, what target audience you are after.

Customers are hard to stereotype. Thus, I have found that the first rule of defining your potential customer base is to build in your mind a composite picture of your typical customer. How old is she? Is she a career woman or a stay-at-home mom? Is she fashion conscious, a "fashion model" type, or a "girl-next-door"?

Obviously, with a little luck you will attract every type of woman. But you can't *serve* every type. In fact, no one can wrap her mind around as nebulous a concept as "all women" or even "all women over fifty." Thus, to repeat myself, I suggest you aim at one woman who is as representative as possible of all the rest. By truly understanding her, you will stay consistent, you will hit the bull's-eye more often and, most important, even when you are not wholly on target, you won't be that far off. If you aim for a woman of twenty-five, and you miss, you will hit women between, say, twenty and thirty-five—still a reasonably cohesive grouping. On the other hand, if you try to aim at women between twenty and forty, chances are your aim will hit both teenagers and women of middle-age. Consequently, because there is little similarity between a teenager and a forty-year-old, you'll have a mishmash.

Once you have defined your iconic woman, buying becomes much more focused, less stressful, and thus easier on you and your customers.

As a very general statement, lower-income customers spend most of their apparel dollars on basics, that is clothes designed for casual wear (as typified by the garments you find in stores like Gap), while higher-income customers will prefer designer clothing. More than half of all women, however, purchase at least one updated, trendy item annually to add some excitement to their wardrobes.

Therefore, the balancing act in being successful in women's apparel is providing customers with enough fashion direction to seem fashionable (and therefore exciting) while also carrying enough basic merchandise to satisfy their everyday needs and so make sure they buy something when they do visit.

You've Found Your Niche!

Let's assume you have decided on the type of women's apparel store you are going to open. You have done your homework by checking out the competition, looking at the marketplace, and identifying a clear need. Whether it is a junior store, a plus-size store, a petite store, a sports related store, a dress-up store, a high fashion boutique, a casual store, or any combination of these and other concepts, the next question is how to maximize your sales and hence the return on your investment.

One way is to add accessories to your mix of products. The advantages of accessories are that they require very little selling space, create more sales per square foot than just about anything else you can sell, and generally carry high markups because they are "blind" items that your customers cannot "price shop." Accessories are an impulse item and are best merchandised close to either the fitting rooms or checkout counters. They are an ideal add-on sale for a customer who has just bought a fashionable garment and who therefore needs to accessorize it. Here is a list of high margin accessories every ready-to-wear (RTW) store should carry:

• Sunglasses
• Small leather goods

- Handbags
- Costume jewelry
- Watches
- Belts
- Scarves
- Hair accessories
- Hosiery

Men's Apparel Store

The good news for owners of men's apparel stores is that men do not change their wardrobes much each year so that (unlike women's clothing) the merchandise tends to stay in style for long periods. The bad news is that men do not change their wardrobes every year and therefore are not good customers for new fashions.

When men get depressed, they don't go shopping—they go to a game or watch sports on television, go running, or watch an action movie. Men as a whole do not particularly enjoy shopping the way women do. They respond less well to flattery (that shirt looks so great because it matches your eyes). They come in knowing what they need, head straight to the area where those items are carried, and start trying them on immediately without browsing. To run a successful men's store, then, keep it as simple as possible, make the atmosphere soothing and easy to understand with simple navigation and well-organized departments, and avoid loud colors, loud music, and loud accessories. Keep the store low-key by painting your walls off white without gimmicky themes.

The sales technique for male customers is to provide service, clarity (so customers know where to find what they need), and fit. Of course, there are trends in men's clothing, but they are much slower than women's, so by keeping up with the periodicals and men's magazines you can pretty much predict the newer fashions you need to have in stock at any one time. To some extent, this may be slowly changing as the "metrosexual" phenomenon gradually spreads. For instance, the idea of "low-rise" jeans for men would have been unthinkable a few years ago. While that idea hardly caught on widely, the very fact that they were marketed at all shows that guys are starting to become more fashion conscious.

Personally, I love the business of men's clothing. My first retail job was as a clerk in a men's store. And later, as a buyer of boy's and then men's wear for a major department store chain, I learned the basics of retailing. I would not exchange these experiences for anything else. In particular, men's clothing stores are rewarding for four reasons:

- They are much less risky than women's apparel. You can predict how many dress shirts or polo shirts or khaki pants you will sell each year, which makes sleeping through the night much easier.
- You do not need to be a fashion maven to open and run a men's apparel business.
- Because it is a more predictable business, you do not have to take as many markdowns or run as many sales, thus driving a higher percentage of profit to the bottom line.
- Whether men are brought into the store kicking and screaming all the way by their womenfolk or wander in on their own, they are a much easier and quicker sale than women. They are less price conscious, and while they tend to buy less, the purchases they make are often more profitable.

Perhaps, after you consider the advantages, you'll feel the same way I do about men's clothing.

Children's Clothing Store

The first decision you need to make when thinking about opening a kids' clothing store is what age group you want to cater to. There is an unbridgeable gap in almost every respect—product, décor, staffing, music, etc.—between toddlers and young teens. They cannot fit into the same store. Since one of your main reasons for deciding to open a kid's clothing store should be your love of children, you'll have to decide what age children you like best. Even so, do not let this warm and fuzzy emotion cloud the most important things to remember when running a kid's apparel store.

First, parents, not children, are the ones with the credit cards and checkbooks. The younger the children, the less influence they have on how those funds are used. Indeed, for very young children, many of the purchases are made by parents without the children even being present. Second, since you cannot cater to kids of all ages (which means you cannot continue to sell to them as they grow up) they cannot become long-term customers. However, their parents may be long-term customers, as they have more children, as they become grandparents, or as they buy clothes for their friends' children. So build your relationship with the parents by keeping in mind that they view their children as tiny extensions of themselves. The way parents dress their children, the degree of style versus basics, is a direct reflection of their own taste. To sell the kid, understand the parent.

In saying that parents are your key kids' clothing customers, you should not forget that the grandparent market is becoming ever more important as baby boomers, growing older, become one of the largest buying segments in our society. There is always a birthday or holiday for which grandma (and sometimes grandpa) can lavish the cutest fashion on their favorite grandchild.

Running a kid's store can be very profitable because kids quickly grow out of their clothing. So, as long as they have not grown beyond your store's age group, growing kids virtually force repeat purchases. Moreover, children's boutiques fill a major service void that big stores either can't compete with or rarely focus on, namely keeping kids entertained during the buying process. Just think about it: How many department stores are staffed to help a child in the dressing room or spend the time to interact with siblings waiting for this experience to finally be over? The result of this service gap is that this segment of the clothing business is one in which it is relatively easy for the service-oriented independent to beat the big guys.

While parents (and sometimes grandparents) make the buying decisions, kids exert a lot of influence on what is bought. They crave peer acceptance and, like their parents, get fashion clues from TV, especially such youth favorites as Nickelodeon and MTV. How many times have you seen a pouting child, arms crossed, refusing to try on the nice outfit mom or dad found? With a little market savvy and TV research, you can be the retailer who saves the day by bringing him something he or she finds cool to wear, and mom finds both affordable and acceptable.

Above all, since children have a limited attention span, the store has to be fun. Fun, of course, is age specific. A colorful window or cartoon-festooned walls may appeal to the younger set, but 'tweens will prefer posters of TV and music stars and the stars' loud music.

Keeping the child interested gives the parents more time to make the right decisions, and helps fulfill the true mission of a kid's store, which is to get the child outfitted as quickly, painlessly (for the parent and you), and profitably as possible. In order to achieve this goal, the store *must* carry the proper mix of basics (underwear, jeans, and pullover tops) to fashion (the latest trends and hot looks). As ever, this is an eternal balancing act in constant motion.

Analyzing the Numbers

Take a look at the charts below that we use at www.dollardays.com to help get clothing stores up and running. Averaging $3,000 in sales a day creates a pre-tax income of over $200,000 a year. We recommend starting in a smaller location to keep your investment manageable and then expanding your space as your customer base grows. Figure 1 gives you an idea of the initial investment for a clothing store. Figure 2a shows what sales per day will do on an annual basis. Figure 2b depicts the operating expenses and potential profit.

Figure 1

WOWPricing Everything Under the Sun

www.dollardays.com
D.E.A.L.
DollarDays Economic Analysis List

FUNDS TO OPEN A CLOTHING STORE

SQUARE FEET	MERCHANDISE	FIXTURES	EXTERIOR SIGN	INTERIOR SIGNS	TOTAL
500	$10,000	$4,000	$3,000	$300	$17,300
750	$15,000	$5,000	$3,000	$300	$23,300
1000	$20,000	$6,000	$3,000	$500	$29,500
1500	$30,000	$7,500	$3,000	$500	$41,000
2000	$40,000	$10,000	$3,000	$500	$53,500
2500	$50,000	$12,500	$3,000	$500	$66,000
3000	$60,000	$15,000	$3,000	$500	$78,500
3500	$70,000	$17,500	$3,000	$750	$91,250
4000	$80,000	$20,000	$3,000	$750	$103,750
4500	$90,000	$22,500	$3,000	$750	$116,250
5000	$100,000	$25,000	$5,000	$1,000	$131,000
5500	$110,000	$27,500	$5,000	$1,000	$143,500
6000	$120,000	$30,000	$5,000	$1,000	$156,000
6500	$130,000	$32,500	$5,000	$1,000	$168,500
7000	$140,000	$35,000	$5,000	$1,000	$181,000
7500	$150,000	$37,500	$5,000	$1,000	$193,500
8000	$160,000	$40,000	$5,000	$1,200	$206,200
8500	$170,000	$42,500	$5,000	$1,200	$218,700
9000	$180,000	$45,000	$5,000	$1,200	$231,200
9500	$190,000	$47,500	$5,000	$1,200	$243,700
10000	$200,000	$50,000	$7,000	$1,500	$258,500
12000	$240,000	$62,500	$7,000	$1,500	$311,000
15000	$300,000	$75,000	$7,000	$1,500	$383,500

Point of Sale Registers are recommended for these stores because of the multiple price points. Systems start in the smaller stores at $3,000 and can go as high as $15,000 in the larger stores.

Figure 2a

www.dollardays.com
D.E.A.L.
DollarDays Economic Analysis List

FUNDS TO OPEN A CLOTHING STORE

OPERATING PLAN

	DAILY	WEEKLY	MONTHLY	YEARLY
Sales	$1,500	$10,500	$45,000	$540,000
Operating Hours	12	84	360	4320
Employee Hours	24	168	720	8640
Sales	$2,000	$14,000	$60,000	$720,000
Operating Hours	12	84	360	4320
Employee Hours	24	168	720	8640
Sales	$3,000	$21,000	$90,000	$1,080,000
Operating Hours	12	84	360	4320
Employee Hours	36	252	1080	12960

Figure 2b

www.dollardays.com
D.E.A.L.
DollarDays Economic Analysis List

YEAR PLAN	$1500 DAY	$2000 DAY	$3000 DAY
Sales	$540,000	$720,000	$1,080,000
Cost of Goods	$270,000	$360,000	$540,000
Gross Profit	$270,000	$360,000	$540,000
OPERATING EXPENSES			
Wages	$86,400	$86,400	$129,600
Payroll Tax	$26,784	$26,784	$40,176
Workers Comp	$1,728	$1,728	$2,592
Rent	$40,000	$40,000	$40,000
Electricity	$4,000	$4,000	$4,000
Telephone	$1,200	$1,200	$1,200
Insurance	$4,000	$4,000	$4,000
Supplies	$1,000	$1,000	$1,000
Advertising	$4,000	$4,000	$4,000
Freight	$54,000	$72,000	$108,000
Total Op Expenses	$223,112	$241,112	$334,568
Gross Profit	$270,000	$360,000	$540,000
Total Op Expenses	$223,112	$241,112	$334,568
Net Income Before Taxes	$46,888	$118,888	$205,432

Retail Detail

Specialty store retail square footage increased 81% during the last decade according to Lazard Freres & Co. analyst Todd Slater. The greatest impact on this growth was to take business away from department stores.

Chapter 13

Retail Alternatives:
From Convenience Stores to Kiosks

No matter what the size of the convenience store—
whether it is a one-store operation or a company
of several thousand—there is one consistent element:
A convenience store is an anchor business to
the neighborhoods of America . . .
—TERI RICHMAN, National Association of Convenience Stores

I F THERE IS ANYTHING the previous chapters should have shown you, it is this retail truism: There is always room for the right kind of store or selling concept. Geographic shifts of large numbers of consumers are characteristic of our ever-mobile population and stores and products need to be wherever people live.

New variations on old retail themes are caused by changing lifestyles, new fashions, increasing concern about health and healthcare, and technological advances. New openings for retailing concepts continue to occur because established merchants retire, sell their businesses, or simply close down. So never forget that the small store with the brilliant new concept you launch today may be the Home Depot or Starbucks of the next decade. Then again, your successful store need not be a "store" at all.

Non-Store Retailing Overview

Currently there is over $125 billion being done in non-store retailing, that is retailing via television, electronic shopping, paper and electronic catalogs, door-to-door selling, in home demonstrations and parties, movable stalls, vending machines, and mail order. Products sold in these ways include most of what traditional retail stores sell, from jewelry to magazines, from books to novelty merchandise. The U.S. Census accounts for over 44,000 non-store retailers in the United States.

The important thing to remember in retail is not to limit yourself: When thinking about how you are going to attack the retail marketplace, think about combining more than one retail opportunity into your long-range plans. For instance if you have a store, think about adding a mail-order catalog or a couple of vending machines for an additional source of revenue.

Temporary Locations

As you travel around this great country of ours, you will often find roadside stands offering all kinds of products, from fresh produce to handicrafts to artwork and souvenirs. Many such businesses sell year round, others are seasonal. Swap meets, garage sales, summer or holiday retail operations, and push carts are just a few more examples of "temporary" operations that can often be continuously profitable. So, as examples of what is possible, let me explore just two of these options, namely temporary seasonal stores and pushcarts.

Seasonal Stores

Just as the successful retail chain Tuesday Mornings is only open for a part of the year, so other seasonal stores provide an exciting opportunity if you want to run a retail store, but want to take some time off from the never-ending effort a year-round retail business entails.

Among my favorite "temporary" retail stores are Christmas stores and closeout stores. With these, you can wait until the last minute to take unfilled space (and just about every mall has some) and only pay rent for the time you are in the store, usually three or four months. Even then, the rent you'll have to pay is usually a steal because the space was going to remain empty. Whatever rent you pay is therefore added, and often unexpected, income for the landlord.

Aside from the attractive rent, the key to success in these types of stores is to get in and out *fast*. If you are working with the right vendors, they can provide an initial shot of merchandise that is small enough to be sold fast, but large enough to fill up your store and make you a handsome profit. Thereafter, you need order only fill-ins for any items that sold faster than expected.

The moment you open, you already need to have a markdown exit plan in place. Just as if you were running a going out of business sale, you do not want any goods left over, to be stored in your garage until next year!

Kiosks and Pushcarts

Kiosks or freestanding carts are now a fixture in most malls. It wasn't always that way. When they first began to appear in malls, retail tenants were outraged because they felt they cheapened the ambience of the mall and introduced new competitors who had the unfair advantage of lower rents.

But landlords persisted in adding kiosks because they let them squeeze out a little more rent money for space not fully occupied by pedestrian traffic. Lo and behold, these kiosks worked so well that the landlords were able to raise rents. In most malls, the rent for a kiosk is now much more per square foot than for standard store locations.

Pushcarts, as our ancestors who hawked products from them in every city in the world well knew, are a brilliant retail concept. Now renamed *freestanding kiosks,* pushcarts are small, efficient, mobile stores, operated by a single person, specializing in just a few products, and easily examined by shoppers from all four sides.

Most kiosks are locally owned and operated, run by entrepreneurs who have taken this chance to get involved in retailing without having to deal with the investment and effort involved in setting up a major store. Some goods found in kiosks such as jewelry, sunglasses, and toys, are sold in other mall outlet stores, but many kiosks are exciting because they handle products sold nowhere else, such as religious clothing, "As Seen On TV" goods, make your own T-shirts, or ethnic products. Studies show that a little over 50% of the mall traffic will at least look at a kiosk, and 6% will actually buy from one. There are over 150,000 kiosks in shopping centers. They have become such a retailing staple that there are also showing up in airports and office buildings.

In contrast to kiosks, an outpost for entrepreneurial endeavor, most regular mall stores are part of national chains. While they are run by local managers, the big decisions about what will be sold, for how much, and how the merchandise will be displayed are made at headquarters, often by men and women who spend little time on the selling floor. Thus, the art of retailing has been largely excluded from the manager's role, and chain stores have become impersonal. Of course, this gives you, as a local, hands-on owner-manager with a survival stake in your store, a huge advantage. This is nowhere more apparent than in the kiosk. Thousands of customers walk by each day, and it falls to you to differentiate yourself from the rest of the mall, to incorporate some drama into your selling effort, add a little fun, perhaps some exotic flavor, and so entice passersby to become customers. You may have seen kiosks sporting a puppeteer beckoning to your children with a talking flamingo, or a remote control helicopter buzzing over your head. Kiosk workers are free to combine a little showmanship with salesmanship. What an exciting opportunity for a good retailer!

If you decide to go this route, however, just make sure that the mall operator is not jamming too many kiosks into his space. Kiosks placed too close together create exasperated shoppers.

Vending Machine Retailing

The first vending machine dates back to 215 BC in ancient Egypt where the mathematician Hero of Alexandria developed a device that would dispense holy water when a coin was deposited. Modern "automatic merchandising," as vending machine retailing is officially designated, has been around for over a century. The first vending operation in the United States began in 1888 when the Adam's Gum Company introduced its penny machines. However, vending really took off after World War II, when suburban growth and cigarette vending machines became ubiquitous. Today, with most of the cigarette machines repurposed for candy and other goods, the vending of snacks and sodas alone generates over $20 billion in sales.

The vending business is appealing because of what I call the three lows: *low* start-up costs, *low* overhead, and *low* working capital needs. At the same time, it is like any other retail concept in that you need to have the right product, at the right price, in the right location, and at the right time. The right product can be anything from candy and snacks, to soft drinks, to fresh flowers, to panty hose, to phone cards, to temporary tattoos, to toys.

If you decide that vending is the entrepreneurial retail approach you favor, you should first understand that you are dealing with two different clients. As always, your ultimate client is the consumer who buys (or fails to buy) the products you are selling. But, in vending, your other

clients are the people or entities that own the space in which you will
locate your machine(s). Convincing them is often a tough sell: they either
already have machines and see no reason to switch to yours, or they don't
want to have machines for any number of reasons—they clutter up the
space, they break down, they disturb people, they don't earn enough.
Here are some of the arguments you can use to overcome these objections:

- The machines provide an important consumer benefit. You can conduct an informal poll of some of the people you meet at the location
  and report back to the landlord that you've interviewed a sample and
  83% said they would appreciate the convenience of your machines.
- Your products are enjoyed by consumers. The manufacturers will give
  you data to support this claim.
- Your machines are modern and look very appealing. You can show pictures to demonstrate how they will spruce up the dull corner where
  you want to place them.
- You can guarantee prompt repair service (although your machines
  rarely break down) because headquarters is nearby.
- Other landlords love your machines. If possible, get some written
  endorsements from satisfied customers.
- And, on the sales volume you anticipate, the landlord can gain some
  valuable incremental income.

Before you put your money into vending, be very cautious. Keep in mind
that 64% of customers say they purchase from a vending machine not
because they want to, but because they have no other alternative. Also,
20% of customers believe that vending machines are unreliable and "eat"
your money without dispensing the product; and 70% believe that, when
this happens, it is too difficult to get a refund. Many customers also
believe vending machines charge a lot more than the same products cost
in your local grocery store. In practice, vending machines do cost more,
which is why consumers buy from vending machines only if the convenience is immediate, the easy availability offsets the extra cost.

Also, be aware that scams in the vending industry hurt hundreds of entrepreneurs every year as vending machine con artists sell them under false pretenses. The problem is so serious that the FTC issued a publication called "Business Opportunities; Avoiding Vending Machine and Display Rack Scams." If you are serious about vending, here are some guidelines to follow before buying vending machines or vending routes:

- Call the Better Business Bureau or Secretary of State and find out how long they have been in business, any business aliases, who are the principals, and if any complaints have been filed against the company or the owners personally.
- Have the company selling you the machine or route substantiate the numbers they quote you by providing them in writing.
- Visit the locations they have promised you. Check out the traffic patterns and competition in these locations.
- Avoid offers that promise there is no selling. In vending, just like other forms of retailing, you are always selling yourself and your product.
- If they are using brand names in their ads, talk to the manufacturer to make sure they are legitimate.
- Compare one vending company to another. Never simply go with the first company that contacts you.
- Do not trust references the company provides unless you are absolutely sure they do not come from a friend, employee, or shill hired to give references. Rather, talk to other people who own machines or routes from the same company. If you can't find any, you'll have learned enough to walk (run!) away.
- Check with the industry publications *Automatic Merchandiser* and *Vending Times* to see if they are legitimate companies. Their Web sites are www.automaticmerchandiser.com and www.vendingtimes.com.
- Talk with those already in the business. You can find them through the industry associations located on the *Automatic Merchandiser* and *Vending Times* Web sites.
- Many of us think we are too smart to be conned, but don't let your pride get in the way. Be very careful before you move forward.

The Vending Business:

Modern Makes It Better

Rest assured, this isn't your father's vending route. In the twenty-first century, just filling machines is no longer good enough. Vending is truly an entrepreneur's business, with 75% of the companies in this industry having sales less than $1 million. Thus, there is always room for a new entrant; but there is a lot of competition. You need to do your homework before filling your first machine.

The first question to ask yourself is: Do you want to take the chance of introducing new products to the vending business, or do you prefer to follow a familiar path and sell existing products in new venues? The first approach involves a potentially higher reward because, with no competitors, there are no venues blocked to you, you will also be less constrained by price. However, there is also the higher risk that the new product will not sell.

The basics required to be successful in the vending business include:

- Control the geographic extent of your market. Don't spread out too far too fast. Most vending machine veterans recommend staying within a thirty-mile radius of your home base.
- Using this thirty-mile rule as a guide, take the time to determine the possible venues for machines in your marketplace: businesses, offices, factories, warehouses, schools, hospitals, residential areas and high-rises. Stop into potential locations and see what is already being vended there. Is there opportunity for more variety or a more targeted product mix? Are the machines clean and well maintained or are they shabby and primed to be replaced by a better vendor? To succeed, you need to know your area intimately. Burn some shoe leather by walking your beat.
- Never forget that you are in the retail business and your competition is all forms of retail. If you are vending candy bars, the local 7-Eleven is

just as much a competitor as another candy bar vending machine.

- Keep in mind that most of your business will come from locations you obtain via referrals. Vending is a relationship-based business. Your personality and willingness to work with clients and suppliers will determine your success.

- Follow the bulldozers. As soon as you see a new building going up, find out who is in charge in order to get your machines in right from the beginning, "from the ground floor," as they say in construction.

- Concentrate on businesses that have night shifts. Their employees are a captive audience for your machines.

- Remember that as a rule, to succeed, vending machines need at least fifty people to pass by each day. Small businesses are prime targets, but not too small.

- Decide whether to start with new or used machines. New machines will obviously cost more, but they may save you money over time because of less repair cost, down time, and sales loss. Also, new machines make it easier to attract new accounts. If you decide to go with used machines, make sure they are no older than 1992 when the electronic phase kicked into vending and they began to computerize the machines. If you are purchasing used equipment, look for a small plaque with a serial number and manufacturing date. Without this plaque you can't tell how old a machine is, and the older it is, the harder it becomes to find replacement parts.

- Check that each one of your machines has a bill- and coin-changing device either in the machine or close by. The average American has 42 cents in their pockets and the average vend is 50 cents. So, a change maker is important!

- Make sure your product mix matches your customer base (this may vary significantly from one location to another). Many consumers will walk away from a machine if it does not have the item they want. Demand does not transfer from one category to another; someone wanting potato chips will not settle for breath mints.

- Remember that variety helps create sales. Regular customers don't want exactly the same thing day after day. Changing products to match the different seasons helps show variety and holds customer's interest. If you are dealing in fresh food, make sure it is changed out several times a week. Your customers know if it has been in the machine a long time. Because you want fresh product, keep track of sales by slot so you can calculate how full each slot needs to be so as not to run out between your visits.

- Decide whether to go with brand names or non-branded products that offer better value—the age-old vending question. Usually vending operations start with brand name products to establish credibility, and then gradually introduce the same type of items in a non-branded variety to give their customers better value and give themselves higher margins.

- Make sure the pricing of your product is fair: Remember that every other retail business is your competitor; the industry standard for goods in established categories is to mark them up to twice their cost. So, while you can charge somewhat more for the convenience you offer, you cannot charge too much. Generally, vending operators price their products at double their cost, selling candy bars for which they paid $0.25 at $0.50. However, if you are introducing a vending category new in your market, for example tattoos or stickers, you may be able to take a higher margin.

- Remember that wherever you place the machines, you will be paying your clients a commission for the use of their space and traffic. Commissions vary from location to location and by vending specialty. As a rule, however, they fall between 10 and 20% of sales.

Should You Buy a Franchise?

Some Questions to Consider

There are basically three different ways to get into retailing:
1. Start a business from scratch.
2. Buy an existing business.

3. Purchase a franchise.

Everyone has heard of franchising, but not everyone knows exactly what it entails. And the franchise rules are complicated and vary by state. Thus, if you are interested in franchising, you should first consult an expert in the field or read one of the many books on the subject. However, to get you started, the following are some basic things you should know about franchising.

The most important thing to understand about franchising is that the franchisor takes on the responsibility of teaching franchisees all about the business, and helps and supports them in getting started. Thus, the franchisor helps franchisees find the right location, provides a full plan for building or outfitting it, often supplies specific equipment, shows franchisees how to do the administration and accounting, and provides marketing materials for franchisees to promote their businesses.

Usually, the franchisor provides a "book" that describes every aspect of the business. Of course, the franchisor cannot guarantee a profit (or, by law, even promise one), but it is in the franchisor's best interest for the individual franchises to be profitable. If franchisees don't do well, neither does the franchisor. Thus, in addition to helping the franchisee start and run the business correctly, the franchisor also conducts marketing campaigns for the franchise group as a whole. Usually, franchisors also run stores of their own so they can test out new products or marketing efforts before they offer them to the franchisees.

In return, the franchisee promises to run the franchise according to the franchisor's rules. That is, they have to keep the store's décor up to the standards set by the franchisor, provide the specified products or services, not sell other products, and so on. If a franchisee fails to follow the rules (which most franchisors police carefully using local management and "mystery shoppers"), the franchisor can withdraw the franchise.

Thus, in net, becoming a franchisee is an easier and generally safer way to start a business. But there is much less freedom—you have to tow the line. And, while you can do well, there is little chance of hitting a homerun since you are constrained by what the franchisor permits. There is also no guarantee that the franchisor will let you open additional locations. There may be none available, or the franchisor may prefer to give the next location to someone else.

There are over 3,000 different franchise opportunities on the current marketplace. But how did it all begin? Singer Sewing Company developed the first franchise opportunity in 1858. Isaac Singer lacked the funds to market his new sewing machine, so he sold the rights to sell his machine to local businesses, which gave him the capital to start production. It also gave the company a manager for each territory and an instant training team to teach people how to use the machine.

Another success story is the Coca-Cola Company. It was able to expand quickly to a national presence at the turn of the twentieth century, shifting the burden of manufacturing, storing, and distributing of its products to local businesses that acquired the bottling rights. By 1921 there were over 2,000 Coca-Cola franchise bottlers, each with exclusive marketing and distribution rights in their territories.

The automobile is really what propelled the franchise business as automobile manufacturers used the capital they gained by franchising the right to sell their cars to tool their assembly lines. Oil companies granted franchises to mom-and-pop convenience stores to sell their gas, and Travelodge franchised its motels to serve this new traveling public.

Not everyone is cut out to own a franchise. First, you need a personality that enjoys working well as part of a larger team. Second, you need to be able to adhere to an operations manual and established procedures, or in other words you need to operate by the book.

The saying of the franchise industry is "in business *for* yourself, but not *by* yourself." You have lots of professionals to consult with and plenty of resources to use when problems arise. Keep in mind, however, that you are purchasing a system already in place, that you will have little or no ability to change it. In the end, many entrepreneurs with the desire to find their own niches and create new products or business practices find franchising too restrictive. If you are an innovator at heart, you may not be happy with a franchise for very long.

The basic question you must ask yourself before you decide to acquire a franchise is: "Am I an entrepreneur or a franchisee?" If you are a true entrepreneur, by trying to force yourself into a franchise (pushing that round peg into a square hole) you may be in for an unhappy and unprofitable journey. I went to a wedding recently for the daughter of my best friend from high school. I cornered his father who, at eighty-one years old still goes to work every day running his family's business.

"Why are you still doing this?" I asked.

Jerome looked me straight in the eye and said, "I love getting up every morning and driving to work. I love the challenge of seeing my decisions affect my family's bottom line. I love being my own boss. The most important thing I have learned in sixty years in my business is you have to like your job."

Real entrepreneurs can't wait to get to work in the morning because they know that each decision they make all day long affects them personally. Jerome could never be a franchise owner because when he sees an opportunity his instinct is to take advantage of it right away. He'd never be happy if he first had to seek agreement from a franchisor. Come to think of it, I could never be a franchise owner, either.

Running a Specialized Business:

A Gift Baskets Example

There are countless specialized businesses you can enter. Each has its own advantages and problems. Obviously, I cannot describe every one of them here, so I have chosen one of those nearly infinite possibilities to give you as an example of what to expect (and look out for) if you choose to enter a specialized business.

Gift baskets is an interesting area. The idea of giving gifts in baskets goes back to the Egyptians who gave beautifully wrapped gifts of oils and perfumes in baskets. Interestingly, this remains one of the hottest gift baskets currently. The theory behind gift baskets is the same today as it was for the ancient Egyptians, namely that the container that holds the products must be desirable in itself and therefore a part of and an enhancement to the gift.

You can start a gift basket business with just some space and a variety of popular products, perhaps beginning as a small seasonal project and gradually expanding into a year-round business. Baskets can be designed for any budget, to fit any occasion, and consist of products for anything you can imagine—cooking, golf, sports, travel, new homes, new babies. The possibilities are endless. As always, however, there are certain business principles to keep in mind:

- **Be visible.** When selling a specialty product such as gift baskets, a vital aspect of your business is to be visible and to achieve that visibility at low cost. Chances are that an advertising campaign won't pay out in sufficient sales; you need a more efficient way to get yourself known. It does make sense to take space in the Yellow Pages. Beyond that, it may make sense to lease a corner of a retail store to show your baskets. Good places to have your product shown include florists, photographers, gourmet food stores, gift shops, and artists' studios. You should sell the space owner the idea that your baskets will attract more customers, and then pay only a percentage of your sales. That way, you can't lose money by overpaying for the space.

- **Make sure your line of gift baskets is easy to understand.** Because most people and companies are too busy to find the perfect gift for themselves, they want to rely on you to provide them with the perfect gift. The last thing they want is to risk giving their crotchety male supplier of gaskets a flowery gift basket laden with fancy soaps and bath oils. Thus, if you make your baskets easy to understand, have an adequate breadth of baskets to satisfy a cross section of recipients, and gain the reputation of being a reliable source, your customers will begin relying on you for many of their gift-giving occasions and reorders will become the mainstay of your business.

- **Know your competition.** While you want your line of baskets to be appropriate for all (or at least most) types of recipients, you do not want them to include the identical products or carry the same themes as competitive gift baskets.

- **Provide great service.** No matter what kind of baskets you are offering, you *always* want to make sure your customer service is better than your competitor's.

- **Ensure privacy first.** If you decide to run this business out of your home, make sure you set up a separate room with a soundproof door where you can work uninterrupted and separate your personal from your professional life. Make sure a business telephone goes into this space, that it has an answering machine, and that no one but you or designated assistants pick it up. Make sure your work area is out of sight, that you have an industrial vacuum to clean up, and that nothing you do (such as parking delivery trucks in the wrong place) annoys your neighbors.

- **Maintain a professional posture.** If your space does not have an office image, rent a post office box from a private mailbox rental facility that offers a street address and suite number. This will give your business a more professional image.

- **Figure out the signed, sealed, and delivered aspects.** Most of your business will involve delivering your gift basket either to the recipients locally, or to post office or Federal Express outlets. Thus, you need to figure out how to make sure these deliveries go to the right place and are on time. However, while you're doing this, you still have to pick up your inventory and supplies, be in your office to take phone orders, and compile your baskets. Thus, the best way to handle deliveries is to hook up with a reliable local courier company, at least until you are large enough to hire your own courier(s).

When dealing with customers and developing your gift basket line, always ask the following questions:

- What is the gift-giving occasion?

- Will recipients be male, female, or mixed?
- What are their age ranges?
- Do the recipients have any dietary restrictions (vegetarian, kosher, allergies, no alcohol, etc.)?
- Do the recipients have any special interests or hobbies such as cooking, gardening, sports, etc?
- What is the budget?

Below are some of the standard gift baskets we sell. I am sure you can customize them for your customers:

- New baby: one for girls and a different one for boys.
- Gourmet food: all kinds of themes centered around French, Italian, Chinese, etc.
- Diet gift basket: jumping on the hottest fads of low-fat, low-carb, etc.
- New home: house warming gifts may include a hammer, night-light, etc.
- Stress-free basket: going back to the original roots of gift baskets from Egyptian culture, this updated version includes aromatherapy products, candles, bath oil, and chocolates.
- Bon Voyage basket: for people taking trips and the travel industry in general.
- New job basket: filled with office supplies, coffee mug, etc.
- Southwest basket: Cowboy theme items.
- East Coast basket: lobster theme.
- All the holidays, birthdays, and anniversaries.

Whereas promotions can often be daunting in other arms of retailing, marketing your gift basket business may be easier than you think because almost everyone you know or meet is a potential long-term customer. Some marketing tips:

- Be able to explain your business within thirty seconds of meeting a new potential customer. Don't bore them with industry statistics and how great you are.

- Give a business card to anyone who expresses any interest in your company.
- Remember that promoting your company by word of mouth is the most cost-effective way. Leads come from your place of worship, school associations, political meetings, health or country clubs, hair salons, alumni associations, and anywhere else people gather. Everyone needs gifts to give, so make everyone aware that you can fill that need.
- Become a member of a gift basket network or exchange where you can bounce ideas off other members, and even get local referrals. One of my favorites is The Gift Basket Exchange, which you can find online at http://gbexchange.net.
- Make personal calls on corporations, many of whom have never had a personal solicitation and will be impressed to talk to a "real person." Corporations can be the most profitable part of your business because they regularly need gifts for customers; employees' birthdays, promotions, etc., but do not have the time to shop for gifts. Moreover, they know exactly how much they are willing to spend per gift, thus reducing the haggling factor.
- Offer to donate your gift baskets at cost to use as table centerpieces for charity or business functions.
- Offer food and beverage manufacturers in your area the opportunity to include their products in your gift baskets as an excellent way for them to launch a new product or expand awareness of an existing one. This could also apply to restaurants, cookbooks, etc. In return, ask them to help publicize your business in various ways.

Developing a Catalog Business

Catalog shopping has turned into a $120 billion business, which represents almost 4% of retail sales in the United States. Despite the increase in postage and paper costs, more catalogs are being sent out than ever before. Mailing costs in the United States alone total $19.5 billion annually.

However, catalog marketing is a different sort of business than other types of retail because it relies principally on statistics. When you run a retail store, you buy the merchandise you think will sell, and if you guess right, you sell it at a profit and repeat the cycle. With catalog selling, you test and test and test again until you find a product (or a group of products) that generates more sales than the cost of printing and mailing the catalog. An executive of one of the country's largest catalog companies told me they test an average of ten products (all of which they think will succeed) in order to find one that makes a profit.

Consider the arithmetic: if a catalog in the mail costs, say, $0.50 and you get a return of 2% (pretty good for most mailings) then sending out 100 copies costs you $50.00, and you make two sales. But to make a $50.00 profit on two sales (even if you make an 80% margin, which is pretty standard in mail order) means you have to sell about $63.00 worth of merchandise just to cover your catalogue and mailing costs, or pushing $100.00 to cover that, your operating costs, and your profits. To sell that much on just two sales is tough and likely to drop your response rate below 2%.

Obviously, I am not saying that a catalog business is not possible or even not potentially profitable. There are 7,000 catalogs in the United States, so obviously this is potentially a very good business. I just want to warn you that to be successful in the catalog business, or in any other direct marketing business, you have to understand and live by the laws of large numbers.

A study from Abacus Direct Corporation found that consumers ages fifty-five to sixty-four spend the most money on mail order retail. However, there are catalogs aimed at every type of consumer. So as you are thinking through the right mail order business to pursue, whether it be a catalog for a special dog breed, or one selling products to cure the aches and pains of the fifty-five- to sixty-four-year-old group, remember that this type of marketing is most successful when it is tightly targeted to a specific cadre of customers. That is one reason why, if you have a special interest or hobby that you think other enthusiasts will share, then that mail order category may be the right opportunity for you.

Once you have the right product mix, the challenge is to find the appropriate mailing lists. There are several mailing services to work with. The largest is Info USA, and you can find it on the Internet at www.infousa.com.

In addition to targeting customers interested in what you are selling, you should also target those geographic areas most isolated and therefore with residents most likely to be interested in using mail order. For example, according to a recent *USA Today* article, the three markets in the United States with the most households that shop by mail are:

• Juneau, Alaska with 81%
• Fairbanks, Alaska with 71%
• Anchorage, Alaska with 65%

Once you have decided on what you want to sell, you should approach the manufacturers and obtain the goods you need *on consignment*. Because so few products succeed, most catalog companies only buy what they have already sold. That is, the manufacturer supplies the goods, the catalog company includes them in their catalogs, sells a certain number, pays the manufacturer for the ones sold, and returns the rest. Many manufacturers will not agree to this approach, but enough do to make it practical. And no catalog could exist if it had to buy the goods and was then stuck with all the unsold merchandise.

As always in retail, there are exceptions. The main one is that if you already run a retail store with a full selection of merchandise, you may want to use a catalog to extend your selling reach. In that case, you will only feature the products you carry in the store and, therefore, you need to do less testing for the catalogue. You only need to figure out whether the sales generated from a catalog are enough to pay for it. Many catalogers use the Internet to enhance their sales, switching their customers from their catalog to their Internet site. To the extent that this is possible, it obviously cuts down the cost of printing and mailing the catalog.

Developing a Direct Selling Business

In the United States, direct selling (the person-to-person sale of a product or service) is a $28 billion industry providing income for more than 13 million people according to the Direct Selling Association.

Home and family care products such as cleaning products, home décor, kitchen storage, and cookware account for 33.5% of the sales; personal care products such as cosmetics, clothing, and jewelry account for 28.2%; and weight loss and nutritional products make up a further 15.4%. That still leaves almost a quarter of direct sales split between a vast number of different products including candles, scrapbook supplies, crystal, expensive fashion goods, and a wide selection of so-called marital aids.

Direct sales have evolved from men selling Fuller Brushes door to door into home-sales parties using a primarily female sales force. This change was started by saleswoman Brownie Wise who began marketing Earl Tupper's line of plastic containers in the 1940s.

Mary Kay, who built her company into a cosmetics giant, started as a single mom without enough time to take a regular job or enough money to hire a nanny to look after her young son. Instead, she started holding in-house parties in neighboring houses, figuring she could leave her eight-year-old alone for an hour or two a day as long as she was nearby. As she tells it, the little boy would await her return, often swinging on the garden gate. The neighbors, walking by, would stop and talk to the boy who was personable and gregarious.

"And where's your mom?" they would say.

"Oh, she's off partying again," the boy would explain.

Mary Kay could never understand why her neighbors gave her such dirty looks!

To be successful in the direct sales business, in addition to putting together a product line that people want, your main task is to retain capable salespeople. Generally, the way this works is that you retain a number of commission reps to work for you. They keep their commission, but you make your income from charging them a little more for the products they sell than you are paying. Then your sales people persuade their friends and acquaintances to become commission salespeople, making a small margin on what they sell. And so, the structure grows until you may have four or five layers of salespeople, and thousands of sellers altogether—and you take a cut from all of them. Of course, only 10 to 20% of all those salespeople actually sell much. The rest of them buy the products mostly for their own use. Still, it's all business to you.

You should understand that the direct sales business is undergoing rapid changes as fewer women in the United States are interested in selling because they have more job opportunities. The main trends in this industry include:

- **Direct sellers moving online.** All seven of the major direct sales retail companies have added online sales to their basic business. In 1999, Amway launched Quixtar, an e-commerce site designed to sell its own, as well as other companies' products. Tupperware also moved online in 1999.
- **Direct sellers moving to traditional retail.** Avon began selling its products in mall kiosks. They created a line called Becoming, which is sold in Sears and JC Penny. Tupperware began selling its line in Target stores and it became so successful that they had to pull it because it was affecting their core party business. In retail, that's what we call a "good problem to have."
- **Overseas expansion driving the business.** Amway entered the Chinese market and captured over $700 million in sales in 2003.

Television Home Shopping

For an entrepreneur just starting out, getting into television home shopping can only be on a local level. Currently home shopping is a $7 billion industry growing at a double-digit rate. It is dominated by two companies: QVC, which does $4.4 billion, and HSN (Home Shopping Network), which does $2.2 billion.

These companies pay the cable operators 5% commission on all sales. Unless you have the capital to invest, this is a retail avenue you will probably want to shy away from. Still, as we have seen from other retail opportunities, you never know. There's always room for one more!

Specialty Store Retailing:

What Are Your Options?

From videos to computers to gourmet food, there are hundreds of specialty stores you can open these days. Rather than going into detail about every one of these specific niches, however, I have picked a few of the larger types of specialty stores to touch upon. The lessons of retailing can be applied across the board to all of them.

Pet Stores

Over sixty-four million households in the United States own pets, with 46% of these owning more than one pet. This has created a $34 billion industry. The pet industry is 60% larger than the toy industry and 33% larger than the candy industry. As more and more people treat pets like children, there exists the opportunity to sell products and services no one had even imagined thirty years ago. Here is a breakdown in the number of pets in U.S. households:

• **Cats:** 77.7 million
• **Dogs:** 65 million
• **Birds:** 17.3 million
• **Reptiles:** 9 million
• **Small animals:** 16.8 million

- **Saltwater fish:** 7 million
- **Freshwater fish:** 185 million

The opportunities in the pet business are far broader than simply opening a pet store. Fifteen million Americans travel with their pets each year, which creates another marketing opportunity. Also, companies such as Paul Mitchell, Omaha Steaks, and Old Navy are selling pet-related versions of their human products.

This is a retail growth industry. Consumers believe that pets reduce stress and lower blood pressure, especially when they become companions to the homebound. As the population ages, baby boomers are buying pets to fill the void left by departed children or spouses.

As pet ownership grows, specialty pet stores will be in greater demand. And, since pet care sales in supermarkets, drugstores, and mass merchants have been declining even as the industry is growing (probably because they cannot provide the specialized care pet owners desire), specialty pet stores seem to be a significant opportunity for enterprising entrepreneurs.

Card and Gift Stores

Seven billion greeting cards are purchased annually. Giftware and collectible items are growing every year. An estimated eleven million households have one or more members who consider themselves "collectors."

There are over 2,000 greeting card publishers and cards can be found in 100,000 retail outlets in the United States. The average U.S. household purchases thirty-five cards a year and 87% of Americans purchase at least one card a year. Women buy 80% of all greeting cards. The average person receives twenty cards a year, 50% of cards are seasonal. This is a huge business, and savvy entrepreneurs can certainly carve out gift store concepts with substantial potential.

Convenience Stores

This industry does $290 billion in annual sales and currently has over 132,000 outlets. Large chains dominate this industry, with 41 companies each operating (or franchising) 200 or more stores. Here is how convenience store sales, exclusive of gasoline, break down:

• **Cigarettes:** 36%
• **Packaged beverages, non-alcoholic:** 12%
• **Foodservice:** 12%
• **Beer:** 11%
• **General Merchandise:** 4%
• **Candy:** 4%
• **Milk products:** 3%
• **Other tobacco products:** 3%
• **Salty snacks:** 3%

Keep in mind that traditional lines of retailing are currently blurring. Drug stores market themselves as convenience stores and convenience stores market themselves as one-stop service with food, car care, banking, and drug store products. So when you open up your entrepreneurial convenience store, what is it *really*?

The National Association of Convenience Stores just released some interesting facts:

• Convenience stores sell nearly 80% of the 100 billion gallons of gas Americans use annually.
• Four out of five convenience stores sell gasoline, with the average store selling 1.3 million gallons a year.
• Coffee is a $3.7 billion category for convenience stores with 54% of consumers who purchase brewed coffee buying it most often at a convenience store and 71% saying they have bought coffee there in the last month.
• Convenience stores sell 21% of all bottles of water.
• ATM services are available in 77% of the stores.

- Money order services are available in 79% of the stores.
- Half of all lottery tickets are sold in convenience stores.
- The vast majority, 76%, of convenience stores are open twenty-four hours.
- Copy and faxing services are available in 32% of convenience stores.

With so many other retailers entering the convenience market, how does a convenience store survive and prosper? The answer lies in three requirements: extended hours, proximity to a neighborhood without an all-night supermarket, and bundling of services together (food, grocery, ATMs, copying, lottery tickets, etc.) to provide many different reasons for local consumers to drop in.

Business travelers, sales professionals, and others on the road are relying more and more on convenience stores to fill all their needs: the morning newspaper, cup of coffee, gas fill-up, but also business needs such as copy and fax machines and e-mail access.

Drug Stores

The U.S. Census Bureau shows retail sales at pharmacy and drug stores to be $191 billion, which is a 4.3 % increase over last year. While 4.3% doesn't sound like much, given this industry's size, it mean an extra $8.2 billion worth of sales! This growth will continue, as aging baby boomers require more drugs. Chains account for 75% of drugstore sales and the number of chain store locations just passed the number of independent stores for the first time. In spite of its size and growth, the industry faces challenges:

- A shortage of pharmacists is haunting this industry.
- Consumers are buying more of their drugs outside the United States to save money. Currently, 7% of Americans have utilized pharmacy operators in Canada and 48% of Americans say they would use sources outside of the United States if it were legal (which it may well become).

- Increased competition from Internet-based and offshore drug stores are causing a loss: 62% of prescription drugs were filled at drug stores in 1998, while this dropped to 54% last year.

So does this mean that there are no opportunities to start your own drug store? Certainly not if you are a pharmacist or believe you can attract one or more to join you in your venture. Even if this is not the case, however, there may be opportunities for you to develop your store into a great general merchandise store first and a drug store second. In that case, the prescriptions will drive traffic into your store, while the rest of the merchandise will drive sales through your register. Here's one example: Fred's was a variety store based out of Memphis, Tennessee and catering to smaller towns in the south. By placing a pharmacist in the back of the store, they created a concept that turned them into a $900 million dollar business with 385 stores.

Summary

Specialty retailing is no different than any other retail business. Success takes good business management, hard work, persistence, and optimism. Whether you want to start a specialty retail store, a vending machine route, a number of kiosks, a catalog, or a direct-selling business, retailing is a hands-on business. The more involved you are, the faster you will be able to stock the right products and choose the right approach for your brand of retail business.

Currently $125 billion of sales are generated by retailers in non-store categories, including television, electronic shopping, paper and electronic catalogs, door-to-door selling, in home demonstrations and parties, movable stalls, vending machines, and mail order. The U.S. Census counts over 44,000 non-store retailers including: temporary locations, seasonal stores, kiosks and pushcarts, gift-basket suppliers, catalog and direct selling businesses, and television home shopping. From videos to computers to gourmet food, there are dozens of specialty store categories including pet, gift and card, convenience, drug, and goodness knows how many others. Amidst this cornucopia of opportunity, surely you will find one that suits you.

Retail Detail

According to Forrester Research, Inc. online retail sales are expected to reach $95.7 billion in 2004. Online retail sales are projected to reach $229.9 billion by 2008, accounting for 10% of total retail sales in the United States. Nearly five million new households will become online shoppers in the next five years, bringing the total of online shoppers to 63 million.

Chapter 14

Internet Marketing:
What Are You Waiting for?

If you do it right, a Web site can enhance your company's image,
build customer loyalty, and get information to customers
and potential customers quickly and cheaply.
If you have a Web site,
it makes your small business look big . . .
—NATALIE SEQUERA, Spokeswoman for Claris Corporation

To MAXIMIZE ITS POTENTIAL, *every* business *must* have an online presence. E-commerce is currently a $54.9 billion industry and growing dramatically. As a modern retailer, you cannot afford not to participate. You need a Web site. Your customers will demand it.

The Internet has become the great equalizer, making it possible for you to reach across town, across the United States, and even across the world and run what amounts to a second business right out of your bricks-and-mortar location.

Not so long ago, a Web site was a novelty. Now it's a necessity. Most new competition within the retail industry has come from products sold over the Internet. Not having a Web site says to savvy consumers: "This company doesn't care enough to provide us with the convenience, savings, and satisfaction of having an online presence. So why should I shop here?"

Moreover, consumers are using the Web just like the Yellow Pages: "Need to find a product, good, or service across the street or across the country? Let your mouse do the walking." The Web today is used largely as a research tool. "But I deal in retail, not research," you might argue. Sure. But what customers are researching is YOU! Once they have found what they want to buy, they will look for where to buy it. And if you are not available on the Web, they will no more buy it from you than if your store were too far away.

Your challenge is to make sure that customers can find the answers to their questions quickly on your Web site. You want to make sure your site is professional, because, much like the shopping experience in the store, the experience a customer has on your Web site reflects directly on your company's reputation.

The most important aspect of your site is that it must be up to date at all times, showing the latest products and prices. People understand if you are sold out of an item that appears on printed material. After all, a catalogue or even a print ad obviously takes time to develop and cannot always be up to date. The beauty of a Web site, however, is that it never has to be out of date—and people know that.

Of course, it should also be professional in all respects; that is, well designed, easy to navigate, well organized with a directory to help people find what they are looking for, with great pictures of your products, and a clear and simple description of how to order them. In addition to the merchandise you have to sell, on your site you should also include:

• Store name, location, and contact information, including phone number, fax number, and e-mail address

- The company's background, its vision statement, and testimonials about its qualities
- Driving directions and hours of operation of your brick-and-mortar store(s)
- Policies regarding returns, warranties, repairs, and shipping options
- Links to non-competing informational sites

As the Web becomes more familiar to more people, as credit card security becomes even more solid, and as more merchants become known for fairness and reliability, customers will incorporate more and more online searching, and eventually shopping, into their daily lives. Therefore, your competition is no longer just the store down the road. It is any store that sells via the Internet and is willing to ship goods to your customer. This raises the level of competition for you and your store, and you must make sure to provide valuable information and images that will induce your customers to buy from you, not your competition.

As we all know, the younger the customer, the more Internet savvy they are likely to be. So, if your product caters to young people, a Web site is an imperative. But senior citizens are learning fast. Thus, your potential online customer base ranges in age very much along the same lines as the customers shopping in your store.

Internet stores (unlike most brick-and-mortar stores) never close. So you can service your customer no matter what time of the day or night they want to shop. However, while that, and the general convenience of shopping online will bring you added sales, don't expect to become the next Amazon or eBay overnight. Rather, look at your Web site as a local marketing tool that will solidify your relationship with your existing customers and expand your customer base. Attracting responses from customers outside your community is icing on the cake.

Creating a Web site:

Why You Should Use a Pro

There are several software programs on the market today that make it easy and affordable to design your own Web site. This is fine for your personal homepage, but for the site that carries your store's reputation and image, I recommend, for at least two reasons, that you work with professionals.

1. **Designing a Web site takes a tremendous amount of time.** You cannot lose focus of the real purpose of your business, which is your retail store. The hours you spend just developing your site could probably be more effectively used to improve your customer's experience in the store.

2. **Designing and maintaining a Web site is *all* about the details.** Once the site is up, how do customers even know you are there? How do you get listed on search engines? How does your site look on different operating systems and different-sized computer screens? These questions, and a dozen more are best handled by a professional Web designer.

Paying Attention to the Front of the Store

All of the pages of your Web site must be sleek, attractive, functional, and easy to read. But you must make especially certain that the "front" of your Web store convinces customers that they want to see more. Your Web store should have the same look and feel as your brick-and-mortar store so your customers have a consistent experience whenever they do business with you. This involves:

• **Color.** Color is what sets the tone for your entire site. Therefore, you should utilize the same colors on your site as in your store. And you must also stay current with your colors.

• **Seasonality.** If your store is decked out in an autumn theme, your Web designer should add the same effect to your Web site.

- **Fonts.** Fonts are the typefaces you use on all of your printed material. They should be consistent in your advertising and mailers. And they should also be reflected in your Web site.
- **Graphics.** Artwork is a major part of every Web site, particularly the pictures of the products you are offering. However, eye-popping graphics may lengthen the time it takes for the Web site to load, a frustration that may cause some consumers to flee the site altogether. With graphics remember the old adage, "less is more."

Choosing a Webmaster or Web Service

When you are seeking a person or company to develop and maintain your Web site, try to find someone who has worked in the retail industry, and therefore understands "sales speak," who is going to be around for a while, and who can become a long-term asset to your business. Don't choose some high school kid, however cheap and brilliant, who neither knows business nor is likely to stay around for long. Also, do not use your ad agency—they will merely subcontract the work so you won't have direct contact with the designer, and the work will cost you more.

If you go to any major search engine like www.google.com, www.yahoo.com, or www.msn.com and enter "retail Web site development," a number of pages listing credible Web developers will magically appear. Pick a few and interview them. (Of course, I am biased in favor of the service provided by my company. You can view it at www.dollar days.com under the tab "Open a Store.")

Selecting a Domain Name

A domain name is your virtual address on the Internet. Like eligible bachelors or loft space in Manhattan, millions of domain names are already taken. In an ideal situation, your domain name should be the same as your store name. In practice, you may have to modify it slightly. Thus, Marc's Men's Store might become www.marcsmenstoreUSA.com. (Remember that you cannot use any punctuation or spaces in the domain name.)

There are several sites on the Internet that help you search for available names. Two of the best are www.register.com and www.godaddy.com. Don't be disappointed if your favorite name is already taken. Sit back, set your head into creative mode, and start typing in words and names. Eventually you will find a name that's free. Now, not everyone can spell or type well. So, once you have chosen your name, you may also want to reserve other names that are very close to your own.

Site Options to Consider

Every Web site offers a number of options. Some are standard, like contact information or useful links, others are less common, such as an e-mail newsletter or book reviews. In the following sections I've gathered the most useful and least taxing Web site options to consider as you go about building your site.

Shopping Cart

Though it should always be informational, your Web site should not be merely informational. Rather, it should generate at least enough income to offset its cost, and there's no reason it cannot become an important source of additional income.

Selling the products you carry in the store gives you an additional opportunity to speed up your turns and it may let you increase your buys and so drive down your cost of goods. Beyond that, the Internet gives you the opportunity to test items that you may not normally carry in your existing store.

Everything the visitor wants to buy can be collected at your site in a shopping cart that you can buy and install on your site. The shopping cart lets consumers make a single payment for all the items they want to purchase. Most shopping carts let buyers pay by all major credit cards or by PayPal, the main currency of the Internet. Just make sure you choose and "test drive" a cart that is easy for consumers to use.

Online Catalog

As I discussed earlier, independent entrepreneurs have always had a tough time getting into the catalog business because of the cost of amassing, printing, and mailing the catalog. However, once you have a Web site where you are offering all the products for sale in your store, you can print a catalog directly from the site and hand it out in the store.

The adage "a picture is worth a thousand words" could not be more appropriate than when applied to your Web store. You need pictures, and they must do your products justice. You have several options to obtain the right pictures:

- **Download pictures from the manufacturer's Web site.** Many suppliers have a section on their site where their customers can download images of their products. Many also have pre-written copy about the product that can easily be added to your site. Take advantage of this cost-efficient offering.

- **Have your supplier give you a disc with all the products and descriptions of their line.** Since most suppliers are printing paper catalogs already, they have their photos on discs that they are usually willing to send their customers.

- **Scan the manufacturer's catalog or have them send you pictures you can scan.** Today's flatbed scanners are so inexpensive that every retailer should have one attached to their computer. (If the preceding sentence is Greek to you, enlist your professional Web developer to hook up a scanner for you and show you how to use it or ask your youngest staffer, who can probably do it in his or her sleep!)

- **Use a digital camera to take pictures of merchandise that you want to feature on the site.** Digital cameras have also come way down in price and are a great help to complete your Web site as they allow you to take pictures of a new product and instantly place it on your Web site.

Affiliate Program

Many companies pay a commission if a customer coming from your site buys something from theirs. This is known as an affiliate program, because you are serving as an affiliate of the Web site to which you are linking.

Naturally, affiliate programs can also work the other way around: you pay another site to send traffic to your site so it becomes your affiliate. To hook up with affiliates, go to any of the major search engines and enter "affiliate programs." Hundreds of different sites will appear. If you build an affiliate program whereby hundreds of other sites direct customers to your site, the incremental business this will drive your way may be an impressive way to expand your business.

To maximize the potential of an affiliate program, you should choose sites that are compatible with the goods you carry. For instance, if you are selling kids' products, contact sites that cater to mothers, families, teachers, or even school administrators.

Once you have sold the potential affiliates on the benefits of the two sites working together, create a banner they can use on their site that quickly explains why someone should click to your site. I've learned that the more you do to facilitate the process, the better the results. Making the banner for the other site to use gives them one less reason to say no. Initially contacting these sites one by one may seem cumbersome, but if you can connect with enough sites that are driving quality traffic to you, your effort will pay off in sales.

Ad Section

Your site should include a section that shows any ads that you run in print media. This is a quick way for customers who missed your ads to keep up to date on the products and deals you are featuring.

Coupons

Coupons (provided they are of sufficient value) can be an effective way of building the number of visitors to your site and, of course, they increase sales. Don't worry about giving away the store: coupon redemptions are generally disappointingly low. But if you get lucky and you achieve a high redemption rate, well, congratulations!, you just built a lot of extra volume.

New Products

Create a section labeled "new products" on the site to feature your hottest current items or to show some new products that are expected into the store shortly. In this way you can create a buzz about new items so customers bookmark your site. It helps if you use language like "updated weekly" or "new items added daily."

Book Review

Giving your personal review of a book related to your industry or the products you carry is a nice touch that establishes you as an expert. After a while, have some of your more bookish employees do reviews as well. This will provide your customers with differing viewpoints, while empowering your employees, especially if you give them bylines.

Bulletin Boards

A bulletin board, a virtual room where viewers can post, read, and respond to messages left by other viewers, can become an active part of your site. Many customers will be experts on a subject, service, or product. The exchange of that knowledge, and any accompanying banter, between customers makes your site an amusing place to go for expert advice.

Feedback

Providing the opportunity for feedback is essential. Customers may think of questions in the middle of the night and, far from being a nuisance, these questions can lead to further sales. As important, the feedback you get lets you know how your site, or store, is performing. If there's a glitch on your site, better to know about it from one customer's annoyed feedback than to lose a dozen customers because you don't learn about the problem. And if there's a problem at your store, a salesperson pushing too hard when you're not around, for instance, customers should be able to complain online. Make sure you answer all feedback honestly and quickly. Eventually, you will be able to hand this duty off to your more experienced and responsible store personnel.

Links

Making it easy for customers to access important related links makes your site a destination for shoppers. Such links should be related sites such as the local chamber of commerce, magazines about the retail industry, or events that affect the products you carry. If you run across a timely article about beauty products or great new kids toys you carry, you should link to that.

Seasonal links are always desirable. For example, you can link to sites that provide seasonal recipes. Holiday poem and story links make your site appear family friendly, while back-to-school links make your site a destination that customers will return to each fall.

Always strive to make your site useful and professional, asking yourself whenever you add a link, book review, graphic, bulletin board, etc., "Will this draw people to my site?" And try to keep your site organized to save your customer's time. If folks like your site, they will forward your pages to friends and family, spreading the word about your site—for *free*!

E-mail Marketing

E-mail marketing is the cheapest and most effective way for retailers to advertise. It has the same effect as sending out regular "snail mail" and it is much less expensive and a million times faster. You come up with a great idea one morning and you can have the e-mail or ad in your customers' hands that afternoon.

In addition to speed, the personalized service e-mail marketing allows is mind boggling. If you know that one of your customers loves a certain brand of clothing, when it comes into your store, you take a digital picture as you are unpacking, e-mail it to your customer, and there you have a personalized, targeted sales message that endears you to your customer—at minimal expense!

A good example of how a Web site can build consumer loyalty is a seafood restaurant I sometimes visit. On one occasion, the owner asked me if I would like to be on his e-mail list. Since my life revolves around the Internet, I said, "Sure, why not?" My initial thinking was, "Okay, every once in a while he will send me an ad or a coupon, and every once in a while I will take advantage of it." Next thing I knew, every Monday I was getting these long e-mails about fish, their habits and their history, and delicious-sounding seafood recipes. Before long, I was hooked on his e-mails! This was not a hard sell for his restaurant, just interesting facts for us trivia buffs and (forgive me) fishionados. Included in his weekly e-mail, he sometimes mentions a special, but I do not feel it is intrusive because his e-mails are interesting, clever, informative—and worth reading. As a result, I am now a very frequent customer.

So, don't be afraid to ask the customers visiting your store for their e-mail addresses. Similarly, ask anyone who visits your store online whether they would like to receive your newsletter. After all, if they came to you through an affiliate program, they already have some interest in what you are doing. Finally, you *can* go out and buy lists of customers with specific interests related to what you are doing, but I would only recommend this once you have exhausted the other means of getting customers interested in your site.

Sending e-mails to your customers is a modern tactic of retailing that, handled aggressively, can provide a level of service achievable in no other way. Also, by having your staff handle your e-mail during the downtime when they are underemployed, you spend very little. So use it in many ways, including:

- Providing advanced information on sales, special events and new products
- Alerting customers that new products have arrived, especially any that are in short supply
- Informing your customers about the latest trends in styles, looks, colors, etc.
- Updating frequent customers on their status in any bonus programs you run
- Sending thank-you notes to customers who make a special purchase
- Sending holiday greetings and birthday wishes
- Providing interesting news about your store

However, be careful to ask customers whether they want your e-mail before sending them too much stuff. You don't want to annoy them with a never-ending bombardment of material in which they have no interest.

What about E-mail Newsletters or E-zines?

An electronic newsletter or "e-zine" sent via e-mail to customers who have said they would like to receive it can be effective, as long as it is meaningful. The stories, articles, and editorials you put in these publications must be short and relevant. To avoid your customers becoming annoyed, make sure they look forward to receiving it because it has great information and is well written and useful. The material in your e-mail newsletter might include:

• Articles about your industry, products, or store.

• Seasonal articles that are relevant to your store or products.

• Weekly tips, hints, or time savers that are general in nature and short in length.

• A regular "From the Editor" column.

• Retail, seasonal, or holiday trivia.

• Local news or a calendar of events.

One important note is to try and make the newsletter interactive. Customers should be encouraged to use their e-mail to ask you questions, reserve or purchase a product, make an appointment, leave a message with a salesperson, critique the store, or offer suggestions for improvements.

Whether the e-mail you receive is feedback from your Web site, response to a mass mailing, or comment on your newsletter, the importance of this feature is that it adds a whole new level to your reputation as a progressive, service-oriented retailer—provided, of course, that you respond to every e-mail the day you receive it. E-mails are instant communicators; you or one of your staff must respond instantly.

Common Mistakes Made with Web sites

For every *right* way to utilize the Internet, there's a wrong way. (Trust me, I'm something of an expert in the wrong way!) To help you avoid the mistakes I and other people have made, the following sections give a sampling of the most common ones.

Ineffective Site

Your site should be a marketing document that sells your products or services. But most current Web sites do *not* have an effective sales function. They have dazzling graphics to wow you, but fail to offer you the information you need to make an informed purchase decision. Your site should be designed to make a sale now or in the future by providing your customer with persuasive, informative editorial content, simply and clearly presented. Thus, your Web site should:

- Include a powerful headline to catch the customer's eye
- Use active language such as "limited time only," "special offer," or "exclusive"
- Use copy that explains the benefits of your product or service from the customer's point of view
- Be error free; nothing says "amateur" like typos, bad grammar, or misspellings
- Build credibility with customer testimonials
- List any awards your store or the products you feature have won
- Include a "Call to Action" phrased as an alternative: "Click here to place product in shopping cart; Here if you would like more information."

Ineffective Advertising

The typical consumer is exposed to nearly 3,000 marketing messages per day! In fact, Americans are so bombarded by advertising that they have learned, by necessity, to tune out a majority of it. The situation on the Internet is no different. There are huge amounts of e-mail, banner ads, and Web sites competing for attention. To cut through the clutter and maximize the exposure your site gets, you can:

- **Buy relevant keywords from the major search engines.** The easiest site from which to quickly buy keywords relevant to your business is www.google.com. Another good site is www.overture.com, which services several search engines. Go onto these sites and sign up in their advertising section. They have an easy, step-by-step tutorial on purchasing keywords that will drive customers to your site. Start out by bidding low ($0.10 to $0.20 for each click that brings customers to your site), and then measure the cost to the sales gained. This is a fascinating new way to advertise and, if you can hone in on words that convert from click to sale, it may become the cheapest advertising you have ever done.

- **Get "spidered" by search engines.** Submit your URL to every search engine you can find. If you don't have time or an employee who can handle it, there are inexpensive services to do the work. One way or the other, to be seen you must be listed, and that is what search engine spiders do. They "crawl" your site and relate what you are doing to key-words being searched by their customers. Make sure before you appoint someone to build your site that they know how to get you listed with search engines.

- **Buy advertising at favorable rates.** In most instances, the price of Internet advertising can be negotiated; never pay list price. Who am I kidding? This book was written for entrepreneurs: *not* paying full price is in your blood!

- **Offer incentives to visit your site.** Rather than merely running a banner ad, offer customers something in return for visiting your site—a monthly sweepstakes or a free sample. To enter the sweepstakes or receive a sample, customers obviously have to tell you their names and e-mail addresses. The resulting list will enable you to educate the customer about your product or service and, ultimately, convince them to buy. Of course, most people will ignore what you are offering; that's the nature of the overcrowded Internet. The people who do accept are clearly interested in you, and therefore, are excellent potential customers.

Incorrect Promotions

The Internet offers you an inexpensive, effective, and fast medium for transferring a large amount of information, but it must be used respect-fully. To that end, you must respect its culture, its intolerance of blatant ads, obvious come-ons, and that great technological sin known as "spam." Unfortunately, spam does work for certain types of products, notably pornography. Otherwise, it wouldn't exist. However, unless you are in some very "specialized" kind of retail business, spam won't work for you. The best way to promote your business on the Internet (and avoid any hint of spam) is to change from an advertising frame of mind to a publicity frame of mind. Here are a few ways to do that:

- Instead of mass promotions, define as precisely as possible the target market or, better yet, an actual *person* you wish to reach. Then direct everything you do at that imagined person.
- Instead of an ad, write an article, or offer free tips.
- Invite reader responses with short story, letter, or other "interactive" contests; post winners on the Web site each week or month.
- Instead of pitching a new item you have for sale, pitch a new contest, event, or free offer.

No Follow-up

Creating repeat customers is crucial to your success on the Internet or in your store. However, with so much talk about getting hits or generating traffic, very little attention has been focused on bringing customers back for repeat visits or purchases. This is a big mistake because this "back end" is usually nicely profitable since you have already spent the heavy money needed to gain a new customer, "the front end." Following up is the key to attracting repeat visits and sales. The methods for doing this include:

- Using a newsletter to reach your clients and prospects regularly without annoying them
- Making your follow-up e-mails personal by having them address individuals and focusing them on the products or interests of particular recipients
- Having special promotions just for prior customers (list these on your site and announce them in your newsletter)

Parting Words

Once you have a Web site that follows the suggestions and avoids the mistakes I have outlined, tell the world about this in as many ways as you can imagine. Here are a few places to try:

- Shopping bags
- Register receipts
- Business cards
- Direct mail
- E-mail
- Newspaper and circular advertising
- Signs in the store
- Yellow Page ads
- Help wanted ads
- Promotional flyers

Don't "over dream" what will happen to your site. Whereas you can count the competitors of your brick-and-mortar store, your competition is worldwide on the Internet. And many competitive sites have full-time employees getting them placed in all the right places.

The Internet is a constantly shifting target, so you can't always keep up with the latest and greatest way to promote your business. However, even if you are not doing thousands of dollars a week on the Internet, do not view this as a failure. Remember that the Net is just another marketing tool to keep you in touch with your customers. Any business beyond that is *gravy*.

Retail Detail

Gen Xers, ages twenty-six to thirty-nine, are 49 million in number and account for an annual consumer expenditure of $735 billion or 18% of the total U.S. consumer spending according to the May 2004 *American Demographics*. As they begin to reach their peak earnings, members of this generation are also the economy's principal family makers. This generation is not as brand loyal as the baby boomers and they will shop at high-end stores as well as discounters. They are also more likely to research items online before going to a store.

Chapter 15

Exit Strategy:
The Beginning or the End?

*. . . Look at your business plan and see if it's likely to tie
into your personal objectives. Is it likely to achieve those?
Develop an exit strategy that ties into the business feasibility
and your personal goals. If it can't do that,
get yourself a different business, because you'll be miserable.*
—PETER ENGEL, excerpt from
*What's Your Exit Strategy:
Seven Ways to Maximize the Value of the Business You've Built*

WHETHER A RETAIL OPERATION is large or small, in a traditional field or selling exclusively via the Internet, the people who own it all have one trait in common: someday, they will leave that business. They may sell it, they may close it down, or they may die in the saddle. But one way or another, exit they will!

This inescapable fact should be the starting point for many of the major business decisions you make as you start your business. In my view, it is axiomatic that the strategic thinking that goes into every aspect of your business should be illuminated by your exit strategy.

Of course, you must consider how to build sales, maximize profitability, attract and hold the right management, and much more. However, if the considerations of how to run the business is where your strategic thinking ends, even though you may build a solid and profitable business, you will fail to maximize your wealth. To put it succinctly, if you build a successful business without a clear exit plan, your business will be "worth less than it's worth"!

The key point that many entrepreneurs starting a new business miss is simply this: just because you build a successful business does not mean that you will become rich. To do that, you also have to find a way to leave your business advantageously. Peter Engel in this book has identified seven main types of exit strategy. They are:

1. Selling to a strategic buyer
2. Selling to a financial buyer
3. Going public
4. Selling to your heirs or employees
5. Liquidating your assets (i.e., milking your business)
6. Being forced to liquidate
7. Managing for life

Not all strategies can apply to all businesses, of course. However, most businesses and business owners will find that they can rationally choose one (or a mixture) of the above exits. It's a choice you can and should make, and it's based not only on what is good for the business, but also on what is good for you. For example, there is no right length of time for you to run your business. Thus, the decision whether you want to sell it to a strategic buyer within a few years or manage it for life is a strictly personal one.

The important point to remember is that the exit strategy you choose will influence many of your business strategies. For example, if you intend to manage for life, you cannot hire entrepreneurial employees who expect to make a killing when you sell the business. As soon as they realize that will never happen, you will lose them. Even more obvious, if you plan to run the business until you retire ten years from now, you probably don't want to hire managers who will want to retire in five. And if you intend to sell the business to your heirs, you will end up with a disgruntled and therefore ineffective management team if you hire men and women who are ambitious to reach the top spot.

Because the exit strategy you choose is so important, I describe each one in some detail in the following sections.

Exit 1: Selling to a Strategic Buyer

A strategic buyer is an individual or a company that makes an acquisition in order to augment its own business. Thus, the buyer may be an actual or potential supplier who views the acquisition as boosting its sales. The purchaser may make the acquisition in order to guarantee itself a sound source of supply. Or, the buyer may feel it can integrate the acquisition into its own operation eliminating duplicated overhead and thus improving profits.

To sell to a strategic buyer at the highest possible price, the seller must structure its business so it fits as smoothly as possible into the buyer's needs. If you intend to sell to a strategic buyer, you should select a short list of the appropriate buyers and then construct your business to be as compatible with those buyers as possible. For example, if your potential buyer is a chain in a comparable business whose stores are located primarily in a single state, you may be well advised to concentrate your stores in a contiguous state. If your buyer has only a very limited health plan for its employees, you should not offer a generous health plan to yours. If you do, when the buyer purchases your company, it will either have to improve its own health plans at great expense, or be in danger of losing many of your employees. In either case, that will reduce the value of your company. Or if your buyers typically own "big box" stores, your value to those buyers is likely to be far less (however much business you do) if you concentrate on shopping mall kiosks.

On the positive side, if your plan is to sell to a supplier, then concentrating all your business with one supplier may be an excellent way to start an auction between that buyer, who won't want to lose your business, and its competitors, who would love to add your business as a new account. Unfortunately, concentrating all your purchasing with one supplier may not be ideal for running your business. The decision of whether to concentrate on one supplier or spread the risk between several becomes a matter of balancing opportunities. If you intend to manage for a long time, you'll opt for several suppliers at least until you're getting close to selling; if you want to sell out in three years, you'll probably concentrate on one.

Exit 2: Selling to a Financial Buyer

A financial buyer is one who brings only money and perhaps management skills to the deal. He is not in the same business. Therefore, making such a sale requires a very different positioning for you as the seller. For financial buyers, there are no synergies between themselves and the seller, so your company has to stand on its own.

For example, you should not create a sophisticated administrative infrastructure if you expect to sell to a strategic buyer who already has one. Conversely, you must develop such a structure if you plan to sell yourself to a financial buyer. That is of particular importance because the financial buyer will be making the acquisition either because he expects to be able to build your company more rapidly than you can, or because he believes he can use your profits or cash flow more effectively than you can. In either case, to maximize the value of your enterprise, your administrative infrastructure should be strong and resilient enough to run independently and withstand the wrenching effects of rapid growth.

Exit 3: Going Public

Going public, that is, making an Initial Public Offering or IPO, is not an immediate exit strategy; it is merely a step in that direction. That is because, with rare exceptions, the underwriters for an IPO won't permit you or any of your key executives to sell their stock for some lengthy period because they want to make sure that all the management that built the business stays with the business. No underwriter will let you and your key managers become so rich as a result of the IPO that you can afford to walk away. However, an IPO is a first step towards your exit. Once you have been public for a few years, you can arrange for a secondary offering, and this time you can sell a large portion of your shares.

There are many structural differences between the company that intends to go public and one that is to be sold privately. These differences range from different accounting practices to very different employment compensation philosophies. For example, to go public, a company usually needs three years of audited financials. Since these are expensive, if you intend to sell privately you can usually limit yourself to one year's audited statement and save money.

If you plan an IPO, you can compensate your key executives with stock options. However, such options have little or no value if you intend to continue to run the company for a long time.

Even more important, in order to go public, in addition to a solid business (which you will want whatever your exit plans), you need two other things: management that is willing to stay with the business and a "dream." If you are selling to a strategic buyer, you do not need loyal management; the buyer will have its own people, but you certainly do need such management if you intend to go public. Moreover, your underwriter will want to see a possibility that the stock will take off and fly high. That's where the dream comes in. You will have to show the investing public not only that you have a sound business, but also that it is on a path that may catapult it to glory.

Exit 4: Selling to Your Heirs or Employees

This exit means that you will be selling to insiders who are intimately familiar with your business and understand its true value. However, such buyers generally don't have the funds to pay you out entirely, nor do they usually have the credit standing to raise the funds. Moreover, for personal reasons you may want to sell to your heirs at less than the business is really worth. For all these reasons, this approach is unlikely to maximize your wealth; rather, it will maximize the wealth of your successors.

If this is your exit strategy, you will probably have to structure the sale so the continuing profits from the business constitute your pay-out. Also, your payout may have to extend over a long time period. Therefore, it is essential that your purchasers are trained and experienced enough to continue to run the business profitably without your presence. To that end, you should make sure that, long before you are ready to sell, you establish a wide-ranging training program for your successors and, as part of that, you let them make more and more independent decisions. This training should continue until you are fully confident that you will be leaving your business in good hands.

The obvious fact you should remember (which business owners too often forget) is that, if you call all the shots until the kids are middle aged, never letting them make a decision of importance, you cannot expect them to become effective, independent entrepreneurs when you finally bow out.

Exit 5: Liquidating Your Assets

Rather than selling your business completely, in some cases you may prefer to sell it off a piece at a time, thus milking it while it is still a viable company. This would apply, for instance, if you have built up a chain of several stores and, rather than selling the whole business, you sell off one store at a time. Sometimes this approach makes sense because the parts add up to more than the whole.

If this is the exit strategy you choose, your business strategies must conform: you must decide which assets you are planning to sell and make sure that they are sufficiently independent of the rest of your business to be saleable, and that their sale will not hurt what you retain.

Exit 6: Being Forced to Liquidate

I hope it never happens to you, but there is always the possibility in any entrepreneurial venture that it fails. Perhaps it descends into Chapter 11 bankruptcy, meaning the business is reorganized but continues. Worse, your creditors may feel the business cannot be saved, and force it into Chapter 7 bankruptcy, meaning it is entirely liquidated and ceases to exist. Obviously failure and enforced liquidation is not a strategic exit decision you make. I include it here only for the sake of completeness.

Exit 7: Managing for Life

Many entrepreneur-owners follow this strategy either because they don't want to think about the fact that their life will eventually end, or (surprisingly) because, until they reach old age or suffer from some major disease, they never think about it. However, in order to maximize the value of the business you leave behind, you should consider managing for life as a planned strategy just as much as selling to a strategic buyer or going public. By knowing that this is your strategy, your employees will know where they stand and operate more confidently and efficiently.

Whichever exit strategy or combination of strategies you choose depends upon your individual situation and needs. No two businesses call for exactly the same strategy, and no two entrepreneurs have the same personal objectives. However, once you understand your own objectives and then choose a strategy that is good for both the business and your own goals, you will be well on the way to maximizing your wealth.

Conclusion

W E'RE FREQUENTLY TOLD that giant chains such as Wal-Mart are driving small retailers out of business. "Their prices are too low." "They buy everything in China." "We can't compete." These are the typical complaints. PBS Television has gone so far as to run a "special" suggesting that Wal-Mart is a main cause for American jobs moving overseas. (They maintain this is a huge problem in spite of the fact that there are more people employed in the United States than ever before, that average incomes in real dollars are at an all-time high, and that the unemployment rate is no higher than it has been on average over the past 15 years or so.)

However, don't worry. If you are smart, energetic, and hard-working, you can prosper even against the largest, toughest competitors. Wal-Mart and those other giant chains should not frighten you. In some ways, especially by "thinning the herd" of other independent competitors, they may actually make your life easier and your business more successful.

Let's admit upfront that there may be some truth in the low price complaints for run-of-the-mill goods because it is true that the giant dis-counters do buy them at lower prices than any independent can obtain. However, when it comes to more specialized (although not necessarily more expensive) merchandise, Wal-Mart and the other giant discounters are actually at a disadvantage to the small retail store. There are three rea-sons for this:

1. While Wal-Mart et.al. can buy in very large quantities, and therefore get the benefit of substantial volume discounts; they cannot buy in small quantities. Thus, they can never benefit from purchasing broken lots, or small amounts left over in a manufacturer's warehouse after a huge discounter's buying spree ends. Nor can they buy from small manufacturers who, having close owner supervision and little overhead, often make excellent products often at more favorable prices than their large competitors.

2. There are many, many products the discounters cannot sell because they cannot buy them in sufficient quantity; the supply is simply too limited.

> One of my friends put himself through college by selling tiny, hand-inlaid tables made by craftspeople on the Italian island of Capri. He sold them very inexpensively—at triple what he paid for them!
>
> "How can you get them so cheaply?" I asked.
>
> "I guarantee to buy their entire output."
>
> "But you only sell about 20 of them every couple of weeks."
>
> "That is their entire output!"
>
> Often, small manufacturers cannot even get an appointment to see a Wal-Mart buyer. Those buyers are looking for carload purchases; they cannot waste their time on companies that produce only dozens.
>
> Moreover, even if some small manufacturers could manage to supply carload quantities, many of them do not want to sell to the giant discounters.
>
> Years ago, a friend of mine owned a company that produced unique, absolutely delectable chocolate-covered cherries. One day his sales manager rushed into his office, elated. "We've just got the biggest order ever. Wal-Mart!" He pronounced the name with all the awe a newly elected congressman might exhibit when first invited for a private chat with the President. Indeed, the size of the order was impressive.
>
> "But that's over two months of our total output," my friend remonstrated, appalled. "What happens next year if they buy from

someone else—while we sit here, without the next Wal-Mart order, and having short-shipped and therefore antagonized a whole bunch of our regular customers?"

"We'll keep selling to Wal-Mart," the sales manager said trying to sound optimistic, his enthusiasm nevertheless waning.

"Will they promise? Or will they switch as soon as another supplier beats our price by a penny or two?"

"No, of course they won't guarantee," the sales manager admitted. "But we make the best chocolate cherries around."

"They've managed without us so far."

"But . . ."

"We'll stay with the customers we have," my friend decreed. "If we have any production capacity left over, Wal-Mart can have it."

"They won't be satisfied with that."

"I'm sure you're right," my friend agreed, smugly turning down the biggest order he'd ever received. "But we'll tell all our loyal customers about what we've done . . . and they'll be even more loyal in the future knowing they can sell the best there is—and that Wal-Mart can't have it."

My friend was right. He relied on small retailers, and his business soared. To this day, fine smaller confectioners are able to sell better tasting chocolate-covered cherries than Wal-Mart can—at prices that are only a few pennies higher (if that) than the inferior, "cheap" cherries that you get at the big discounters.

3. Small retailers may beat the giants in another price related factor: their overheads may be considerably lower. Instead of a whole management superstructure, teams of buyers, batteries of lawyers (to fight the incessant lawsuits leveled against Wal-Mart), cadres of store designers, layers of accountants, passels of marketers and public-relations spokespeople, as well as all the store clerks, supervisors, merchandisers, managers, vice presidents, executive vice presidents, and who knows what all, as an independent retailer, you may get by with a couple of store sales personnel, a part-time bookkeeper, and perhaps your spouse and

teenage kids on busy holidays. Sure you may pay a little more for the merchandise, but you need a far lower margin to cover your overhead than even the most efficient discounters can live with. As a result, your actual selling price may end up being even lower than theirs.

Price isn't by any means the only factor in retailing. Sure it's important, but so is the choice of merchandise and, perhaps above all, the quality of service you can supply to your customers. And here the small retailer wins over the big box store hands down.

In spite of their best efforts, neither Wal-Mart nor any other giant retailer can match the personal service you, as an independent operator, can offer your customers. It's all very well to have the Wal-Mart greeters smile at customers when they enter the store. But the fact remains that they don't know those customers from Adam or Eve. On the other hand, when your customers come into your store, you do know them. You can often greet them by name. Even if you can't remember their names, you can introduce yourself and, in doing so, find out their names. "Hi, welcome to my store. I'm Harry Schmolowitz." Said with an extended hand and a questioning smile, this usually elicits a return smile and a mumbled, "Joe Smith." And if that doesn't work, why, you can always ask.

Once you have your customer's name, your computer, correctly programmed, should supply the rest of the information you need. "How is that sweater you bought last year holding up? We have some new ones that just came in." "Young Johnny still playing football? We're running a contest for two seats at the Super Bowl."

No customer can long withstand that sort of personalization. And no giant retailer can match it. Wal-Mart, eat your heart out!

None of this is to say that the chain stores do not offer serious competition. Of course they do. But then I don't know of any business, retail or otherwise, that is without competitive push back. The point is that, contrary to the complaints you hear from retailers driven out by Wal-Mart, even the largest, most aggressive chain store is nowhere near strong enough to stop you if you know what you are doing.

The retailers who have been driven out by Wal-Mart were capitalizing on their local monopoly by selling ordinary merchandise at exalted prices. When Wal-Mart came in, they found themselves undersold. Customers who had been forced to pay through the nose because they had the bad luck to live in areas where there were no competitors, suddenly found themselves able to buy at fair prices. It's hard to see why that is so unfair. "Wal-Mart has stopped me from exploiting my customers," hardly seems a valid reason for small retailers to complain.

Indeed, if you find an area with an adequate population base in which no giant retailer has yet landed (perhaps inhibited by local political opposition), you might be well advised to rush in with a store that undercuts the competition by offering fair prices. Of course, your competitors would consider you to be the "bad guy" who builds a solid, profitable business by offering your customers a better deal than they have been getting up to now. Maybe your competitors will hate you. But you can be assured that your customers will love you—and there are more of them!

Even if there are giant retailers on all four corners of a giant shopping mall, there is still ample opportunity for you to open your new retail establishment and be glowingly successful.

Your giant competitors will be spending huge sums to bring customers to your very doorstep. Once there, they are yours for the taking. Offer them: unique merchandise they cannot get at the giants; lower prices (if necessary even loss leaders) on a few, limited-supply closeouts or production tag ends (to drive home the point that you are not high priced); and impeccable customer service, and I assure you, your business will grow, thrive, and be profitable. Soon you will be able to open a second and a third store. Maybe you'll turn into a giant chain yourself. But if you do, beware! There will always be ambitious, small retail entrepreneurs—just like you are now—ready, willing and able to steal your customers and build their own retail empires off the back of yours.

So go for it. And good luck!

Appendix

Retail Glossary

2/10 Net 30: 2% is the discount rate if payment is made within ten days. Otherwise, payment is due in 30 days.

3/10 ROG: 3% discount is allowed within 10 days of receipt of goods.

8/10 EOM: 8% discount is allowed if the invoice is paid within 10 days from the end of the month.

Add on sale: Additional items customers buy due to in-store suggestions or promotions.

Ad slicks: Camera-ready ad, usually on glossy paper. Many vendors supply these for newspaper ads.

Advertising: Paid message communicated through various forms of media and designed to influence the purchase behavior and thought patterns of the audience.

Allocation: Suppliers determination of how much of (usually) scarce merchandise to assign to their customers.

Allowance: Any price reduction given by suppliers to retailers for various reasons (late delivery, damaged merchandise, below standard quality, overstock, etc.).

Anchor tenants: Major stores that serve as the primary draw of customers to a shopping center.

As is: Merchandise sold in its current, often slightly flawed, condition.

Assets: Those items of value the company owns such as cash in the checking account, accounts receivable, inventory, equipment, and property.

Assignment: The transfer of title, right, or interest in certain real property. For example, if you sell your business and turn over your lease agreement to the new owner, that is an assignment.

Authorized shares: The total number of shares the corporation is permitted to issue.

Automatic ordering: A feature in certain software systems of stores to automatically create suggested orders based on preset criteria for minimum and maximum stocking levels.

Average margin: The difference between what you pay for all the goods you sell during a specific period, and what you buy them for, calculated as a percentage of the selling price of the goods.

Average markup: The difference between what you pay for goods and what you sell them for during a specific period, calculated as a percentage.

Back haul: Trucks that have delivered merchandise to a buyer and are now empty are available to back haul material to their home base.

Back order: When an order cannot be filled because the products are not in stock, the order is left open until the goods arrive.

Bad debt ratio: The amount of money you believe the customers will never pay, also called uncollectible funds, divided by the total sales, expressed as a percent.

Balanced tenancy: The mix of stores in a planned shopping center chosen to meet the full range of consumers' shopping needs.

Balance sheet: Financial statement that shows the company's assets, liabilities, and owner's equity. The value of the assets must equal the value of the liabilities plus equity.

Base rent: Minimum monthly rent payments excluding pass-through, percentage rents, and all other charges.

Basics: Merchandise that customers need all the time.

Beginning of the month (BOM) inventory: The inventory in the store at the beginning of the month.

Big box store: A large store focused on a broad selection and low prices of a specific category of goods. Big box stores typically have few frills.

Billed cost: Manufacturer's price for goods.

Board of directors: Group of business leaders, typically including a company's CEO and other senior executives, who serve as advisors or supervisors of the company. In a private company, the board has little operating control. However, in a public company, the board represents the shareholders and may be called upon to make major strategic decisions including hiring or firing the CEO, making acquisitions or divestitures, etc. In return they receive either cash or shares of stock.

Book value: Net value of a company as shown on the balance sheets. In successful companies book value is often much less than actual value.

Bottom feeders: Customers who buy clearance merchandise, distressed companies in trouble, etc., at rock bottom prices.

Boutique: Upscale shop designed to present usually expensive merchandise tailored to a specific customer mix.

Breadth: The extent of the selection of merchandise in a department such as, for instance, the number of different styles, colors, sizes, etc.

Breakpack: Process of pulling inner packs from a master carton in order to ship smaller quantities to stores.

Brick-and-mortar: Traditional retailing in a physical business location as opposed to virtual retailing conducted online.

Business plan: Detailed road map of where a business is going and how it is going to get there.

Buying groups: Organizations that coordinate or pool the buying needs of many small retailers into a larger order with manufacturers or suppliers in order to negotiate better pricing, delivery, and payment terms.

Call tag: A freight carrier's written authorization for customers to return merchandise to the retailer at no cost.

Cash discount: Deductions taken from the cost of goods for performance of prearranged terms of payments. For example, 2/10 means payments within ten days can deduct 2% off the invoice.

Cash flow analysis: Financial statement showing how much money the company had at the beginning of the month, how much money came in through sales and payments, and how much went out as payments to create what was left over at the end of the month.

The cash flow statement may differ greatly from the profit and loss (P & L) statement. For example, a major capital purchase may deplete cash but not impact profit because it has merely converted one form of asset (cash) into another form (the capital good).

Cash on delivery (COD): Goods that are delivered to the store only upon immediate payment for them to the deliverer.

Cash wrap: Shelving and stands surrounding the cash registers.

C corporation: Standard corporation structure that establishes the company as an independent legal entity.

Charge back: Deductions on an invoice taken by the retailer for shortages, damages, freight allowances, etc.

Clearance: Selling inventory at reduced prices at the end of a season or life cycle to move excess stock.

Clipping service: Companies that are paid to read a broad selection of newspapers and magazines and cut out articles that reference specific subjects.

Closely held corporation: Company controlled by one or a small number of owners.

Closeouts: Merchandise that is no longer being manufactured that is sold at reduced prices to clear out remaining inventory.

Comp store: Comparison of this year's business to last year's in stores that have been open at least one year.

Consideration: For a contract to be valid, the requirement of one party to pay or do something must be countered by the other contracting party giving or doing something (the consideration).

Consignment merchandise: Merchandise that is placed in a store but remains the property of the supplier and is paid for by the retailer only when it is sold. Consignment merchandise usually may be returned to the supplier whenever the retailer wishes.

Cooperative Advertising: Retail advertising for which the supplier pays the retailer's cost.

Cost per thousand (CPM): Term used in media buying that refers to the cost of reaching a thousand people in your target market. (The Roman numeral for one thousand is M.)

Cross merchandising: Using different lines of goods to help sell each other, for example by displaying them together.

Current assets: Company assets that are liquid or can be converted to cash in less than one year.

Customer base: The customers who shop in your store.

Debt financing: Financially, supporting a business with borrowed money that costs interest and, per its terms, has to be repaid. In contrast, equity financing supports a business with invested money that remains in the business, carries no interest expenses, but reduces the percentage of the owner's share of the business.

Deep and narrow: Large quantities of a small selection of merchandise.

Defectives: Merchandise that is incomplete or faulty.

Demographics: Set of objective characteristics that describe a group of people. Includes characteristics such as age, home ownership, number of children, marital status, residence, location, job function, and many other criteria.

Depreciation: The amount an asset is assumed to fall in value each year. This amount may be an actual reduction in the asset's value (such as when a car is expected to wear out in a certain number of years) or set by accounting standards for purposes of collecting profit or taxable profit, even though its value may increase (such as a house).

Depth: The number of pieces of merchandise of a specific item or category in stock.

Distribution: The system by which goods move to retailers from manufacturers via importers, wholesalers, etc.

Dividends: Money from corporate profits paid to shareholders in proportion to their investment.

Doing business as (DBA): The name the business uses for its operations, as distinct from the name under which it is registered.

Earnings before interests, taxes, depreciation, and amortization (EBITDA): This figure is of key importance when buying or selling a business in that it tells the buyer what he can expect his pre-tax profit to be, assuming he funds the business so it pays no interest.

E-commerce: Buying and selling products over the Internet.

Electronic Data Interchange (EDI): Method by which orders are transmitted from the buyer to the seller via e-mail.

Employee manual: Document prepared by the company and issued to employees indicating the company's policies and procedures.

Employer Identification Number (EIN): An IRS-assigned number used by the government to make sure your business pays the required payroll withholding taxes for your employees.

Endcap: Display at the end of an aisle.

End of month (EOM) inventory: The inventory in the store at the end of the month.

Equity financing: See Debt financing.

Event marketing: Promotional plans built around outside events (sporting, charitable, local, etc.).

Face out: Merchandise is presented on the shelf with its front showing on the shelf. The advantage is that the product is more visible; the disadvantage is it uses up more shelf space.

Factor: A bank or finance company that buys the receivables from a manufacturer at a discount from their face value. The amount of the discount depends on the percentage of the debt the factor expects to collect. If the receivable is from firms with a strong credit rating, the factor will pay more than if the receivable is shaky. Retailers then pay the factor, not the vendor, for the merchandise.

Federal Trade Commission (FTC): The government agency responsible for enforcing antitrust laws.

Finish out: Structural, mechanical, electrical, and decorating costs involved in transforming a new or previously occupied retail space into a new store.

First cost: The cost of goods before duties and transportation, the true cost of imported merchandise.

Fiscal year: An accounting period of twelve months. Can be the calendar year or a twelve-month period chosen by an organization.

Fixed costs: Costs that, at least in the short run, do not vary in relationship to sales.

FOB factory: Retailer pays all shipping and other charges for transportation, insurance, etc., from the seller's factory onwards.

FOB warehouse: Seller pays all shipping and other charges for transportation, insurance, etc., to the buyer's warehouse.

Franchisor: Business operation that sells the rights to its name, concept, and trade know-how for a limited geographic area to an independent buyer known as the franchisee.

Freelance: An independent individual or company that works, under their own auspices, for one or more companies that assign them specific tasks but provide only general supervision. Like a consultant, they are paid a set rate with no benefits.

Freight companies: Transportation companies who move goods.

Freight on board (FOB): The point where the shipping costs become the responsibility of the retailer rather than the vendor. Title of the merchandise passes from the seller to the buyer at the FOB point.

Freight out: Freight costs for merchandise sent out.

Frontage: Section of the store facing the street or pedestrian walkway.

Generic merchandise: Non-branded products, often copied from branded merchandise but selling for less.

Guaranteed sale: The vendor's promise to take back unsold merchandise and issue a refund or credit.

Independent contractor: A supplier of services who is not an employee and from whose remuneration the employer does not withhold taxes. These are paid by the independent contractor. To qualify as an independent contractor, you have to work independently, use your own tools of the trade, be under only general supervision of the employer, and (usually, but not necessarily) work for several different employers. Commission sales reps who work for several firms and workmen such as plumbers and carpenters who are retained for specific jobs are typical of independent contractors.

Independent retailer: Stores not associated with a chain.

Industrial espionage: Practice of collecting information about competitors through devious methods. Using public information sources is not espionage, but obtaining it from a competitor's employee is.

Initial markup: Difference between cost of goods and the original retail price.

Inventory: The dollar value of the stock on hand at the store and at the warehouse. Taking inventory is the act of physically counting and recording the quantities of merchandise on hand.

Jobber: A distributor or middleman who buys merchandise to be resold to retailers.

Job description: Detailed listing of the duties to be performed by the person filling the job. This is an important benchmark against which to measure future performance, especially if lack of performance forces you to fire an employee.

Keystone: Retailing term that sets a selling price for merchandise at double its cost. If you buy an item at $10.00 and sell is at $20.00, you are marking it up at keystone. If you are selling at $30.00, that's double keystone.

Kiosk: Booth or stall set up in a shopping center to sell goods. May be temporary or permanent.

Landed cost: The total cost of imported merchandise once it arrives in the country. Landed cost includes first cost from the manufacturer, duties, transportation, and insurance.

Layaway: Storing merchandise for a customer for a later purchase usually requiring a deposit and a time limit for complete payment to be made.

Letter of credit (L/C): An agreement from the bank assuring a vendor that it will be paid for the merchandise once it is delivered according to preset specifications regardless of the buyer's financial condition, thus eliminating the seller's risk. The buyer has to have adequate credit to satisfy the bank and pays the bank a small commission for this guarantee.

Liabilities: Amount owed including accounts payable, loans, credit card debt, taxes due, etc. Short-term liabilities are those that have to be paid within twelve months. Long-term liabilities are those due in more than twelve months.

Licensing: Fee paid to use a name, product, or know-how for a given period of time and in a specified geographical area.

Life cycle: Many products go through four phases between market introduction and eventual demise: introduction (birth); maturity (middle age); decline (old age); and death. Thus, like people, products have a lifecycle.

Limited Liability Company (LLC): Form of corporate structure that provides business owners with personal liability protection but taxes corporate profits or losses at the individual level.

Limited partner: A partner who invests money but does not participate in the daily operations of the business. This partner is liable only for the amount of money invested. The general partner runs the business and is paid for his services.

Liquid assets: Anything the company owns that can be quickly turned into cash, such as accounts receivable, current finished goods inventory, and financial instruments (e.g., stocks and bonds).

Logo: The stylized representation of the name of a business.

Loss leader: Product intentionally sold at a loss to attract customers.

Maintained markup: The average markup of an item sustained over a period of time, usually six months or longer.

Markdown: The difference between the original retail price and the reduced price.

Marketing: Process associated with the selling of goods or services to more people than you can approach personally. The art and science of marketing includes product development, package and logo design, pricing, market research (to determine the consumer acceptance of these aspects of the product), advertising, sales promotion, merchandising, and public relations to make people aware of the product.

Market niche: Defined segment of the market with a need for a particular product or service.

Market share: Sales of a company or product as a percentage of total sales of that category of products in a defined area (i.e., a single store, a town, state, country, etc.).

Market trip: Organized visit by a buyer to the place from whence they are buying their products.

Merchandising: Selecting, pricing, displaying, and advertising items for sale in a retail store.

Merchants' association: Organization formed and controlled by a group of merchants (often the tenants of a single mall or other group location) to plan promotions and advertising to benefit all the businesses in the area.

Minimum: Smallest amount of goods a supplier will allow you to purchase, expressed either as a dollar amount or a physical quantity.

Mom-and-pop store: A store that is small and operated by people who appear to be members of a family.

Net income: Money left over after all expenses.

Net 30: Credit terms extended by a supplier where the retailer pays the full amount of the purchase within 30 days of shipment.

Non-compete clause: An agreement employees or suppliers sign indicating they won't use your ideas or business methods on behalf of a competitor or start their own business in direct competition to you. Non-competes are tricky. If you try to tie an employee up too tightly, the courts may hold that you are depriving that employee of the ability to earn a livelihood, and will strike down the contract. Generally, the more you pay the employee for the non-compete and the more limited its scope, the more enforceable it will be.

Off price: Merchandise that is purchased for less than regular price.

Off-price retailing: Stores offering well-known brands of merchandise at substantially lower prices compared to conventional stores handling the same brands.

Open to Buy: Most retailers establish a maximum level of inventory they can afford to have on hand. The Open to Buy is the amount of merchandise the retailer can still buy before reaching that ceiling.

Opportunistic buy: Buying products at far below their original price because a vendor is overstocked.

Outsourcing: Contracting with outside people or companies to provide services that were previously performed in-house by employees.

Partnership: Formed when two or more people share ownership of a business.

Planogram: Structured plan for displaying a line of merchandise on the shelf so as to maximize their visibility and sale. For example, a store might have a planogram for its detergents that would specify that Tide (its bestseller) had, say, ten shelf facings while lesser brands had fewer. By following the planogram, restocking shelves remains orderly and as planned.

Point of Sale (POS): Computer register system used to record sales by item, department, etc. The information is used to help make merchandising decisions and capture financial information.

Power retailers: Merchants with sufficient financial strength, marketing skills, and desirable content to enter any market they want.

Pre-paid: Vendor pays freight to store.

Price point: Various price categories. For example, one price may be for good products, another for better products, and a third for best products.

Price sensitive: Tendency for the demand for an item to be strongly affected by its price.

Price war: When two or more competitors try to beat each other's prices, possibly intending to drive the weaker competitor out of business or, at least, reduce their business substantially. They undercut each other's prices systematically, sometimes to such an extent that they are losing substantial sums of money on the price war "footballed" items.

Private label: Brands owned by a retailer or retail group rather than by a manufacturer.

Profit and loss statement (P & L): An accounting report that shows revenues, costs of goods, gross profit, expenses by major category (including depreciation and amortization), pre-tax profits, taxes, and after-tax profit.

Purchase order: The form used to place an order and give written authorization to a vendor to deliver specified merchandise at a stipulated price. Once accepted by the vendor, the purchase order becomes a legally binding purchase contract.

Rate card: The price list used primarily in advertising that lists costs based on the size of the ad, the length of a commercial, the positions of the advertising within its medium, and how often it is repeated.

Reach: Number of persons exposed at least once to a message during an ad campaign.

Receiving: The physical process of taking possession of merchandise.

Resale number: State issued identification number that permits retailers to buy merchandise without the vendor having to pay sales tax. When the retailer then sells to a person or entity that has no resale number, the seller is required to collect the tax from the purchaser and pass it on to the state.

Returns: Products sent back to the vendor for refund or credit against future sales.

Run of paper (ROP): Newspaper advertising term that applies to advertisements that the publisher can place anywhere in the paper.

Sales rep: Person or company representing the manufacturer in the sale of its goods.

S corporation: A corporation whose profits and losses pass directly through its owner(s).

Seasonal merchandise: Goods designed to sell only during specified seasons. *Seasonal* may be literal (such as summer clothing) or figurative, such as the Christmas or Easter seasons.

Secured line of credit: Line of credit that is guaranteed with collateral.

Short-term loan: Loan due within one year.

Show special: A price incentive offered by manufacturers to induce buyers to place orders at a trade show.

Shrinkage: Loss of merchandise at retail caused by shoplifting, internal theft, or bookkeeping errors.

Slotting fee: The price retail chains demand to stock an item they do not carry. The amount of the slotting fee may vary with the space, display, and promotional support to be allotted to the new item.

Small Business Administration (SBA): The government office that provides counseling and business plan evaluation for small businesses. While it does not lend money, it guarantees bank loans for small business people who could not otherwise qualify for them.

Sole proprietorship: Business is transacted for which the single owner is personally responsible (as compared to a corporation, the debts of which are normally not the responsibility of its owners, even if there is only a single owner).

Special order: An order for products not in stock.

Stock keeping unit (SKU): An individual item of merchandise. Each item is normally recorded in the retailer's books by manufacturer, style, number, size, color, and unit price.

Substitution: When a vendor substitutes one style for another on an order. This can happen with or without the retailer's permission. However, retailers are not obligated to accept the substitute product if they have not approved it.

Suggested Retail Price (SRP): The retail price suggested by the manufacturer.

Terms: The payment schedule for goods received.

Trade area: Geographic area from which a store or shopping center will obtain most of its customers.

Traffic department: These vendor departments optimize cost of freight and keep track of shipments to their customers.

Triple net: Name applied to a payment for leased space that includes rent, taxes, insurance, and common-area maintenance charges.

Turnover: Number of times the average investment in merchandise is bought and sold during a given time.

Universal Product Code (UPC): The bar coding system for merchandise.

Unsecured line of credit: Line of credit that is not backed by a specific piece of collateral.

Volume: Dollar sales of goods sold during a given period of time.

About the Author

MARC JOSEPH started his retail career working his way through college at an independently owned men's clothing store where he learned the art of selling, stocking, and customer service.

Following his graduation from Miami University in Oxford, Ohio, Marc began his professional career with Burdines, the Florida-based division of Federated Department Stores. He spent thirteen years there. Starting as an assistant buyer in electronics, he was promoted sequentially to buyer of children's wear, senior buyer of men's wear, divisional merchandise manager in women's wear, and finally store manager at several Florida stores.

Marc was recruited away from Burdines to become the General Merchandise Manager of BDS, a chain of variety stores based in Jackson, Mississippi. Located in small towns in thirteen Southern states, these stores were akin to mini-Wal-Marts. When Marc joined BDS, there were 220 stores, by the time he left there were 551 stores.

Marc next accepted the position of General Merchandise Manager of the pioneering chain in the new dollar store concept called Everything's A Dollar (EAD), based out of Milwaukee. When Marc joined EAD there were sixty stores; when he left there were 424 stores. While at EAD, Marc started a second chain of stores where everything was priced at either $5 or $10. These stores, named The $5 & $10 Store, were located near the Everything's a Dollar stores to let shoppers find higher-priced merchandise, but still at great values.

Marc then joined Action Industries in Pittsburgh as Senior Vice President of Merchandising and Marketing. Action was the largest supplier of promotional merchandise to the grocery, drug, and discount industry with Wal-Mart as their largest account. Action industries owned factories all over the world to manufacture "closeouts," and combined these goods with real closeouts from American manufacturers to provide chains with a regular flow of merchandise for both everyday and seasonal promotions.

Following his stint at Action, Marc joined Crown Book Stores in Washington, DC as the Senior Vice President of Merchandising and Marketing, responsible for building the new, larger Crown Super Stores concept and expanding the smaller stores into the large big box bookstores that are now the industry standard.

Wanting to get back to his entrepreneurial roots, Marc moved to Phoenix, Arizona and started a chain of hair salons called Hair Today. The concept behind this chain is that many trading areas have a need for both a budget hair salon and an upscale salon. Based on this insight, Marc would open a budget salon at one end of the shopping center, and a better salon on the other, thus capturing all the customers shopping in the area. He started with one store and built it into an eleven-store chain before selling it in 2002.

At the same time, Marc co-founded DollarDays International that has become the largest business-to-business site on the Internet. DDI sells over 30,000 items by the case to stores in all fifty states and thirty foreign countries. Over 350,000 users, including gift shops, drug stores, convenience stores, grocery stores, discount stores, dollar stores, women and men's clothing stores, children's apparel stores, pet stores, eBay traders, flea market merchants, and many other types of sellers are registered at www.dollardays.com. The company's business has more than tripled each year since its inception.

It is safe to say that Marc Joseph has in-depth experience with every type of and every aspect of retailing. During his career, he has attended just about every type of industry trade show including:
- American Book Sellers (ABA)
- American International Toy Fair
- Associated Food Stores Show
- Association of Surplus Dealers (ASD) and Associated Merchandise Dealers (AMD)

- Atlanta Gift & Accessories Show
- Canton Fair (China)
- Comdex (technology show)
- Consumer Electronics Show (CES)
- Dollar Store Expo
- Fancy Food Show
- General Merchandise for Supermarket, Mass, Drug and Convenience Stores (GMDC)
- International Housewares Show
- Magic Show (Men's and now WWD Women's Apparel Show)
- National Hardware Show
- National Stationary Show
- New York Home Textiles Show
- New York International Gift Fair
- The Off Price Specialist Show
- Philadelphia Gift Show
- School, Home & Office Show
- The Super Show (sporting goods show)
- Transworld Merchandise Show
- Variety Merchandise Show

RUSTY FISCHER is a business writer living in Orlando.